BY ELLEN VORA

The Anatomy of Anxiety:
Understanding and Overcoming the
Body's Fear Response

Season of the Witch:
A Psychiatrist's Case for Magic

SEASON
OF
THE
WITCH

SEASON OF THE WITCH

A Psychiatrist's Case for Magic

ELLEN VORA, MD

THE DIAL PRESS
NEW YORK

The Dial Press
An imprint of Random House
A division of Penguin Random House LLC
1745 Broadway, New York, NY 10019
randomhousebooks.com
penguinrandomhouse.com

Grateful acknowledgment is made to the following for permission to reprint previously published material:
Copper Canyon Press: "If we're not supposed to dance/Why all this music?" from *Concerning the Book That Is the Body of My Beloved* by Gregory Orr, copyright © 2005 by Gregory Orr. Reprinted by permission of Copper Canyon Press c/o The Permissions Company.
Andrea Gibson Poetry: Excerpts from the following essays by Andrea Gibson from her Substack *Things Don't Suck:* "Love Letter from the Afterlife" (December 21, 2023) and "Post-Election Letter to a Friend" (November 14, 2024). Reprinted by permission of Andrea Gibson Poetry.
Hope Publishing House: Excerpt from *If You Can't Break the Wall, Be the Grass That Grows Through the Cracks: What to Do When You Feel Powerless But Refuse to Be Silent* by Mya Zin, copyright © 2025 by Hope Publishing. Reprinted by permission.
The Anaïs Nin Foundation: Excerpt from *The Diary of Anaïs Nin, Volume 4: 1944–1947*, copyright © 1971 by Anaïs Nin. Reprinted by permission of The Anaïs Nin Foundation. All rights reserved.
W. W. Norton & Co.: Excerpt from poem on pg. 97 by e.e. cummings from *Complete Poems, 1904–1962* by e.e. cummings, edited by George J. Firmage. Reprinted by permission.
Pantheon Books, an imprint of Penguin Random House LLC: Excerpt from *The Book: On the Taboo Against Knowing Who You Are* by Alan Watts, copyright © 1966 by Alan Watts. Reprinted by permission of Pantheon Books, an imprint of Penguin Random House LLC.
The Charlotte Sheedy Literary Agency as agent for the author: "Where Does the Temple Begin, Where Does It End?" from *Why I Wake Early* by Mary Oliver, copyright © 2004, 2005, 2017 by Mary Oliver with permission of Bill Reichblum. Reprinted by permission of The Charlotte Sheedy Literary Agency as agent for the author.

Hardcover ISBN 978-0-593-97758-3
Ebook ISBN 978-0-593-97760-6
1st Printing
Printed in the United States of America

1st Printing

First Edition

BOOK TEAM: Production editor: Luke Epplin • Managing editor: Leah Sims • Production manager: Meghan O'Leary • Copy editor: Mimi Lipson • Proofreaders: Barbara Jatkola, Pam Feinstein, Claire Maby

Book design by Jo Anne Metsch

The authorized representative in the EU for product safety and compliance is Penguin Random House Ireland, Morrison Chambers, 32 Nassau Street, Dublin D02 YH68, Ireland. https://eu-contact.penguin.ie

FOR MY DAD

A thing is about to happen here that has not happened since the Elder Days. The Ents are going to wake up and find that they are strong.

—J.R.R. TOLKIEN, *The Two Towers*

Witch:

/wiCH/

noun

Any woman who has reclaimed the intuitive, mystical, and embodied ways of knowing that our culture tries to shame and suppress.

CONTENTS

AUTHOR'S NOTE

In this book, I use terms like "women" and "feminine" when I explore cultural patterns related to intuition and the stories we live inside. My perspective is shaped by my experience as someone who was born female and has navigated the world as a woman, but I recognize that womanhood encompasses experiences far more diverse than my own. In my psychiatric practice, I have also observed recurring themes in how our culture shapes the experiences of anyone who moves through the world as a woman, regardless of how they arrived at that identity.

When I reference feminine and masculine energies, I am speaking in generalities, not absolutes. We all contain both, and there are countless exceptions to any broad observation about gender. Still, I believe it is useful to explore cultural tendencies through a gendered lens, as imperfect as that lens may be.

I also want to acknowledge that some people who identify as men or as nonbinary may resonate with the invitation to reclaim their "witchiness"—their intuitive gifts and connection to mystery. While I write from my own lived experience as a woman, this invitation to trust our deeper ways of knowing extends to all—especially to anyone who has been taught to devalue their intuitive nature or shun a connection to magic. Though I cannot speak to every person's experience, I believe the journey back to wholeness has relevance for all who have felt they needed to hide or apologize for parts of themselves.

The stories in this book draw from my personal life and my work as a psychiatrist. All patient anecdotes have been anonymized, and identifying details have been altered. To protect confidentiality, many stories are composites of multiple cases. Consent has been obtained from all individuals whose stories appear in this book.

Content note: Some sections discuss sensitive topics, including sexual trauma and pregnancy loss. Please feel free to skip these sections if they feel too activating.

This book is for informational purposes only and does not constitute medical advice.

INTRODUCTION

Very suddenly, a decade ago, my mom had a pulmonary embolism and died. She and my dad were on a road trip. It was my husband's birthday. I was six months pregnant.

That acute phase of grief was painful in the physical sense of the word—my head throbbed, my chest ached, I barely slept for weeks. I would try to focus on work, only to find myself collapsed on the living room floor, sobbing. I would bend over my pregnant belly in the shower, hands on knees, heaving guttural pleas. The tears felt involuntary, like a primitive survival instinct. My voice reached for my mom the way an infant cries for its caregiver. My body was saying, "Mom, please come to me, I need you."

In the weeks that followed, I was consumed by the questions of grief: *Why did this have to happen? How will I get by without her?* But in that collision of pregnancy and mourning, one singular question cracked me open: *Does my mom still exist in some form, or is loss absolute?*

WHO KNEW?

A few weeks after my mom's death, I was receiving acupuncture in a sunny Flatiron office from a practitioner named Momoko. She had been recommended by a friend to support my grieving process. As I lay on the treatment table, needles precisely placed, my eyelids grew heavy and my psyche took flight through memories. Fragments of childhood came flooding back—the musty smell of our coat closet, my mom at the kitchen table over a bowl of minestrone, the plastic crinkle of library book covers. I had a vision of the Seattle Space Needle—where she was when she passed. My imagination attempted to piece together what she must have gone through in the last moments of her life. A flash of suffocation passed through me.

Toward the end of the treatment, my thoughts began their slow ascent from the depths. Eventually, my mind drifted to the book I'd been reading at the time—*Fifty Shades of Kale* by my friend and colleague Drew Ramsey, MD. I found myself feeling envious. Would I ever write a book? Was I falling behind in my career? With grief and a growing fetus weighing me down, ambition felt like something from my past.

With a gentle clearing of the throat, Momoko pierced the sunny afternoon silence: "I have a message coming through from your mom, if it's okay to share?" Momoko was known for her intuitive abilities—her capacity to receive messages from spirit. In my fuzzy state, I stumbled over my words. "What? Oh. Please, yes, of course."

"Your mom says," Momoko began tentatively, "'It's time to stop reading books and start writing books'—if that makes any sense to you?"

Goose bumps sprung up around the needles. It felt so much like my mom's parlance. And the fact that my mom was speaking to the very thought I was having in that moment was uncanny. My mind fluttered with excitement. *Could this be real? Could she be here, in spirit form, sensing my thoughts and giving me advice?* This was, of course, immediately followed by doubts. *That's impossible. Who am I kidding? Even if she does exist, how can she know my thoughts? I've lost my mind.*

As Momoko began to remove the needles, she offered, "Do you have anything you want to ask her?"

Did I have anything I wanted to ask my mom? I wanted to ask her everything. Where are you? Did you suffer? Are you okay? Will I be okay? Does God exist? Should I use soap when I wash my cast-iron pan?

I should explain: I grew up half Jewish in what one might call a high holiday secular style, dipping into holiday traditions while remaining coolly detached about the whole business. Instead of holding any religious beliefs, my friends and I worshipped at the altar of science. Skepticism was seen as a virtue. Country music about Jesus made us roll our eyes. It was understood that we were all atheists.

When I was in middle school, already a perfectionist chasing straight A's, I worked up the nerve to ask my mom if I could quit Hebrew school. She was driving me to my afternoon lesson and I explained that I wanted that time back for academics. Without a word of protest, she simply flipped on her turn signal and turned the car around. My mom always kept a healthy distance from religion. If I had to guess, I think that my mom would have called herself an atheist. We'd never had lengthy conversations about faith—it hadn't been a topic much on my mind until I lost her. But now, as I lay sobbing on Momoko's table, desperate for a framework to make sense of my mom's death, I wondered if our devout skepticism had left me unprepared.

Did I have anything I wanted to ask her? I sensed that my hour was up and that Momoko, seeing the tears streaming down my face, was being generous. I knew I'd better consolidate my questions into one.

"Could you ask her," I ventured, "'If you're really here, sending me a message, then what do you make of the fact that you . . . still exist?'"

Momoko went silent for a moment, then said, "Ha," with the inbreath of someone caught off guard. "Your mom is funny," she said. Like a radio receiver, Momoko picked up my mom's response and amplified it to me—words that reverberate through my psyche to this day.

"Your mom is laughing. She's saying: 'Who knew?'"

Who knew. Here was my mom—the woman who had turned the car around when I wanted to quit Hebrew school, who had renounced her own Presbyterian upbringing, who had raised me in our secular household where skepticism was a virtue—revealing the ultimate plot twist. I could feel her say, "Who knew that I could die and still be here?"—amused at her own ongoing existence. "What a pleasant surprise. Who knew?"

I desperately wanted to believe that this exchange was real. As I left Momoko's office, something came into focus that would carry me through grief and on to the next part of my story: an openness to mystery. I would build on that foundation. I could accept this loss. And at the same time, I could feel my mom's presence, be guided by her, trust in divine timing. The alternative was utter devastation: A world where the end is the end. Random, bleak, and cruel.

You can call this a variant on denial, but in that moment, I chose to trust that something vast, something beyond our comprehension, is playing out in this galaxy. At first, it was indeed a *choice*. I decided that I preferred to live in a world where perhaps my mom continued to exist in some form. This choice softened the ache of grief.

Who knew? In two simple words, my mom had captured the essence of what continues to intrigue me. That small phrase—signifying an openness to mystery and magic—transformed how I metabolize loss and move through the world—and in time, how I practice medicine too.

But first, let me step back and explain how someone who had been vaccinated against believing in God at a young age could even entertain such a choice.

PROUDLY LOW-MAINTENANCE

On paper, I'm a board-certified psychiatrist, medical acupuncturist, yoga teacher, and writer. I followed the instructions my whole life—I was good at school, and it served me well. Yale undergraduate, Columbia medical school. But credentials don't tell the whole story.

I spent the first three decades of my life performing a particular version of myself: rational, shrewd, proudly low-maintenance. My ultimate aspiration was to be the chill girl—the kind who could hang with the guys without causing any inconvenience. I learned early that to be accepted, especially by boys, I needed to be undemanding and unfussy.

Being "high-maintenance"—a phrase loaded with misogynistic disdain—was a cardinal sin. High-maintenance girls took forever to get ready, they wore uncomfortable footwear, they were bad at parallel parking, and they took offense at jokes. They had hormone swings and bodies that demanded attention. They acted "crazy" around their periods. I, on the other hand, prided myself on being easygoing, low-key, and impossible to offend. Okay, so maybe I was ignoring my body's signals and pushing through discomfort or indignation with a smile. But surely that was a sign of strength and good character.

This performance of chillness won me approval (mostly from men, who held the power to approve), but it came at a cost. From the moment puberty sets in, there's actually nothing chill about the machinery of the female body. I realize now that anytime a girl is perceived as chill rather than high-maintenance, we should be concerned: She may be denying her body's needs. Her chillness is likely the product of an unconscious calculation she made to get by in a culture that has little patience for the complex demands of female bodies. I ran that same calculation: *If I could just be one of the guys*, I thought, *perhaps I'll be respected.* So I dutifully performed the masculine side of myself.

This calculated denial is savvy, but is it worth it? Each time I pushed aside my discomfort for the sake of being low-maintenance, I was creating rifts with myself—small acts of self-betrayal. I was learning to silence my body's intelligence and training my body to expect to be ignored.

I used to judge other women if I felt like they arrived at a different calculation—I'd scoff at their sensitivity, math hesitancy, or multitangent stories. Something inside of me clenched when women seemed too emotional or woo-woo, or if they spoke openly about "the energy in the room." *Get it together*, I would think. *You're making us all look bad.*

I went decades proudly abstaining from anything woo-woo—hanging with a crowd of doctors, engineers, and tech bros in the city. I understood the assignment: rational thinking was celebrated, while intuition was suspect. So I buried any intuitive nature that I had and crafted a more acceptable persona: the logical, low-maintenance woman who could parallel park and who never caused a fuss.

Looking back, I recognize this performance for what it was—what internet culture now calls "pick-me girl" behavior. I was unconsciously distancing myself from other women, emphasizing how I was "not like the other girls" in a bid for male validation. It's not something I'm proud of, but I understand now that I was simply trying to get my needs met in a world that often feels like a game of musical chairs mixed with an episode of *The Bachelor*. I was choosing the version of womanhood that seemed to offer the most safety.

So many women feel the same pressure to perform. Maybe you've experienced moments of this yourself: you sense something beneath the surface of a situation, an energy at play, but rather than giving it voice, you silence yourself. Saying what you sense might be met with resistance, skepticism, or even an eye roll. And so you tuck it away, or try to talk yourself out of it meaning anything at all.

Some women double down fiercely on rationality. They appreciate data, they read Nate Silver, they feel contempt for astrology and life coaches. These highly "rational-identified" women are often the most successful in the room; they wear their skepticism as a badge of honor. They're not aware that they're estranged from their mystical side—they might even deny that they had it to begin with. Perhaps they dismiss what we call "intuition" as nothing more than unconscious pattern recognition. And they come by this denial honestly. After all, they hit the mark: In a world where power, respect, and safety belong to those who can prove their intelligent rationality, what choice do we have?

A CRACK IN THE FAÇADE

By the time I was a psychiatry resident in my early thirties, with several years of training under my belt, I started to feel a dissonance between rationality and intuition. I'd had a few moments when these buried "woo-woo" parts of me began to show up in unexpectedly helpful ways. There were treatment decisions where the data couldn't steer me one way or the other and I'd have to tune in to something subtler—a gut sense of what a particular patient needed. And in my personal life, there were moments—like the seemingly orchestrated way my husband and I got together—that felt unusually synchronistic. Were they mere coincidences? Something about it all felt a bit out of the ordinary, perhaps even guided. I would look at the man who would become my husband and have the distinct if illogical thought: *You're familiar to me from my future.* I was glimpsing cracks in my own rational façade.

Meanwhile, the benefits of my coveted membership in the boys' club were proving thin, insubstantial. However "chill" I managed to be, was I ever fully welcomed into those clubs? It began to dawn on me that, in certain circles, true respect was never actually on tap. I was compromising myself for a prize that didn't exist. So what was all this self-betrayal for? As mythologist, writer, and professor Joseph Campbell put it, I had "climbed to the top of the ladder and found it's against the wrong wall."

Something essential in me began to gnaw and chafe—a disavowed part of me that was long forgotten. My dormant intuition was stirring.

As a burned-out med student, I found myself drawn toward practices I'd previously dismissed. First came yoga. Med students are runners—there was no time for something as unproductive as yoga. But when I got my gym schedule mixed up one day and found myself walking into Beginner Hatha instead of Cardio Burn, even though I preferred grunting and control over surrender and slow breathing, I heard a quiet voice inside that said, "Just give it a try." Well, it was that and the fact that I'm far too much of a people pleaser to stand up and walk out of a gym class. I stayed.

I sank awkwardly into that first experience, hiding in the back row. Everything about yoga was foreign. I hadn't a clue about listening to my body. The teacher said, "Lengthen your side body," and I thought smugly: *I'm pretty sure there's no such body part.* Yet it also felt oddly spacious. I could feel the movements loosening my controlling grip on the world and tempering my restless anxiety. For the first time, I felt how breath could be used to maintain equanimity even in the face of struggle.

Then came Chinese medicine. I had heard about an outlier rotation in the Bronx. They were teaching med students how to use acupuncture to complement twelve-step meetings for patients in recovery from substance addiction. Like yoga, it was many degrees off from my conventional medical training. But I felt another distinct tug from somewhere that wasn't my logical mind. I knew I had to learn this discipline. During that rotation, I witnessed my patients shift from a state of disturbance to peace; out of despair and into hope. I was hooked. I went on to do formal training in medical acupuncture, then specialized further in auricular (ear) acupuncture. As I gained expertise and started to treat mental health conditions, the skeptic in me kept thinking, *Show me the research,* and *It's probably just a placebo effect.* But I couldn't deny what was happening—treatment-resistant conditions were improving after just a few acupuncture sessions. It made me a believer in the effects of things I could not see, things I couldn't measure with conventional tools.

In my last year of residency, I decided to use my elective time to become a yoga teacher. There were plenty of programs available within easy reach of my apartment, but I found myself scanning the globe instead. When my eye landed on a program in Bali—the farthest time zone away—I felt that inner "yes" again. I realize how this sounds: privileged American seeks enlightenment in exotic locale. What spiritual awakening would be complete without the obligatory pilgrimage to Bali? Even then, the cliché wasn't lost on me, but despite many good reasons not to, I found myself stuffing my orange yoga mat into the overhead bin of a plane out of JFK bound for Denpasar.

It was there, in that sensual Indonesian landscape, having my city defenses softened by daily meditation and rippling rice paddies, that I had an experience that would change everything. I was studying with an energy worker, a magnetic woman named Daniela. During a healing session, she put me under a spell of sorts.

The minute I lay down on her table I dropped into a liminal trance. After the hour-long treatment, I lay resting in a hazy state of calm when Daniela broke the humid stillness.

"So." She spoke as if she were a doctor delivering a diagnosis. "You're a witch."

"I beg your pardon?" I managed to reply. Part of me wanted to nervously laugh at this new age jargon, but another part—the part that had been quietly growing stronger—felt oddly thrilled.

"Don't worry," Daniela chortled. "It's a good thing. I'm a witch, my mother's a witch, and you're a witch."

I wouldn't fully understand what this meant for some time. But something had been named in me, something I'd been moving toward without realizing it.

After Bali, I returned to the waxy hospital hallways to finish my residency. I wasn't ready to call myself a witch, but something had shifted. I found myself trying on a watered-down spiritual worldview rooted in yoga philosophy. I held it with a light grip, but it was a distinct departure from worshipping at the altar of science.

Once I graduated and became a newly minted psychiatrist, I began practicing differently than most of my colleagues. I specialized in what I called "holistic psychiatry"—a functional-medicine approach to mental health, meaning that I addressed problems at the root rather than reflexively suppressing symptoms. In practice, that meant treating the body as a whole system, addressing the ways that physical health impacts mental health, and acknowledging the primacy of our psychospiritual needs—such as our needs for community and purpose.

I brought diet, lifestyle, and mind-body medicine to the fore of care. I talked to patients about their sleep and digestion, identified autoimmune and hormonal issues underlying their mental suffering, and treated gut issues that drove inflammation in the brain. I taught stress management through yoga, mindfulness, and breath work. Where most mainstream psychiatrists focused on prescribing ever more medications, I offered a less invasive whole-body approach.

For several years, this integration of Eastern and Western approaches sustained me beautifully. I had built a practice that honored both scientific rigor and ancient wisdom. My patients were healing in ways that I hadn't seen in my conventional training. My work felt purposeful and alive.

THE BREAKING POINT

Those first few years of practice, I straddled the worlds of science and soul, holding my rational mind and nascent spiritual inklings in an easy truce. Whatever openness I had to existential meaning was a diluted spirituality, loosely gripped. The gaps and contradictions didn't trouble me—"maybe" was answer enough.

But loss has a way of demanding resolution. When my mom died, none of it—not my traditional medical training, not even this carefully constructed bridge between East and West—was enough to meet the moment. Now uncertainty felt unbearable. I found myself seeking answers with a new desperation, cornering every rabbi, priest, and healer I could find with the same burning questions: *Is God real? Does my mom still exist? Please tell me what you know.* The philosophical had become personal, and "maybe" no longer felt good enough.

My burgeoning spiritual worldview faced its critical test: Would I retreat to the safer rational worldview I had been raised with, which gained me respect from others but left me defenseless against grief? Or would I open up to a spiritual perspective that could hold the magnitude of loss?

And that was where I was as I lay on Momoko's table. My medical training, my rational thinking, even my light spirituality expressed through yoga and acupuncture weren't working to alleviate my pain. I felt I'd lost my way. Rudderless and prone to second-guessing myself, I was struggling to make decisions. I was anxious and controlling—everything felt fragile, and I couldn't release into sleep or joy. I was quick to anger, short-tempered with friends and loved ones. It all felt so unfair, but who was there to blame? I couldn't seem to get out of my own way.

But my mom's uncanny "Who knew?" shook loose my rational scaffolding.

From deep in the undertow of grief, something surfaced in me—an invitation to engage with the possibility of magic.

Despite my longtime disavowal of all things irrational, I found myself unwilling to accept that my mom's death was an absolute loss in a senseless and random universe. Instead, I felt a strong preference for an expanded perspective—one that included the possibility of her ongoing existence. For the first time, I opened. Like ligaments softening before labor, my worldview began to stretch—making room for the possibility that something beyond comprehension was at work, that my mom might still exist in some form.

In choosing that—and then actually *feeling* like things were occurring that corroborated it—I found something I'd been missing my entire life. It was more than comfort, though the comfort was immense. There was guidance in this perspective. Meaning. Transcendence. It cushioned the blow of grief in a way nothing else could. That choice transformed how I move through the world. I began to live with my heart open to magic.

When I say magic I mean the miraculous, the mystical, the uncanny—the inexplicable sense that there's some meaning and order in our cosmos. Magic transcends rationality, inviting us to embrace the mystery of existence and trust forces beyond our understanding. It's the acknowledgment that not everything can be measured or explained, and that when we stop reflexively dismissing what cannot be proven, we make space for an expanded version of reality.

Once I opened myself to this possibility, synchronicities began to occur around me. Even though I was a psychiatrist trained in the rigors of evidence-based medicine, I began having experiences that defied explanation. I began to receive messages from my mom.

One gray afternoon, I found myself at the end of the Christopher Street Pier on the Hudson River. In the past, I had taken walks there with my mom. Now it was a place I would go to feel close to her—where the boundary between worlds seemed thinner. As I stood there alone, my grief was sharp and consuming. I closed my eyes and spoke into the wind coming off the river, "Please, Mom, send me a sign."

When I opened my eyes, I saw only the river's cold expanse and boats passing indifferently by. My heart contracted with familiar pain. *I knew this was foolish,* I thought bitterly. *It's time to accept that she's gone.* But then something made me pause. Gliding close to the pier was a boat, unremarkable except for the words written in stark blue letters against its white hull: SPIRIT CRUISES.

These signs became more frequent as I learned to notice them. The song "Spirit in the Sky," which had held special significance for my mom and me, would play in grocery stores just as I was wishing I could ask her about ingredients for a family recipe, or in cafés anytime my sister and I got together. The word "spirit" would appear in books falling open to just the right page—my mom was, after all, a librarian. She would visit me in my dreams. Each time, I felt her presence, her gentle reminder: *I'm right here. Who knew?* In a moment when I could have disappeared into my grief, I chose to see those signs. To let them in. As I logged these uncanny experiences, a magical worldview became less of a choice and more of a *knowing.*

Losing my mom at such a vulnerable time was an initiation. Magic was what I needed in that moment, but rather than feeling like something altogether new, it felt like a homecoming. I was finally understanding what Daniela had recognized in me years earlier in Bali. I was proud to be a woman fully alive to mystery—one who sensed the invisible currents that connect us all, trusted the whispers of her intuition, and was unafraid to believe in what cannot be proven.

I was a witch.

The altar of rationality I had grown up with was no longer enough. The holistic therapeutic approaches were good and helpful, but even they had not been enough to meet that moment of devastation. When everything else failed me—when all my training and carefully constructed approaches crumbled in the face of sudden loss—the only thing that could sustain me was a witch's radical openness to mystery. A willingness to believe in unmappable forces, in love that transcends death, in a universe far more magical than I had ever allowed myself to imagine. Claiming my witchiness was the medicine I needed.

PART I

SEEING CLEARLY

To build a case for magic, we must first understand what we've lost—and how we lost it. For centuries, women have been systematically severed from our deepest ways of knowing. Our mystical side has been pathologized and driven underground through both overt persecution and subtle cultural conditioning.

This was never an accident. It served a purpose: women who trust their inner knowing are harder to control, exploit, or dismiss. A woman connected to her power doesn't need external corroboration to know what she knows. She becomes an inconvenience to systems built on compliance and self-doubt. Understanding how we got here is the first step toward reclaiming our wholeness.

Chapter 1

THE MEDICINE OF MAGIC

Your first act of rebellion is to see clearly.

—MYA ZIN, *If You Can't Break the Wall, Become the Grass That Grows Through Its Cracks*

I've observed that patients who view the world as random, material, and devoid of divinity tend to slip more easily into demoralization and depression, especially when facing difficult circumstances like loneliness, moral injury, or loss. Those with a spiritual orientation, on the other hand, seem to be protected. This protective effect particularly shines in the face of challenge.

Dr. Lisa Miller, a professor of psychology and education at Columbia University, has pioneered groundbreaking studies on the relationship between spirituality and mental health. Her research reveals that individuals with a strong sense of spirituality—defined not as religious doctrine but as a personal connection to something greater than themselves—are 90 percent less likely to experience major depression compared to those who don't consider spirituality important.

This kind of spirituality—sometimes called secular spirituality—doesn't require adherence to any religion or dogma. It's simply an openness to mystery, a sense that the universe holds meaning. Research consistently shows that this orientation correlates with increased happiness and lower rates of depression and suicide. What's most fascinating is that this isn't just psychological but also biological. Miller's neuroimaging studies show that individuals with strong spiritual or religious commitment have measurably thicker cortical regions in areas associated with emotional regulation and resilience.

But this isn't something you can force. You can't fake your way into genuine belief, and I wouldn't ask you to try. What I will invite you to consider is this: If you view spirituality with skepticism, is that skepticism truly yours, or have you internalized a cultural skepticism? Do you have an openness to mystery that's buried beneath layers of social conditioning? Many of us carry a latent receptivity to magic that we've learned to suppress. And in suppressing it, we may be missing out on what spiritual openness has to offer. That was certainly my experience.

As the steward of many people's mental health, I know the benefits and limitations of medication and therapy. I've come to appreciate that, no matter how well medicated and therapized we are, at some point we all must grapple with existence itself: *What is happening here? Is the fabric of the universe purposeful or random, benevolent or cruel?* Where we land on those questions has an outsized impact on daily mental health. In our quiet moments, do we trust that everything will be okay in the end? As the nineteenth-century thinker Frederic W. H. Myers recognized, the most important question we can ask may be: "Is the universe friendly?" Einstein grappled with this same fundamental question and arrived at his own conclusion: "Subtle is the Lord, but malicious He is not."

If we believe this world is random, that potential catastrophe lurks around every corner, how can we not live in a state of vigilance? This can foster anxiety, or even an overwhelming fear of death. A purely materialist outlook leaves little room for meaning in the unfoldings of our lives. Anytime something seemingly magical does occur, we force ourselves to sober up and explain it away. And grief can feel untenable when we believe that the end is the end, and that loss is senseless. An openness to magic holds us when life feels heavy, anchoring us to a more hopeful and trusting narrative. When we might otherwise despair, magic helps us find meaning in our challenges.

There are other ways a connection to magic shapes my practice, even if I don't typically speak openly about them. Though I grew up in the suburbs of New York City rolling my eyes at country songs about

Jesus, I now begin every patient session and speaking engagement with a silent prayer, asking to be a conduit for source (universal intelligence) to work through me in service of everyone's highest good. Before writing, I light a candle and pray. These practices have been transformative. My writing pours forth more easily, I show up with more honesty in front of audiences, and insights arise with patients that feel beyond my training or intellect. I even weave energy work into clinical sessions alongside traditional dialogue. The more I practice this way, the better my work flows.

And this isn't just about my work—it's about allowing my witchiness to pervade all of me. No more walling off my witchy self from my doctor self, pretending I don't pray to ancestors for wisdom. No more deflecting my connection to magic with self-deprecating jokes about crystals or astrology. No more fearing loss of credibility as punishment for speaking from my intuitive knowing. This book is, in essence, a coming out of the closet. These fractured parts can finally become one integrated whole.

But perhaps most importantly, I've learned that it's not enough for *me* to believe in magic. What I ultimately want is to empower my patients and readers to discover and trust their own connection to the mystery—to become their own witches. I have seen that when they do, they walk through the world with a quiet conviction that wasn't there before. They feel less easily shaken by life's inevitable challenges, more anchored in their own knowing than swayed by external pressures—especially those that don't have their best interests in mind. They develop the qualities that Brené Brown captures in her phrase "strong back, soft front, wild heart"—they move through the world resilient and empathetic, grounded yet open to change, fierce. Most importantly, they begin to trust that they are whole unto themselves.

THE FIVE PRACTICES OF A MODERN WITCH

Women today are caught in a crisis of disconnection—from themselves, from one another, and from the deeper currents of meaning that could sustain them. We've absorbed a cultural script, performing a sanitized version of ourselves that prioritizes linear thinking while betraying our intuitive nature. The cost of this self-betrayal shows up everywhere: in our bodies, which cry out with digestive issues, painful periods, and autoimmune conditions as we force our cyclical feminine rhythms into rigid masculine structures; in our relationships, where we've lost the circles of sisterhood that once held us; and in our daily experience, where we feel rudderless and anxious. We outsource countless intimate decisions because we've learned to distrust our own inner knowing.

When loss inevitably comes, we're left defenseless. We're forced to navigate grief in a culture that offers little ritual or preparation for this underworld journey—a culture that cuts us off from an ongoing relationship with our loved ones that could transform our devastation.

The deeper wound is that we've internalized centuries of conditioning that tells us the witchy way of knowing—intuitive, holistic, embodied, ineffable—is inferior. Some of us are not even aware that there's a problem. We have absorbed society's value system so completely that we join the ranks who see "woo-woo" as a dirty word. Our feminine intelligence is so thoroughly suppressed, and we are proud to be the "right" way: rational and skeptical.

In our desperation to be taken seriously in a world that values only one narrow slice of intelligence, we've lost touch with our witchiness.

This conditioning stems from the belief that rationality is superior to intuition—that logical, linear thinking (characteristic of the left hemisphere of the brain) is intelligent, while intuitive knowing (more characteristic of the right hemisphere) is unreliable and untrustworthy. When logic became king, it shaped our culture from the inside out—privileging the material over the mysterious, the head over the heart.

To reclaim magic, we need strategies to push back against these biases. Through years of careful attention, I've developed five practices that serve as antidotes to our culture's most limiting patterns. These practices took shape first through my work as a psychiatrist, as I noticed strikingly similar patterns in how women described feeling stuck and disconnected despite vastly different circumstances; then through my training across diverse healing modalities, from Chinese medicine and acupuncture to yoga. They crystallized through my own journey of chafing against cultural forces that felt hostile to my nature. But perhaps most importantly, they arose from the very orientation this book advocates: one of intuition and of listening for what wants to emerge. Each of these five practices counters a cultural bias that pulls us away from magic.

THE FIVE PRACTICES

1. Embodiment
   Our culture disconnects us from our bodies at every turn, teaching us to numb ourselves and live from the neck up. A witch practices embodiment—inhabiting her body fully, trusting its intelligence, and relearning how to truly feel.

2. Presence
   Our culture fragments our attention and pulls us out of sovereignty. A witch refuses this by cultivating presence—being fully aware of the present moment, alert and awake to what drives her.

3. Valuing Yin
   Our culture glorifies yang energy—action, productivity, endless doing—while devaluing yin energy of receptivity and rest. A witch honors both energies, moving fluidly between doing and being. And she knows that yin is where the magic happens.

4. Opening to Mystery
   Our culture privileges the material, trusting only what's "backed by science" and dismissing anything that can't be measured as unworthy of serious consideration. A witch leaves space for mystery. She's willing to be surprised by the inexplicable, recognizing there's more to reality than what can currently be explained.

5. Serving the Collective
   Our culture prioritizes individual achievement and self-optimization while losing sight of our interconnectedness and responsibility to the larger whole. A witch serves the collective because she feels a

vital connection to her ancestors, the earth, and the larger web of sentient beings.

These five practices serve as a road map for resisting the cultural forces that will otherwise pull us off our paths. They are our way back to feeling whole, anchored in ourselves, connected to our communities, and fully alive to the mysteries threaded through our existence.

THE BIASES BEHIND THE PRACTICES

The disconnection created by these cultural biases is not making headlines in psychiatric circles, nor is it working its way into the peer-reviewed research on women's health or diseases. It's a silent crisis, unseen and little known. But from the front lines of my work with women, I observe it daily. I see women struggling with a nameless unease—they feel unmoored, unhappy, unworthy, unwell. Women at the end of their rope from burnout and not tending to their bodies' cries for rest (but also not seeing a realistic path toward that rest). Women caught in patterns of overworking or numbing themselves with alcohol, shopping, or endless scrolling because the truth of their experience feels like a bottomless abyss. Women mired in chronic over-giving because they can't tune in to their boundaries, and because society praises them for this behavior. Women stuck in toxic relationships because of a thousand micromoments where they didn't feel worthy of demanding what they deserved. Women seeking reassurance and deferring to those around them because they doubt their own knowing. Behind their symptoms often lies a state of fragmentation: the disavowal of an essential, witchy part of themselves.

Our culture has taught us that our mystical parts are unacceptable—shadow aspects to be ashamed of. So we suppress, molding ourselves into the acceptable form. But suppressed parts don't go down without a fight. Whether we examine this through Internal Family Systems—a therapeutic approach that works to integrate the different parts within us—or through a Freudian lens of making the unconscious conscious, the core principle remains the same. We need our wholeness. When we reject parts of ourselves, we become trapped in patterns of self-betrayal and fragmentation, unable to fully relax into ourselves.

Then there's the rudderlessness. So many of my patients are living their lives in their heads, cut off from their hearts, fumbling through life without the clarity and conviction that comes from embodied knowing. They can analyze every angle of a decision and fill an entire therapy session listing pros and cons, but they can't *feel* what's right for them. It's as if they have dropped their compass over the side of the boat, and it has plummeted into the depths. They look up at me with pleading eyes, as if they half expect me to make decisions for them. Unable to access guidance from within, they make choices from a frazzled, neurotic place. They can't sense their body's "yes" or "no," which keeps them stuck in the wrong relationships, unfulfilling careers, and patterns that drain their life force. With their deepest insights shut down and silenced, self-doubt proliferates. They believe the answers lie outside, rather than recognizing that they are the experts on themselves—and the only ones who can chart their own paths.

Many of my patients have learned how to play the game of life, appeasing the world while ignoring the rumblings of what is true for them inside. I think of Chaya, who spent decades in selfless service to everyone around her—managing her aging mother's care, supporting her husband's career moves, being the office mom and a short-order cook for her kids, and volunteering for every school committee. When she finally decided to set boundaries and reclaim her energy, she sat in my office and said, "I have no idea what *I* actually want." I see it in the successful type A's who have squeezed themselves into patriarchal models of success, and in the sensitive souls who carry crushing shame because they struggle to thrive. I believe this self-abandonment traces back to our disavowal of our woo-woo parts.

Perhaps the most heartbreaking effect of our estrangement from magic is when we miss the opportunity for an ongoing connection with deceased loved ones. I work with a woman whose father died when she was very young. She feels his presence regularly, but she dismisses these experiences because she feels foolish believing them. She desperately wants the comfort of that connection, but she talks herself out of it, shutting it down. Another patient has experienced multiple pregnancy losses and sometimes dreams about the spirits of her unborn babies. Though it would bring her immense comfort to believe that they're still in her life in some form, she discards these experiences as wishful thinking. With both patients, our work centers on beginning to trust what they sense—to stop betraying their own knowing just because our culture tells them it's unfounded.

This is what I want for everyone: Not to adopt my specific beliefs but to discover their own authentic relationship with mystery. To trust the soft voice of intuition when it speaks. To notice the signs and synchronicities weaving their way into our lives. To honor the dreams that arrive with messages and the gut feelings that know truths our minds haven't yet grasped. To understand that embracing our witchiness isn't about abandoning reason—it's about reclaiming the full spectrum of our intelligence.

THE SEASON OF THE WITCH

Why now, in this particular moment, are women being called to step out of hiding and reclaim our magical nature? The answer lies in a convergence of necessity and opportunity that has never existed before.

We're ready now because women are more platformed and empowered than ever. We have our own money and legal protections, we're living in the post–Me Too era, and women outperform men in college admission and graduation rates. Social media has created unprecedented forums for public conversation where we can carry one another forward, building networks of support that span the globe. Though it's going down kicking and screaming, the patriarchy is losing its stranglehold on power.

And beyond being resourced, we're simply done. Done being fragmented, done feeling "less than," done disavowing an essential part of ourselves. We're done apologizing for our intuitive gifts, done assuming that what comes naturally to us—our cyclical rhythms, our emotional intelligence, our capacity for seeing the whole picture, even our multi-tangent stories—is somehow wrong or inferior to the linear, rational way of being that our culture celebrates. We're done with the exhausting performance of being "low-maintenance," done with the self-betrayal and self-denial that has kept us small. We're done pretending that our sensitivity is weakness, that our embodied knowledge is somehow less valid than provable facts, that our way of moving through the world needs constant justification. The generation of women rising now refuses to continue hiding half of who we are to gain acceptance in a world that was never built for our wholeness.

There's another urgent reason why this moment demands our emergence: truth itself has become increasingly elusive. In an era of media manipulation, echo chambers, deepfake technology, and AI-generated videos and voices, we are living through an unprecedented assault on our ability to discern reality. Now more than ever, we need access to a different type of knowing—one that cuts through manufactured narratives. Our ability to sense beyond the surface and feel truth in our bodies becomes our protection against manipulation.

But perhaps even more urgently, now is the season of the witch because we cannot afford to wait any longer. The world desperately needs the wisdom and power that witches hold. Our planet is careening toward disaster precisely because we've privileged extraction over regeneration, competition over collaboration, rational analysis over the kind of attuned listening that can sense what the collective truly needs. We do not have the luxury of time to hesitate until it feels absolutely safe to come out of hiding, because we hold what the planet is sorely missing: reverence for nature and the fierce understanding, as mothers and caretakers of the world's children, that the most vulnerable populations must be considered and protected. When we reclaim our witchiness, we don't only heal ourselves; we model a different way of being. We need to emerge from hiding, speak our truth, and save what sits at the precipice of utter destruction before it's too late.

No pressure.

Each of us has a different role in the ecosystem of planetary healing. Some will serve marginalized communities or champion environmental causes. Some will create art to awaken cultural consciousness, some will be healers, while others will run for office. Some will force their way into boardrooms, bringing a feminine perspective to all-male tables, while others will bypass those tables and build their own boardrooms. Some will tend to their families—profoundly important work that shapes the future. But each of us needs to step into these roles as fully integrated witches: women who refuse the cultural conditioning that rational trumps intuitive; that we should be distracted and disconnected from our bodies; that doing matters more than being; that only the measurable is real; and that the individual exists separate from the collective. We must live rebelliously and reclaim the magic that these biases would steal from us.

THE RECLAMATION

When we reclaim our connection to magic, life becomes infused with purpose. We feel guided, able to sense the invisible currents steering us and able to access states of transcendence. We learn to trust our convictions and, for once, recognize what our hearts truly desire—this by itself is revolutionary for women who are conditioned to live tirelessly in service of others.

The transformation extends to our physical health as well. We attune to our bodies' communications, sensing what we need before symptoms become crises. We allow for the natural balance between activity and rest, giving and receiving. We stop betraying our bodies' signals in service of being "low-maintenance" and instead honor the complex, rhythmic symphony of the female body.

Trusting in magic helps us shift out of our anxious minds and into our hearts; out of fear and into love. And nothing could be more consequential. When enough of us emit the frequency of the heart, this creates a ripple effect of peace on the planet.

A magical orientation places us in a stance of reverence—toward the sacred intelligence of nature, the guidance of ancestors, the vast mystery of it all. From this place of humility and wonder, we stop grasping for control and learn to collaborate with forces infinitely greater than ourselves.

A connection to magic transforms how we navigate grief. Believing in my mom's continued existence didn't erase the devastation of loss, but it fundamentally altered my experience of it. Instead of drowning in a senseless, random universe, I found a way to feel an ongoing connection to her. In many ways, she is even more present in my moment-to-moment life now than when she lived a train ride away. I began to experience the truth in the words of the late poet Andrea Gibson: "Dying is the opposite of leaving. . . . I am more here than I ever was before."

When we begin to honor both our analytical and our intuitive intelligence, we access a fuller spectrum of our human capacity. It starts by inviting the witchy self back from where she was sent—cast out, lost, burned, abandoned, or shunned—and opening to her medicine. The woman who embraces her inner witch stops asking permission to know what she knows. She stops seeking constant external validation and starts trusting the elegant guidance system that lives within her. She becomes a woman dialed in to mystery—sensing, trusting, and drawing meaning from the universe's knowing wink.

I dream of a world where women move through life unapologetically trusting mystery. Where we're in constant dialogue with source, spirit, guides, and ancestors. Where we no longer shrink from what others dismiss as woo-woo. Where we find ourselves held by the loving intelligence that underlies all existence, and we touch rapture—that ecstatic recognition of being part of something vast and wondrous.

We are all witches. We always have been. When we reclaim our witchiness, we reclaim our birthright to a life of meaning and magic. The world is calling for this magic now—not Hollywood spells but the deep magic of women who know their worth, trust their intuition, and embrace the mystical without apology or shame.

This book is the story of how I learned to stop betraying myself in countless small ways and discovered that the parts of myself I'd been taught to disavow were actually gifts to be claimed, and the very foundation of my purpose. It's an invitation for you to reclaim those same gifts.

I understand I could be deluded. This could be a senseless, random universe. Perhaps when we die, in the blackout of nonexistence, it turns out there was nothing more than our material existence. That was it. If so, color me surprised! But for the journey between now and then, I'm getting immense comfort and guidance from my magical worldview. And I wish the same for you.

Don't miss the magic.

You are a witch. This is a magical universe. And it's time to come home to yourself.

Chapter 2

THE WITCH WOUND

> To conclude. All witchcraft comes from carnal lust, which is in women insatiable. . . . Wherefore for the sake of fulfilling their lusts they consort even with devils. . . . It is no matter for wonder that there are more women than men found infected with the heresy of witchcraft. . . . And blessed be the Highest Who has so far preserved the male sex from so great a crime.
>
> —HEINRICH KRAMER, *Malleus Maleficarum*

What images arise for you when you hear the word "witch"? Most likely, it's an older woman cloaked in black, hunched over a bubbling cauldron with a pointed hat and a broomstick nearby. Perhaps you see the three weird sisters from *Macbeth*, stirring their pot while chanting "Double, double toil and trouble," or the Wicked Witch of the West melting under Dorothy's water bucket. As Wiccan priestess and journalist Margot Adler observed in *Drawing Down the Moon*, "The very power of the word ['witch'] lies in its imprecision. It is not merely a word, but an archetype, a cluster of powerful images."

These images crystallized over centuries, shaped by fairy tales that warned children about women who lived alone in the woods, by Disney films that taught us to fear older women with gnarled features, and by Halloween costumes that reduced the witch to something cartoonish. This folklore isn't uniquely Western—across cultures, independent women with spiritual authority have been cast as dangerous. But nowhere has the witch archetype taken root quite like in the West. Even our modern entertainment continues this legacy, from the slapstick caricature of the Sanderson sisters in *Hocus Pocus*, which flattens Salem's tragedy into camp, to the subversive reimagining of Elphaba in *Wicked*—who dares to defy both gravity and societal expectations.

The cultural inheritance of the witch is a strange alchemy of entertainment and historical trauma. Our collective imagination blends Salem's gallows with Hogwarts, and the very real persecution of women with our fantasies about magical empowerment. The witch has simultaneously become the villain in our cautionary tales and the hero of our fantasies about being able to bend the world to our will. The layered mythology of witches captures our deepest anxieties about women who step outside prescribed roles and refuse control.

Understanding where our ideas about witches come from is the first step toward understanding what it might mean to reclaim the word.

THE SHADOW OF HISTORY

The very word "witch" reveals how the idea has been distorted over time. Some argue that it's originally from the Old English *wicce* (wise woman), a term of reverence for female healers. As Clarissa Pinkola Estés writes, "Like the word *wild*, the word *witch* has come to be understood as a pejorative, but long ago, it was an appellation given to both old and young women healers, the word *witch* deriving from the word *wit*, meaning wise." By the 1200s, church records had redefined "witch" as "heretic in league with the Devil"—a deliberate transformation of wisdom into wickedness.

As writer Elise Loehnen reflects in her book *On Our Best Behavior*, "A wizened woman clutching a cauldron and broom is who we commemorate in our Halloween costumes." Yet, Loehnen reminds us, "both artifacts are symbols of a housewife." The cauldron cooked meals and brewed healing teas. The broom swept floors. It was the ultimate weaponization of domesticity: turning the very tools of women's care and labor into evidence of their supposed evil. The old woman with her herbs and cats wasn't a supernatural menace but, often, a village healer, a midwife, or simply a woman who remained single by choice. The rebranding of these domestic artifacts became a way to mark as dangerous any woman who threatened existing power structures. Nonconformists, independent widows, rebellious women who wouldn't submit to the authority of church or state or doctor—all were recast as threats to be feared and cast out.

The witch hunts emerged from a perfect storm of social upheaval, plague, and the age-old need to find someone to blame. As Loehnen documents, the persecution began with the Inquisition's systematic targeting of anyone who questioned church authority. But when the bubonic plague ravaged Europe, killing between twenty-five and fifty million people, the need for scapegoats intensified. The plague was seen as divine punishment, and those deemed "other" became convenient targets for society's collective panic. Loehnen explains:

> The first hunted were the "crones," the wise women, the elders, typically widows who refused to remarry or had no options to do so. These women had long been the keepers of powerful traditions—they were the culture's healers, prophets, and midwives; they initiated young girls into the rites of womanhood; they mentored mothers; and they carried intergenerational stories and wisdom. But beginning in the middle of the fifteenth century (dramatically peaking from 1560 to 1760), these women, too old to be seen as sexual objects, and possessing knowledge and skills the church viewed as threatening, were persecuted as witches.

The 1486 treatise *Malleus Maleficarum* ("The Hammer of the Witches"), written by Dominican monk Heinrich Kramer, codified the persecution and provided detailed instructions for identifying, interrogating, and torturing suspected witches. Its central premise is that women are inherently more susceptible to the devil's influence due to their "lustfulness" and weak moral character. The document, though later condemned, spread like wildfire across Europe, becoming the blueprint for centuries of violence against women. The persecution also served economic interests: widowed women who inherited property became prime targets, as their executions allowed land to be handed over to male relatives or the church.

The witch hunts of Europe and colonial America claimed the lives of an estimated forty to sixty thousand people—predominantly women. But the psychological impact extended far beyond the direct victims. The message was clear: women who knew too much, healed too well, or saw too deeply were dangerous. The very qualities that had once made them respected healers and wisdom keepers became sources of suspicion and shame.

While European witch hunts represent a particularly violent expression of it, this pattern of suppressing women's healing powers isn't unique to Western history. Colonial expansion spread this perspective globally. Indigenous and non-Western cultures that once honored female healers—from curanderas in Latin America to shamans across various traditions—saw these practices undermined through colonization.

But the even more insidious inheritance had to do with the methodology of persecution. As Loehnen explains: "Female friendships were specifically targeted. . . . Under extreme torture, women were forced to betray each other—friends turned on friends, daughters their mothers." The ancient tradition of women supporting other women through life's passages was reframed as conspiracy. Loehnen muses, "I have to wonder if the emotional sediment of this is one of the reasons women today can be wary of each other and are often willing to watch each other get cut down."

Only three or four hundred years ago, women who displayed intuitive gifts were branded as witches and subjected to unthinkable violence. What we often frame as distant historical events—sanitized for Disney films or relegated to Halloween costumes—actually represent a living wound in our collective unconscious that survives in our language, power structures, and internalized shame. Each time a woman is dismissed as irrational or crazy, each time traditional healing practices are labeled "alternative" or unscientific, every time a woman mocks astrology or distances herself from the mystical, we witness the modern expression of this ancient suppression.

Somewhere in our cellular memory, many of us carry a faint knowing: in previous eras, bad things happened to women who saw in the dark. Some call this cellular memory the "witch wound," and I believe it manifests today as that subtle unease we feel when our inner knowing pushes against the boundaries of what's deemed acceptable. When we second-guess ourselves before sharing anything off-center, we feel the weight of generations of women who learned to silence their truth in order to stay safe.

From a more scientific perspective, trauma specialists understand how collective experiences can reverberate through generations. We carry this trauma in our DNA, in what researchers now recognize as epigenetic inheritance—the biological passing down of traumatic experiences through generations. (It's worth noting that, while epigenetic effects of trauma are well documented in animal studies, research on epigenetic inheritance in humans is still emerging, with evidence primarily coming from observational studies of populations exposed to stressors like famine and war.)

When we witness a woman undermining her knowing with "I don't know, I just feel like maybe . . . ," or when she experiences a flutter of unease before speaking about a hunch she can't logically prove, I believe she's feeling the ripples of this historical wound.

I see this frequently in my practice. Women will share insights or premonitions, then quickly retreat: "I'm sorry, I'm not usually into woo-woo things" or "I know this sounds crazy." While at first glance these might seem like innocuous social niceties, they're actually protective behaviors, unconscious attempts to avoid the fate of our forebears who dared to claim their intuitive power openly.

Understanding this historical context helps explain why the pressure to be "rational" feels so existentially threatening to many women. It's not just about fitting in, being taken seriously, or succeeding in our careers; somewhere in our collective psyche, there's a memory of much darker consequences for straying from accepted ways of knowing.

This is how we got here—to a place where we apologize for believing something we can't explain, where we've learned to dismiss ourselves before anyone else has the chance to. The witch wound runs so deep that we don't typically recognize it as a wound. We simply accept that rationality is superior, that logic trumps intuition, that whoever provides citations wins the argument.

The witch hunts established a template that endures: when women claim knowledge outside patriarchal authority or trust our bodies over institutions, we are perceived as a threat. We become witches. And witches, we learned, must hide. The witch trials may have ended, but the witch wound lives on in generations of women who learned to feel shame for their magic and disavow their true nature. We are the daughters of women who survived by hiding their light.

BOTH/AND

Contemporary scholarship often emphasizes an important insight: the women killed in witch hunts weren't practicing supernatural magic—they were simply women. Widows with property, healers whose herbs competed with emerging medical establishments. There were economic and political motives behind the persecution, and accusations of witchcraft served as convenient cover for seizing land and consolidating power.

But I bristle at how this narrative can swing too far toward dismissing women's actual power, as if pointing out the historical injustice requires secularizing women's abilities. The subtext often seems to be: "Of course these women weren't really witches, because magic isn't real." But what if both can be true? What if, at times, these women were targeted precisely because they *did* possess something genuinely powerful—expressions of the very embodied knowing and mystical connection that I believe *all* women carry?

Yes, they were "just women." And women, it turns out, can be pretty magical. The witch hunts succeeded in part because they made women themselves complicit in disowning their magic. Today, when we insist that historical "witches" had nothing magical about them, we are inadvertently perpetuating a materialist view—that this is a random universe, that belief in magic is foolish.

Perhaps the most accurate understanding holds space for both truths: these women were killed for being inconvenient to patriarchal systems, *and* they carried forms of knowing that were genuinely formidable.

IT'S NO ACCIDENT

The patriarchal campaign to cast magic as dangerous and woo-woo as foolish isn't accidental—it's a deliberate tactic of control. The cultural pressure to disavow certain parts of our feminine nature isn't some weird glitch in the zeitgeist. For women living in our modern, hyper-rational world, our intuitive intelligence, our connection to the mysterious and nonmaterial aspects of life—our magic—has been *systematically* diminished and downgraded. Convincing us to feel shame and self-doubt is a clever strategy to maintain the status quo.

Women come coded with a unique ability to tap into the subtler levels of life. This was once our primary intelligence—it was innate and ancient, a way of knowing that guided us through the centuries. And, in a way that changed the course of history, it was recognized as a threat.

So what was it about these abilities that provoked such fear?

A woman connected to her magic is inherently threatening to established power structures. Our ancestral mothers had access to guidance and conviction that made them impossible to control. After all, if a woman has a direct connection to source, what need does she have for religious intermediaries? Women who possessed knowledge of healing, midwifery, and natural medicine threatened the emerging male-dominated medical establishment. Women who lived independently challenged patriarchal control. If a woman trusts her own knowing, how easily will she submit to authority? A woman firmly rooted in her magical nature is neither easily swayed nor readily governed. She's a rebellious employee, a bad customer, a religious heretic, and a defiant wife. She stands as an obstacle to complete patriarchal control—too sovereign in her power to be easily dominated. Our ancestors' connection to the nonmaterial world gave them a quiet confidence, a power that existed outside the bounds of conventional authority.

The establishment response seems calculated: transform women's greatest strength into a source of shame. Through persecution and public humiliation, women's gifts were driven underground. Women were made to fear their own power, question their own knowing, and worse, scrutinize and betray one another's intuitive nature.

When our patriarchal society tells us belief in magic is foolish, what they actually mean is: they don't understand it, they can't control it, and it threatens their power.

As author and therapist Dené Logan writes in *Sovereign Love*, "I don't believe that any of the ways society conditions women to self-abandon are a coincidence." Intuition and mystical wisdom have always threatened the patriarchy precisely because they can't be controlled through physical dominance or rational argument. In response, those in power have discredited healers, stripped credentials from midwives, and violently suppressed those who worshipped nature during religious rites, branding them as devil worshippers. As a result, we've been taught to believe that true healing comes only from those in white coats with prescription pads and industry-approved guidelines, and that spirituality should be mediated through male-dominated organizations.

What's most insidious about this dynamic isn't the skepticism from those around us—it's how deeply we've internalized it. Many women carry a persistent, low-grade shame about their latent woo-woo tendencies. We've learned to second-guess ourselves, to apologize for our beliefs before anyone has a chance to challenge them. We've wholeheartedly adopted the belief that rational thought is superior to intuition, never questioning why we've learned to deny these essential parts of ourselves. Like a fish unaware of water, we never see the invisible conditioning all around us. But it's there, privileging evidence over intuitive knowing and keeping us disconnected from our magical inheritance. Our estrangement from magic has been an act of survival and self-preservation in a world built by and for men. While the overt persecution has ended, every time we silence our intuition for fear of being dismissed or ridiculed, we're responding to this ancient wound that lives on in our collective psyche.

WHAT IT MEANS TO BE A WITCH TODAY

If we're all witches—as I believe we are—then what does that actually mean? When I claim this identity for myself and invite you to do the same, I'm not talking about the Hollywood version of witchcraft with wands and spell casting, or even the religious practice of Wicca, though

I deeply respect that spiritual tradition. I'm talking about something more fundamental: reclaiming a way of being that our culture has taught us to abandon.

In my understanding, a witch is a woman who has stepped back into the fullness of her intelligence. She has learned to inhabit multiple ways of knowing simultaneously. While she can draw on her rational mind as needed, she also trusts the wisdom that flows through her from sources she can't name or prove. She moves through the world embodied and receptive, noticing the magic that shows up in even the most mundane moments.

The modern witch isn't necessarily living deep in the forest or mixing potions by moonlight—though she may be. She's the executive who pauses before signing a contract because something in her body signals, "Wait." The mother who senses her child's distress hours before any outward signs appear. The friend who calls you at the exact moment you need her. She's the descendant who dialogues with her ancestors during prayer, and the artist whose creations channel something from the beyond. She is every woman who notices the intricate web of connections running through her seemingly ordinary life.

A witch is someone who sees through the cultural conditioning and calls BS. She recognizes that we've been pushed to disconnect from our bodies and stay constantly distracted. She knows that we've been taught to believe that only what can be measured and proven deserves our trust. A witch understands that these messages are lies designed to protect a broken status quo. She reclaims the very qualities our culture has taught us to dismiss—her intuition, her presence and embodied wisdom, her cyclical nature, her connection to mystery, and her interconnectedness with all beings. Rather than choosing one way of knowing over another, she integrates them all, moving fluidly between rational analysis and intuitive guidance, between doing and being, between the measurable and the magical.

Being a witch means reclaiming sovereignty over her own body and trusting that she is the ultimate authority on what she needs, especially when faced with systems—political, institutional—that claim to know better. While she remains open to feedback and insights from those around her, she doesn't constantly seek counsel or reassurance from others because she has developed conviction in her inner compass. She's begun to notice that anytime she overrules her intuition—whether with pure cerebral logic or outsourced advice—she is led astray.

A witch experiences guidance. She feels when something larger orchestrates events—the goose bumps of recognition when greater forces seem to be pulling the strings. She sees what I call the wink of the universe—those moments of synchronicity and uncanny coincidence that leave us in awe. She has learned to trust and surrender to this presence, spinning meaning from life's unfoldings. This doesn't mean she bypasses straight to "everything happens for a reason," but that she can derive lessons and growth from events that might otherwise feel random or unwelcome.

Most importantly, a witch is open to the mystery of existence. She knows there's more to reality than what can be explained. She understands that her intentions and where she directs her life force can influence events, and she wants to use this power for good—to help shift the planet out of extraction and toward regeneration, out of fear and into love.

A witch's power is gentle yet tremendous, like water wearing away stone. Her power doesn't seek to dominate but to connect—to source, to nature, to those around her. When I say source, I mean the infinite essence from which all existence arises—what some might call the divine, universal consciousness, or the fundamental fabric of the universe. A witch is intertwined with nature itself, taking her cues from its rhythms—the turning of the seasons and the phases of the moon that mirror the tides of her own body.

I invite you to consider "witch" even more broadly, as an archetypal energy within women that has always existed but has been made taboo. A current within us that has been written off as dark or dangerous, ugly and villainous, precisely because it's powerful and difficult to control.

The witch is an aspect of the feminine psyche where the shadowy, hard-to-fathom parts of women's wisdom reside. It is the part of us that is more yin—inward, sensing, and receptive—rather than bright, productive, efficient yang. It's home to our intuition and our innate belonging to the world of spirit. It is the part of us that is connected to the invisible realms.

A witch approaches life from a place of reverence and humility. She can hold the full spectrum of human experience, touching the depths of grief while maintaining an unshakable trust in the larger order. This is what true witchiness looks like: not an escape from reality but a deeper way of being in it.

Chapter 3

MEN ARE RIGHT, WOMEN ARE CRAZY (OR SO WE BELIEVE)

The heart has its reasons which reason knows nothing of.

—BLAISE PASCAL, *Pensées*

At the root of our severing from magic is our unconscious belief that rational, linear thinking—characteristic of the left hemisphere of the brain—represents the gold standard of intelligence, while intuitive knowing—characteristic of the right hemisphere—is dismissed as airy-fairy delusion. We've absorbed this hierarchy so completely that we police ourselves, second-guessing our gut instincts and apologizing for sounding too woo-woo. We've learned to worship at the altar of data and logic as the only true way of knowing. Once you start to see how thoroughly this bias has colonized your mind—how often you dismiss your own wisdom in favor of what sounds more "reasonable"—you'll begin to spot it everywhere.

INTUITION: THE WITCH'S COMPASS

At the heart of witchiness lies our relationship with intuition. While intuition is often reduced to sophisticated pattern recognition or elevated to some rare psychic gift, I believe it's actually a universal and innate ability.

Scientists would say that intuition is nothing more than the brain's ability to detect patterns and synthesize information below the threshold of conscious awareness—that it delivers insights that only *seem* to arise from nowhere. Yet I experience it as something more mystical: a bridge between our conscious minds and the larger intelligence that flows through all existence. Whether we call that larger intelligence source, the divine, or simply the subtle wisdom of our bodies, intuition is how we access guidance that transcends what our rational minds can compute.

Some neuroscience points to the possibility that intuition has to do with picking up on signals from the right hemisphere of the brain. I think of the right hemisphere as a receiver, constantly detecting body signals and environmental cues, while the left hemisphere acts as the interpreter, demanding logical explanations. The witchy woman has learned to honor her right hemisphere's insights without reflexively letting her left brain dismiss them as illogical.

Intuition speaks through physical sensations, such as the tightness in our stomach when something feels off, or the expansion or warmth in our chest when something feels right. It communicates through dreams, through images popping into our awareness, through the stream of consciousness that flows when we put pen to paper.

The witch understands that this internal guidance system is as valid and valuable as any data set. She has learned to feel the difference between anxiety (which contracts) and intuitive warning (which expands even as it alerts). She knows the distinction between ego-driven desires (which have a grasping quality) and soul-level guidance (which arrives with a sense of peace, even when it's pointing toward something challenging).

The woman who embraces her inner witch can stop seeking constant external counsel, because she has started trusting this elegant internal compass. Intuition is a little piece of source consciousness that exists within us, waiting to be acknowledged and trusted. Ever present yet inexplicable, I think of intuition as the gateway drug to magic.

INSTRUMENTS OVER INSTINCTS

The low murmur of Sunday afternoon chatter filled the café as Mark and Audrey settled their tab. Audrey hesitated before signing the check, her mind momentarily blank at the prospect of calculating 15 percent. She turned to Mark, who confidently produced the number without a second thought. It was a small moment, barely worth noticing, but it was representative of so many exchanges in their relationship.

Later that evening, they were having dinner with another couple when the conversation turned to music. "What kind of music are you into?" their friend asked.

Mark cleared his throat and responded, "Audrey's into show tunes," and was that a slight smirk that crossed his face? "Not my thing." He continued, "I'm into jazz—but Audrey doesn't *get* jazz." The casual dismissal stung. Why was it that he was allowed to simply *dislike* her music, while her lack of enthusiasm for his meant she didn't *get* it? As if musical taste were a matter of intelligence rather than preference. After a glass of wine, Audrey was feeling animated. She launched into a story about an eventful subway commute. As she incorporated entertaining anecdotes and multiple side references, Mark interrupted her with a nudge, "Land the plane, Aud."

This subtle pattern had been running in the background of their relationship for years, but it became most pronounced during Audrey's pregnancy. At thirty-four weeks, she began experiencing what she could only describe as a deep bodily knowing that something was wrong. Not cramping, not bleeding—nothing the pregnancy books warned about. Just an insistent nudge from somewhere deeper than logic that said, *Pay attention.*

When she brought her concerns to Mark, he pulled up her latest test results on his phone. "Look at the numbers, Aud. Everything's normal. Your blood pressure was fine, protein levels were good. The data says you're fine." Mark's background as an aerospace engineer had trained him to trust instruments over instincts. "You're just anxious because, you know . . . pregnancy hormones."

But Audrey's unease only intensified. When she pressed her doctor for additional monitoring, he was initially dismissive. "You were just here, and everything looked great."

The subtext was clear: she was being hormonal, anxious, high-strung, needy. They might as well have called her hysterical.

Partly out of caution, and partly because dismissing a pregnant patient carries medicolegal risks, Audrey's obstetrician agreed to bring her in. It turned out her blood pressure was concerningly high. She was sent straight from his office to the hospital with preeclampsia—a condition that could have had grave consequences if left undetected. As she was watching her nurse place an IV, Audrey felt a strange cocktail of emotions: fear for the outcome, vindication in her intuition, shame for being seen as hysterical, and indignant rage that everyone had dismissed her.

In the end, Audrey and her baby were both fine. But she remained troubled by the lasting effect of having her intuitive knowing dismissed. She'd been written off by her medical provider and her husband. She had even doubted herself for a fleeting moment. Yet she knew she wasn't hysterical. Pregnant and more attuned than ever to her body's signals, she had seen through the veil. And she'd been right—like a modern-day Cassandra, cursed to speak truths that others refused to hear.

What infuriated Audrey wasn't just the dismissal of her knowing, but how the world around her continued to validate Mark's rationality while pathologizing her intuition. When they would tell friends the birth story, the emphasis was always on the wonders of modern obstetrics—how they were able to save Audrey and the baby just in time. While it was miraculous indeed, the dissonance was maddening: here was concrete proof of Audrey's ability to listen to subtle messages from within, yet her husband and doctors reframed the entire experience as simply a triumph of modern medicine.

THE CASSANDRA COMPLEX

In Greek mythology, Cassandra was gifted with the power of prophecy by Apollo, but when she rejected his advances, he cursed her so that no one would believe her predictions, even though they always came true. The Cassandra complex describes the psychological phenomenon of experiencing accurate intuitive insights that are disbelieved. Like the mythical Cassandra, many women find themselves trapped in a maddening cycle: they see clearly and speak truthfully, yet they're met with skepticism, patronization, or outright dismissal. The complex captures the frustration of being right but unheard, and hints at the toll of living in a world that consistently invalidates subtler ways of knowing.

PASS THE TEST

This dynamic isn't unique to Audrey's relationship—it belongs to countless women who have learned to doubt their way of knowing the world. We live in a culture that has spent centuries telling us that the rational way of perceiving truth is the only valid option. The "smart" people, we are told, are the ones who can quickly calculate tips in their heads and cite double-blind studies. Those of us who feel energy, who read signs in the stars, who sense patterns in seeming coincidences? We're dismissed as ungrounded. So we second-guess ourselves and feel "less than" when compared with our rational counterparts. And beyond the resentment lies an insidious sense of shame about our connection to anything mystical, magical, or woo-woo.

I remember sitting across from a medical fellowship interviewer, his suit pressed, his smile professionally calibrated. The fluorescent lights hummed overhead, casting that familiar institutional glow that made everything feel just a bit dystopian. When he asked how I typically made clinical decisions, pen poised above his notepad, I had the passing awareness that I was more guided by intuition than I cared to admit: that I sense the undercurrents in a situation, feel the rightness or wrongness of a choice in my body before my mind can articulate why. I thought of all the times my "irrational" hunches had proven right, how my intuition had guided me through complex problems like a compass pointing true north.

But I knew better than to say any of this. I'd learned that words like "intuition" and "feeling" were coded feminine, dismissed as soft and unreliable. People in positions of power in our culture want algorithms, not instincts.

So I straightened in my chair and delivered what I knew he wanted to hear: "I take a data-driven approach, reviewing the medical literature and letting evidence guide my clinical decisions." I watched his face brighten with approval, pen scratching across the page. I'd passed the test, proven myself suitably logical, appropriately disconnected from those messy, mystical ways of knowing.

Looking back, that interview was the culmination of years of learning how to "pass the test." In her seminal book *The Heroine's Journey*, Maureen Murdock talks about the conditioning of being a "father's daughter"—how a woman grows up observing her father's power and prestige, and she wants that for herself. So she contorts herself to mimic his way of being. Our culture still equates a "good mind" with traditionally masculine traits such as logical thinking and analytical precision. Meanwhile, intuitive wisdom—what we've long called "a mother's intuition"—gets treated as somehow less legitimate. Even if we don't consciously shape our persona to fit this model, we all absorb the message that rational qualities are intrinsically more valuable.

Many of the qualities we valorize as drivers of society—linear thinking, analytical rigor—have long been associated with masculinity. During the Enlightenment, when objective reasoning was held up as the supreme path to truth, empirical evidence became the holy grail of civilization. But you don't need to take a tour of ancient history to see examples of this pervasive bias. In everyday life, we nod approvingly at a slide deck with data-driven information. We're persuaded by a TED

Talk when evidence is cited from the medical literature. We gravitate to podcasts offering solutions that are backed by science—better yet, through double-blind, placebo-controlled trials.

When it comes to something counter to these qualities—say, anecdotal evidence or Indigenous knowledge—we draw back, arms crossed, eyebrows raised. Should someone share their hunch about what to do in a tricky bind—that's when the smirks come in. It remains common in mixed-gender settings for the group to nod in agreement with the logical, unemotional man while subtly dismissing—or even scorning—the sensitive, emotion-forward woman next to him. And it's often women who are the first to pile on.

Unless you've been fortunate enough to be raised in some kind of matriarchal coven, or maybe Northern California, you likely know this pressure yourself. For most of us, the journey through early childhood, into education, and out into the workplace involves constantly learning that she who arrives at her conclusion with objective evidence wins.

THE NEUROSCIENCE OF KNOWING: WHEN LEFT BELIEVES IT'S "RIGHT"

The bias toward rational thinking over intuitive knowing is wired into how our brains work. When I discovered the work of Dr. Iain McGilchrist, British psychiatrist and author of *The Master and His Emissary*, I finally understood our culture's worship of rational thinking, and why that creates such internal conflict for some of us. Our society has been constructed on a cultural preference for left-brain thinking—a preference that has reinforced itself over time by creating institutions that reward rational thinking, making that the ultimate measure of intelligence.

McGilchrist's scholarship reveals that our brain hemispheres not only perform different functions but have fundamentally different ways of experiencing the world. The left hemisphere focuses on details, categorizes information, and excels at linear thinking. It's the part of our brain that helps us analyze data, follow step-by-step instructions, and create systems. It thrives on explicit instruction and logical sequences.

This is the part of our brain that has given us the triumphs of the rational age—scientific advancements, technology, medicine, and the understanding of the material universe. It gives us the ability to calculate a 15 percent tip on the fly. Through the power of logical, data-driven thinking, humans have had breakthroughs that have helped eradicate diseases, extend lifespans, and create technologies that would seem like magic to our ancestors.

The right hemisphere, in contrast, sees the big picture. It understands context, makes unexpected connections, and grasps the implicit. It excels at pattern recognition, helps us make sense of complex systems, and learns by experience, not instruction. It's the hemisphere that fires up when a composer assembles musical notes into a unified symphony. It's also key to our emotional intelligence, allowing us to pick up on subtle cues, read between the lines in social situations, and connect deeply with others.

The right hemisphere traffics in realms too profound to be neatly described in words. It does not have the same command of words as the left hemisphere, so it speaks the language of metaphor, myth, and imagery. This is why art, music, and storytelling can often convey revelations that logical arguments can't reach—they are accessing the ineffable insights of the right hemisphere. As Jill Bolte Taylor describes in her TED Talk "My Stroke of Insight," when a stroke temporarily silenced her left hemisphere, she found herself immersed in "the enormous collage of the present moment . . . connected to the energy all around" her. With her left brain's linear thinking and incessant "I am" narration quieted, she entered a wordless awareness of interconnection, timelessness, and peace. It's as though the right hemisphere translates the deeper truths of the universe, while the left hemisphere gatekeeps those insights to preserve our ability to function in our quotidian lives. After all, it's hard to do your taxes while contemplating the nondual nature of reality.

McGilchrist describes a crucial characteristic of the left hemisphere: *It believes it's right.* It is characterized by certainty and a tendency to deny, dismiss, and rationalize away information that doesn't fit its existing model of the world. The right hemisphere, in contrast, is more open to new information and more comfortable with ambiguity. As McGilchrist explains further, "The left hemisphere tends to be much more sure of itself, beyond anything that the evidence would support, whereas the right hemisphere tends, if anything, to be particularly aware that it might be mistaken—even though it is much more likely to be correct."

Most crucially, the left hemisphere speaks on behalf of both hemispheres. It dominates expressive language, while the right hemisphere struggles to articulate its insights verbally. Or, as McGilchrist puts it, "the left hemisphere is the speaking hemisphere. The right hemisphere has literally no voice."

In other words, the left hemisphere not only dismisses the diffuse metaphorical insights of the right hemisphere, it goes on to mansplain them away.

One interesting difference between male and female brains is that female brains, on average, show more functional connectivity across the corpus callosum, the bridge connecting the left and right hemispheres. That is to say, we have more communication between the logical left and the intuitive right. The implications of these differences are complex, and it is difficult to draw firm conclusions. But research suggests that while male brains are optimized for *intra*hemispheric communication—stronger connections within each hemisphere—female brains are optimized for *inter*hemispheric communication, integrating the analytical with the intuitive. Translation: men's brains are wired for single-mode tasks, while women may be more naturally oriented toward connecting the dots between different types of thinking.

This tidbit of neuroscience is actually a powerful metaphor for what witches can bring to our world. While the male brain is "structured to facilitate connectivity between perception and coordinated action" (think: catching a Frisbee, backing into a parking space), women's brains have different strengths. In the researchers' words, "female brains are designed to facilitate communication between analytical and intuitive processing modes." I find myself wondering if this connectivity may position us to more easily bridge the material and the mysterious.

This kind of integrated intelligence is beginning to be valued across all sectors, including in traditionally left-brain industries. As Jensen Huang, CEO of NVIDIA (a leading tech company) explains: "My personal definition of smart is someone who sits at that intersection of being technically astute . . . and having the ability to infer the unspoken . . . [to] feel the vibe . . . and the vibe came from a combination of data, analysis, first principle, life experience, wisdom, sensing other people." Huang goes on to describe this type of intelligence as the seemingly preternatural ability to "see around corners."

In many ways, the left hemisphere represents a more yang way of knowing—the ability to assess situations and arrive at clear-cut answers through analysis and logic. The right hemisphere embodies a more yin way of knowing—it deals in the ineffable aspects of life, speaking through myth, imagery, and intuitive hits. But because the right hemisphere lacks language, it cannot advocate for its own insights. This is where witches have a potential role: we can serve as stewards of the right hemisphere's wisdom, committed to translating its holistic insights into the world of words and action.

On the microcosmic level within our own brains, the left hemisphere dominates and silences the right. On the macrocosmic level, this same pattern plays out in our relationships and in society: Mark's data trumps Audrey's intuition, and our hyperrational culture devalues the ineffable ways of knowing. When faced with complex issues, the left hemisphere is often impatient to arrive at a simple conclusion. When presented with ambiguous, mystical insights, the cultural response is reflexive dismissal. Just like the left hemisphere itself, our culture lacks the neurological compunction that might cause it to question its certainty. But as witches, we can listen for the nudges from the right hemisphere saying, "Actually, it's not so simple."

The ability to incorporate the insights of the right hemisphere becomes even more crucial as we enter the age of artificial intelligence. AI represents the ultimate expression of left-brain thinking. As it increasingly takes over left-brain tasks, the right-hemisphere capacities that AI cannot replicate become even more precious: intuition, diffuse awareness, and connection to the mysterious. Our witchy ways of knowing may be among the last uniquely human abilities.

Of course, both men and women possess each form of intelligence. But Western culture increasingly reinforces the rational worldview. The story of patriarchal and capitalist society might be read as the triumph of left-brain dominance, leading to the marginalization of right-brain wisdom. This profound imbalance has left witchy women questioning our intuition and feeling a sense of inferiority about our ways of knowing.

To reclaim our inner witch, we must stop gatekeeping our own right-hemisphere insights. We need to cultivate trust in the wisdom that flows through our corpus callosum—those flashes of knowing that our left brains can't immediately explain. The same dynamic that plays out between our hemispheres repeats across every level: left hemisphere silences right hemisphere, rational overrules intuitive, doctors override healers, simple explanations overshadow the ineffable. In each case, the louder, more verbal, more socially validated force drowns out the quieter, more subtle, but often wiser way of knowing. As witches, we must recognize this pattern and refuse to participate in our own silencing. We must stand firm in honoring both dimensions of human intelligence.

HOW CAN IT BE REAL?

The right hemisphere understands the whole picture with wisdom, but struggles to articulate those insights in words. This is why practices that work through metaphor—storytelling, poetry, dream interpretation, tarot, and astrology—can be so powerful. They open up lines of communication with our right brain.

The right hemisphere can't tell us directly what it knows, but it can generate an image or a feeling. When a tarot card presents you with a picture and you feel a certain way about what you see, that automatic response may be your right hemisphere speaking in its wordless way.

Left-brain folks often dismiss these practices as having no basis. They point out that professional astrologers can't reliably guess people's star signs, thinking Q.E.D.—they've won the argument. But if you're thinking of tarot and astrology as fortune-telling, you're asking the wrong question. The question that matters is not "How can it be real?" but instead "Can it benefit us?" I believe it can, because it creates an inroad to what we subtly know but struggle to articulate. What we call magic may simply be a conduit to the right side of our brain.

KEEPING OURSELVES HONEST

Before we go further, I want to pause to acknowledge something important: there is such a thing as going too far toward believing in magic. Opening to mystery can run the risk of ascribing significance to every coincidence, leading us into delusional belief systems where we make major life decisions based on signs that may not be there. If you're someone who's already overindexed on right-hemisphere, magical thinking—if you tend toward the dreamy and whimsical, or find yourself dismissing practical concerns in favor of mystical interpretations—these are beautiful qualities, but you might benefit from a bit more grounding. Perhaps you'd find value in balancing some of your hunches with left-brain analysis and concrete considerations. We would all do well to meet somewhere in the middle.

I also want to clear something up: there's nothing inherently wrong with left-hemisphere thinking or the gifts of rational analysis. The Enlightenment's emphasis on logic and scientific method has given us extraordinary advances. The left and right hemispheres are equally valid—that's the point. The issue isn't that left-brain thinking is bad—it's that we've been culturally skewed toward these values for several centuries, creating an imbalance. My call to reclaim our inner witch isn't a refutation of analytical thinking but rather an invitation to *restore balance* by appreciating the value of right-hemisphere wisdom. We all benefit from both: the sharp focus of logic and the expansive vision of intuition.

But the reality for most women is that we've been living in the wake of decades of learning to silence our intuition. We feel shame for our woo-woo inclinations, and this is causing us to feel less-than while missing out on the potential magic in our lives—the guidance, comfort, transcendence, and ongoing connection with mystery that could enrich our existence. Whenever we get lost in either extreme, we can always return to the yin-yang symbol, which reminds us of the essential balance between mystery and materiality, intuition and data, right-hemisphere sensing and left-hemisphere reasoning. The goal isn't to abandon logic but to reclaim the wisdom we've been taught to dismiss.

We also need to keep ourselves honest about what we're actually experiencing. It's easy to mistake overthinking for intuition. I'm someone who thinks through every possible outcome of a situation—if there's an eventuality, I've probably considered it. When something I anticipated actually comes to pass, it's tempting to think, *Whoa, I intuited that!* But let's be real: if you've thought of *everything*, of course some of your thoughts will line up with what unfolds. This is not psychic ability but a simple probability effect. When you generate enough predictions, some are bound to line up with reality due to chance alone. True intuitive knowing feels different from anticipating myriad possibilities; it's more like a quiet certainty that arises from the body rather than through exhaustive mental calculation.

Beyond mistaking analysis for intuition, there's another way we can go astray in our relationship with mystery. An openness to magic is not about spiritual bypassing or claiming that everything happens for a reason. As Kate Bowler—writer, historian, and professor at Duke Divinity School who faced stage-four cancer at age thirty-five—powerfully articulates in her work, the "everything happens for a reason" narrative can be a cruel oversimplification of life's deepest sorrows. Through her own confrontation with mortality, she discovered that true faith isn't about finding neat explanations for suffering but about holding both the beautiful and the terrible at once.

I believe we need both medicines: the ability to sit with pain and difficulty without trying to make it okay, and the capacity to make meaning from the unfoldings of our lives. We may never know why there are horrible tragedies or why there is suffering. We have to be okay with that remaining unknowable. And yet, as Bowler wisely concludes, life can still feel deeply meaningful.

WHEN LEFT RULES THE WORLD

Our culture values left-hemisphere rationality in ways that create hidden hierarchies, which show up in how we choose our careers and nudge our children along their paths.

Consider this: in a viral video of a kindergarten classroom, a teacher asks students to draw a firefighter, a pilot, and a surgeon. Predictably, all the children—boys and girls alike—draw men. Then come the visitors: a firefighter, pilot, and surgeon file in, all women. The children's surprise creates a heartwarming moment to focus on gender equality and representation.

But beneath this seemingly progressive message lies a deeper inequity. While we owe immense gratitude to the women who fought for our right to enter these professions, the underlying message remains troubling: traditionally male professions are framed as inherently more valuable, more prestigious, more worth aspiring to. This messaging suggests that now that women have proven ourselves to be "just as good as men," we should naturally gravitate toward historically male professions. After all, these roles command higher salaries and greater respect.

But what if we've gotten the equation backwards? What we label as better or more important work has not necessarily been harder or more valuable—just more left-brain, and therefore more prestigious in our patriarchal world.

Our society systematically places higher value on left-brain professions while undervaluing right-brain contributions. Caregiving, social work, and being an art teacher are less remunerative than banking, accounting, and software engineering. But are they truly less important? Or are they simply less left-brain? Perhaps a good metric for a profession's worth might be: How difficult is the work, how high are the stakes, and how essential is it to society? Consider childcare. Have you ever taken care of children for eight straight hours? If there was ever a skilled and difficult job that is critical to society, it's that.

The evidence of this warped valuation system surrounds us: when traditionally male professions become predominantly female—like psychology, pediatrics, or public relations—salaries decline in lockstep.

Meanwhile, when traditionally female work like cooking in professional kitchens becomes male dominated, we see the rise of celebrity chefs (with gilded salaries to match). When female-dominated fields like teaching *remain* predominantly female, they remain undervalued. Yet traditionally masculine fields that continue to be male dominated, like orthopedic surgery and finance, maintain their high status and compensation. Though these are only correlations, it would seem that our society inadvertently devalues work as it becomes associated with women.

This diminishment of female-associated activities shows up in the stories we tell our children where the "exceptional" female protagonist is celebrated specifically for rejecting traditional feminine interests in favor of masculine pursuits—she's praised for choosing swordplay over embroidery, battle skills over debutante balls. I love to cheer on Mulan and Merida as much as anyone, but I can't help but notice that these narratives subtly reinforce the idea that masculine traits and ambitions are inherently more worthy, while dismissing traditionally feminine interests as unimportant or limiting.

While we think we've been progressing toward freedom, over time, the "shoulds" of gender roles have merely shifted, not disappeared. Whereas in the 1950s we told girls they "should" be ladylike, today's girls get the memo that they "should" be engineers. Modern parents feel a certain self-righteous pride anytime we arrive at the girl's birthday party with a STEM toy rather than a doll. Though we're making progress, we're still just replacing one "should" with another. And I can't help but notice the trend among grown women toward hobbies like needlepoint and crochet—as though they've had enough of pretending that they prefer swordplay.

We can't ignore that our system remunerates masculine professions more generously, so it's only logical that well-meaning adults will push girls into STEM fields to help ensure their financial security. But here is a radical suggestion: What if, instead of putting the burden of the "should" du jour on young girls, we valued all passions and interests? What if, instead of forcing girls into careers or hobbies that we believe are better, we paid caregivers, social workers, and teachers what their work is truly worth? If we could rectify our cultural bias toward left-brain thinking, then people could follow their calling without economic or social penalty.

Each time we nudge someone away from their authentic interests toward what society deems prestigious or valuable, we systematically train them to lose connection with themselves—and by extension, their intuition and inner witch. The path to equality isn't about "shoulding" women out of their interests, nor is it about losing ground and forcing women back into "tradwife" roles. Rather, it's about recognizing and properly valuing all forms of contribution to society—whether they align with left- or right-brain strengths—and ensuring all choices carry a reasonable amount of dignity and worth.

Rebalancing our cultural bias toward rationality requires:

- Valuing both analytical and intuitive intelligence equally
- Decoupling left-hemisphere skills from prestige and pay
- Stopping the systematic undervaluing of caregiving fields
- Paying nurturing professions commensurate with their true difficulty, skill, and value
- Dropping all the "shoulds" and honoring whatever passions arise

The devaluation of right-brain interests and callings has led countless women to find themselves in adulthood with objectively successful careers, yet feeling miles away from their authentic passions—often unable to even remember what once sparked their joy and sense of purpose. The path back to reclaiming that inner knowing can feel uncertain when we've spent years learning to dismiss our deepest yearnings as impractical or somehow less-than.

BALANCING LEFT AND RIGHT

In the early years of raising their daughter, Audrey and Mark would clash over parenting decisions: how to approach mealtime struggles, sleep training, even when to give Tylenol. Mark always had firm, outspoken opinions backed by research, while Audrey relied on intuitive senses guiding her choices. At times, Audrey considered defending her perspective. But Mark's arguments were impeccable—fortified with citations from medical journals, delivered with the kind of authority that makes dissent feel foolish. Audrey began to feel that every conversation about her intuitive insights ended the same way. Like the left hemisphere dismissing the right, Mark didn't see their differences as equally valid viewpoints—to him, there was only right and wrong, rational and irrational. So Audrey stayed silent. Over the years, her voice grew quieter, and the weight of shame for her way of knowing grew heavier.

But silencing our intuitive wisdom comes at a tremendous cost—not just to individual women like Audrey, but to our collective capacity for wisdom. The complex challenges we face today—from environmental crisis to mental health epidemics—cannot be solved through purely rational approaches. They require us to sense the patterns, to understand the whole rather than just the parts. I'm not saying the solution is to reject rationality, but rather, to reclaim the full spectrum of our intelligence. When we begin to honor both our analytical and our intuitive intelligence, we access a fuller range of our human capacity.

In the rare instances when Mark and Audrey were able to integrate Mark's data with Audrey's instincts, they made their best and most harmonious decisions. We can only imagine what might shift if leaders around the globe learned to integrate data with embodied insights. This journey starts with noticing each moment when we silence our deeper knowing—when we shrink inward as the brute force of logic threatens to undermine our intuition. And it continues each time we voice our right-hemisphere insights. True wisdom comes from integration, not division.

PART II

THE FIVE PRACTICES

The women who sit on the couch of my psychiatric practice are grappling with a fundamental disconnection from their own knowing. They can rationalize their way through decisions but can't *feel* what's right for them. They doubt themselves, and they rarely feel they've arrived at a place of conviction, contentment, or self-worth.

As I trace this unease back to its source, I find the same root cause surfacing again and again: a centuries-old elevation of cerebral analysis over embodied knowing—one that has driven us toward relentless productivity, seeded distrust in anything that can't be measured, and convinced us that we're separate from one another and from the earth. This shift created five fundamental biases that now invisibly shape how we move through the world. To reclaim our witchiness—to integrate both logic and the wisdom that arises from subtler sources—we must actively resist each one.

FIRST PRACTICE: EMBODIMENT

Our Culture Wants Us Dissociated. A Witch Is Embodied.

From the moment I entered puberty, I carried a premonition of my mother's death. For some twenty years, this knowing lived in my body—a shadow I couldn't explain but couldn't shake. It felt like remembering the ending of a movie I'd already seen—a hair-standing-on-end certainty that I somehow knew how this story would unfold. I'd have flashes of visions: car accidents, ambulance lights refracted through raindrops on windshields. I developed rituals—I had to tell her "Drive safely, see you later, I love you" before any trip, feeling as if my words were the only thing holding back an oracle from coming due. In middle school, I had constant anxiety about her safety, compulsively praying for her safe return from even the most mundane outings—her commute from work, a trip to the grocery store. Decades later, when she passed—suddenly, without warning—it felt *familiar*, something my cells had long anticipated.

In the years since, as I've grappled with questions of consciousness, spirit, and what lies beyond our material understanding, I've come to see that our bodies are exquisitely sensitive instruments—radio receivers capable of tuning in to frequencies that seem to defy time and space. Though most of us have learned to dismiss these signals, trading embodied wisdom for the supposed reliability of rational thought, I've reopened the case. Perhaps our bodies, the most material aspect of our existence, may be the very instrument through which we connect to the immaterial.

This kind of inexplicable bodily knowing isn't unique to premonitions of loss. This is the body speaking in its native tongue. The body can't talk, but, in my experience, it has a lot to say. Its language is one of somatic sensations—a vocabulary of expansion and contraction, tension and ease, warmth and chill. Our bodies are constantly sending these signals: We say yes to a project at work, and our body immediately contracts, communicating a clear "no" in its own language; that knot in your stomach during a conversation with a co-dependent family member or while hearing a misleading sales pitch; the subtle ease in your chest when you're finally on the right path; the goose bumps on your arms when someone's words ring true. These sensations are our first language, our most direct line to intuitive knowing. When we truly inhabit our bodies, intuition comes through as a clear signal.

If we want to be connected to our intuition and receive insights from source, we need to be embodied. That is, fully present in our physical experience—aware of sensations, patterns of breath, and tension—rather than dissociating into mental chatter, numbing behaviors, or living from the neck up.

After glimpsing the invisible waters we've been swimming in—the ways we've been conditioned to prize rationality and doubt the insights of our right hemisphere—we're ready to turn toward our first practice: embodiment. This is where we remove everything that blocks our magic from flowing freely. We'll explore how to clear the static from our physical channels so we can better receive messages from the unseen realm. Whether through healing our bodies from inflammation or reclaiming our power from systems of control, each step we take strengthens our connection to source.

I believe women's bodies are uniquely coded with an ability to tap into life's quieter dimensions. Our more complex hormonal systems make us more sensitive to environmental cues than men. As mentioned, our brains show more functional connectivity between hemispheres, allowing us to integrate logical and intuitive information more fluidly. This heightened sensitivity served an evolutionary purpose. As the ones potentially carrying the next generation, women needed keen awareness of various threats, like the emotional tone of a group and whether food or water was safe to consume. We developed what anthropologists call "diffuse awareness"—the ability to track multiple subtle signals at once and sense the undercurrents in a situation. Think about those stories that so many mothers have—waking up at 2 A.M. with an inexplicable urge to check on a teenager who turned out to be in a precarious situation, or canceling plans because something felt "off" about a child, only to discover they were coming down with an illness. We have to be comfortable with knowing without knowing how we know.

But how exactly does this sensing work? Perhaps the answer lies in the sophistication of our cellular intelligence. Each of our thirty to forty trillion cells can contain tens of thousands of receptors, with some specialized cells having up to one hundred thousand or more, constantly processing information. This vast network of cellular communications hums beneath the surface, gathering and processing information far beyond the bandwidth capabilities of our conscious minds.

Dr. Azra Bertrand, an innovative voice in integrative medicine and founder of Biomancy University, has drawn attention to the cerebellum—what he calls the Mother Mind—an ancient brain structure that takes up only 10 percent of brain volume but houses a remarkable 80 percent of its neurons. I remember learning only two things about the cerebellum in medical school: that it's involved in coordination, and that it's especially vulnerable to alcohol (hence our loss of coordination when we're drunk). But emerging neuroscience is beginning to explore a more complex role. Though long overlooked, this "back brain" may serve as a powerful processing center for emotion and sensory input. It works largely below conscious awareness, computing staggering amounts of data in parallel with our more verbal cerebrum.

Recall Audrey, who sensed something wasn't right during her pregnancy. Perhaps this decentralized intelligence can explain why we sometimes "just know" things without being able to explain how. When we have a gut feeling, could we be accessing this ancient processing center that operates outside conscious thought?

Despite having these sophisticated instruments for knowing, we live in a culture designed to dampen our senses. From our constant stream of addictive distractions to the substances that numb our pain and check us out of our lives, we are barely at home in our bodies. This disconnection shows up along a spectrum—from being unaware of the body's subtle sensations and needs to steamrolling over the bodily messages we *do* hear, all the way to dissociation, where it's as though we are disembodied altogether. This last one is often an adaptive strategy for coping with trauma—it's as though the body decides it's safer to be entirely severed from sensation rather than live in an unbearable reality. Regardless of our degree of disconnection, the way we protect and promote our ability to "hear" somatic information is through embodiment.

While most of us experience somatic "knowings" constantly, we've been conditioned to override them, defaulting to the familiar territory of the rational mind. Tuning in to these frequencies requires us to land back in our bodies. In the chapters that follow, we'll explore both sides of embodiment—how to recognize our somatic intelligence, and how to navigate the cultural forces that pull us away from it.

Chapter 4

THE GUT: A SUPERHIGHWAY TO OUR INTUITION

Trust my gut? The thing that can't even tolerate dairy?

—Internet meme

Olivia was sitting on her couch scrolling Instagram after a long day. She hovered over a post that read "Hot girl tummy issues" and thought to herself: *You have my attention.* She swiped through the carousel about the epidemic of digestive problems among young women. After ten years of yo-yo dieting, veganism, and an obsession with wellness that masked a sublimated eating disorder, Olivia felt seen by this trending topic. But what she didn't yet realize was how her compromised gut health connected to her inability to access her deeper truth.

For Olivia, the disconnection from her gut wisdom started early. During our time working together, I learned that she had recurrent ear infections as a toddler and received her first few courses of antibiotics before her third birthday, followed by countless more rounds throughout childhood. It would be decades before she discovered that dairy intolerance was the real culprit behind those infections—her body had been trying to tell her something all along, but modern medicine's quick fixes had drowned out the message.

By her twenties, Olivia's relationship with her body had become downright adversarial. Her digestion was so compromised that she lived in yoga pants, the mere thought of a waistband against her perpetually distended abdomen enough to make her want to hide under the covers. In college, she opted for a nuclear option for her acne—a combination of birth control pills, antibiotics, and Accutane that cleared her skin but further devastated her gut lining and her microbiome. Though she noticed concerning changes—crying spells and increasingly erratic digestion—she never thought to connect it to her meds. There is ample evidence that birth control impacts mood, libido, vaginal lubrication, and gut health; that Accutane carries a host of potential adverse effects; and that antibiotics decimate the gut flora. Yet our medical system is happy to napalm acne, even when it devastates everything else in the process. And I believe the cascade of interventions that disrupted her body's delicate ecosystems also had a more insidious impact: it disconnected her from her ability to sense what she needed.

"I literally have no idea what I want," Olivia told me in our first session together. She had come seeking help for what she called her mental health trifecta—depression, anxiety, and ADHD. But what struck me most was her profound disconnection from her own knowing. Whether discussing her unfulfilling job as a sales rep, her lukewarm "situationship," or even what she wanted for dinner, Olivia had lost access to her internal compass.

"Does he make you laugh? Does he make you feel safe?" I asked about the man she was dating.

"I mean . . . I guess? Sometimes? I'm not sure," she replied, demonstrating the same uncertainty that characterized all her attempts at self-reflection.

The parallel was clear: just as her compromised gut could no longer properly discern what to absorb and what to eliminate, Olivia had lost her ability to sense what served her and what didn't. She'd tried everything to fix her physical symptoms—probiotics, prebiotics, parasite cleanses, elimination diets, colonics, even coffee enemas. Yet she remained stuck in a cycle of constipation and bloating, her body as confused about how to process food as her mind was about how to process life decisions.

According to her mom, Olivia had been a headstrong, passionate child who knew exactly what she wanted. But that clear-knowing girl was nowhere to be seen. The twenty-seven-year-old sitting in my office was a perfectionist and people pleaser, so disconnected from her own truth that she couldn't even tell if she liked her job or her boyfriend.

A SUPERHIGHWAY IN DISREPAIR

The stories of my patients often reveal a striking pattern—when our physical body is out of balance, our intuitive capacity dims. Perhaps nowhere is this connection more evident than with the gut, our body's ancient instrument for discernment.

Throughout history and across cultures, we've recognized the gut as a second brain—a source of deep, emotional knowing. It's no accident that we speak of gut feelings, gut instincts, and gut wisdom. That thirty-foot-long tube running through our core isn't just processing our food—it's processing information about our world, helping us sense what nourishes us and what harms us. It's an interface between the outside world and our inner terrain, and it's where our immune system surveys the horizon for potential pathogens. The enteric nervous system, the network of neurons lining our digestive tract, contains more nerve cells than our spinal cord. Our gut produces most of our body's serotonin and houses the microorganisms that influence everything from our mood and cravings to our metabolism, and perhaps our inner compass as well. The gut is the superhighway to our intuition. When this system is compromised, we lose more than just digestive comfort—we lose a vital channel of inner knowing.

The numbers tell a sobering story: between 30 and 50 percent of Americans suffer from some form of digestive disturbance, whether it's irritable bowel syndrome (IBS), acid reflux, inflammatory bowel disease, or chronic bloating. Much of this comes down to the changes occurring with our gut microbiota. Gut bacteria outnumber human cells ten to one, making us more microbial than human. We are, quite literally, one and the same with these tiny organisms.

Yet modern life wages constant war on this delicate ecosystem—from multiple courses of antibiotics and chlorinated tap water to pesticides like Roundup that damage the gut lining. At the same time, we've lost our traditional exposures to diverse, beneficial bacteria that we once got through contact with soil, livestock, fermented foods, and the natural environment. Instead of playing in the dirt, we sanitize our hands, disconnecting ourselves from the microbial world that could support our physical and emotional well-being.

Perhaps nowhere is the ubiquity of poor gut health more evident than in the rising rates of IBS, particularly among women. Recent research reveals a fascinating biological basis for IBS. Studies from UCLA and McGill University have found that women with IBS show distinct structural differences in the insular cortex—the brain region responsible for processing visceral sensations (sensations from deep within the body). That is, these women are "listening" to their internal landscape in a different way than others. Rather than viewing IBS purely as gut dysfunction, we might understand it as a marker of an overall state of heightened internal perception. And perhaps evolution didn't make a mistake by creating a subset of the population with bad stomachs—perhaps evolution selected for some people to be particularly perceptive. These folks serve as the canaries in the coal mine that identify poisons before the rest of us catch wind of them, and gut discomfort just happens to be an undesirable side effect of this overall trait. These women with IBS aren't "too sensitive"—they're exquisitely attuned to their inner terrain. In essence, these sensitive stomachs may actually be sophisticated warning systems, alerting us to imbalances—from noxious pesticides to broader ecological disturbances—that less sensitive individuals might miss. This reframes what the medical establishment pathologizes as a disorder into what it might actually be: a heightened capacity for awareness and discernment.

HOW DO YOU KNOW IF YOU HAVE GUT ISSUES?

Signs Your Gut Is Working Well

- Regular bowel movements (well-formed stool, easy to pass, at least once daily)

- No bloating or abdominal discomfort
- Minimal food sensitivities
- Clear skin, no rashes
- Consistently good energy, stable mood, mental clarity

Clues You May Have Gut Dysfunction

- Constipation, diarrhea, or alternating between the two
- Abdominal bloating or distension
- Reflux or heartburn
- Frequent belching or flatulence
- Hemorrhoids
- Abdominal pain or cramping
- Persistent nausea
- Mucus or blood in stool (seek immediate medical attention)
- Skin issues like eczema, rashes, or acne
- Food intolerances, brain fog, fatigue, joint pain, or autoimmune conditions

Note: Gut issues don't always show up in the gut. Symptoms can be systemic—showing up in the skin, the immune or endocrine systems, even the emotions.

What Should You Do If You Suspect Gut Issues?

- Start with gentle changes like adjusting your diet, supplementing with probiotics, prioritizing sleep, and managing stress.
- If symptoms persist or worsen, consider working with a functional medicine doctor, naturopath, or gastroenterologist.
- Testing may include:
  - **Stool test** (to assess microbiome, parasites, inflammation)
  - **Breath test** (for SIBO—small-intestinal bacterial overgrowth)

- **Blood work** (to check for anemia, signs of infection, nutrient deficiencies, food sensitivities, and inflammation)

Rather than starting Olivia on the cocktail of psychotropic medications she thought she needed, we began with healing her gut. A comprehensive stool test revealed what years of medical intervention had wrought: an overgrowth of pathogenic bacteria and yeast, and a deficiency of beneficial bacteria. Her gut was as crowded with unwelcome influences as her life was with other people's opinions and expectations.

Working with a naturopath, we began the careful process of clearing the pathogens using antimicrobial herbs, then rebuilding her microbiome with probiotics and fermented foods. She incorporated gut-healing nutrients like collagen, glutamine, beta-glucan, lactoferrin, and butyrate (found in ghee). We eliminated inflammatory triggers like conventional gluten and dairy while introducing nourishing traditional foods like bone broth. A simple tool—the Squatty Potty—helped restore proper elimination mechanics almost overnight.

But the most challenging prescription was the one Olivia resisted most: *rest.* True healing requires the body to be in a parasympathetic state—what's known as "rest, digest, and repair" mode. Olivia's life of rushing from work to workouts to evening social obligations left no space for this essential restoration.

For two months, she committed to creating pockets of deep rest in her daily life. And slowly, as her digestion normalized, something else began to shift. Creative impulses bubbled up—she found herself drawn to dance classes, something she hadn't done since childhood. She began to recognize which relationships energized her and which depleted her. One day, she walked into my office with an unmistakable clarity in her eyes.

"I'm going back to school," she announced, a mix of terror and exhilaration in her voice. "And I ended things with Anthony. I knew. For the first time in as long as I can remember, I can feel what's right for me."

When I asked her to elaborate, she said, "Whether something is a yes or a no, I don't have to think it through a million times anymore. I just know."

The transformation wasn't only in Olivia's symptoms—though those, including her mental health symptoms, had improved considerably—but in her entire way of being. As her gut health was restored, so was her gut wisdom. She had rediscovered her internal barometer for truth, that intuitive sense that tells us what to absorb and what to eliminate, not just physically but in all aspects of life.

HOW TO HEAL YOUR GUT

Healing the gut is often a multistep, highly individual process, ideally guided by a functional medicine practitioner or naturopath. But the big picture follows a clear arc:

Step 1: Remove or Reduce What's Irritating the Gut

- **Universal irritants:** alcohol, conventional gluten, industrial seed oils (a hotly debated topic, and I'm open to changing my mind, but this is where I currently lean)
- **Individual food sensitivities:** dairy, eggs, corn, soy, nuts, nightshades (e.g., tomatoes, potatoes, peppers, eggplants)
- **Gut-disruptive medications** (under medical guidance):
    - **NSAIDs** (e.g., ibuprofen, naproxen): damage gut lining, increase permeability
    - **Antibiotics:** wipe out beneficial microbiota
    - **Antacids/PPIs** (e.g., omeprazole): reduce stomach acid, alter microbiota balance
    - **Hormonal contraceptives:** linked to altered microbiota, inflammatory bowel disease risk in some studies
    - **Psychiatric meds** (e.g., SSRIs, stimulants, antipsychotics): microbiome effects, motility changes (how quickly food moves through the gut)

- **Steroids:** increase gut permeability, alter immune-gut interaction

- **Overgrown microbes** (under medical supervision, use herbal or conventional antimicrobials to address):
  - SIBO
  - Parasites
  - Dysbiosis (imbalance in gut flora)

Step 2: Add In What Soothes the Gut

- **Foods** that support gut repair:
  - Bone broth
  - Fermented foods: sauerkraut, kimchi, yogurt, kefir, beet kvass, apple cider vinegar
  - Starchy tubers: sweet potatoes, plantains, white potatoes, taro, yucca
  - Ghee (clarified butter)

- **Supplements** that promote healing:
  - **For gut lining:** collagen, L-glutamine, lactoferrin, beta-glucan, bovine colostrum, DGL (deglycyrrhizinated licorice)
  - **For microbiome:** probiotics and prebiotics
  - **For regularity:** magnesium glycinate or citrate, fiber, hydration, kiwi, triphala, aloe

Step 3: Create the Conditions for the Gut to Heal

- **Rest:** Healing happens in a parasympathetic (rest-and-digest) state.
- **Start your day** with ~16 oz. room-temperature water to encourage elimination.
- **Tone the vagus nerve:** chanting, humming, gargling.
- **Regulate the nervous system:** meditation, breath work, yoga, qigong, tai chi.

- **Use a Squatty Potty** or footstool for optimal pooping posture.

For a deeper dive into gut healing and its connection to mental health, see Chapter 8 of my book The Anatomy of Anxiety.

Chapter 5

BETTER DATA THAN A WEARABLE CAN PROVIDE: TUNING IN TO THE BODY

> Coming back into relationship with our bodies becomes the first step in reclaiming our relationship with the inner feminine we were programmed to reject early on.
>
> —DENÉ LOGAN, *Sovereign Love*

Our bodies are our primary channel for connecting to our intuition. They are sophisticated radio receivers that speak to us through goose bumps, gut feelings, or the hair rising on the back of our necks. But if you're like most women I work with, you might be wondering, *If I have this incredible antenna, why can't I hear the signal?* A capacity for somatic knowing is our birthright. Yet, for many of us, the signal has grown faint.

The problem is not an absence of transmission but the presence of interference. Static surrounds us—some of it technological, some cultural, some embedded in the very systems meant to support our well-being. From our guts to our wombs, modern life has created interference patterns that cloud our connection to our innate wisdom. As I experienced for years when I was physically inflamed and my hormones were helter-skelter, when this receiver is compromised, our inner knowing becomes distorted, and we lose our intuitive frequency. It becomes harder to distinguish the signal from the noise.

If we want to reclaim our inner witch, we must understand: dissociation from our bodies blocks our access to magic. When we're disconnected from our physical selves, we can't feel the subtle sensations that help us hear our intuition. To reclaim our magic, we must reclaim our bodies. The path back to our intuitive gifts begins with clearing the static so we can once again have a hotline to our intuition.

THE OUTSOURCING OF BODILY WISDOM

When my husband, Vimal, wakes each morning, I ask him how he slept. He used to pause, tune in to his body, and respond with a felt sense of his rest ("Pretty good"). Now he glances at his wearable and says, "I don't know—let me check the app." This small moment captures a profound shift in how we relate to our bodies: we've outsourced our knowing, trading embodied wisdom for data.

The trend extends far beyond sleep tracking. We no longer trust ourselves to know the state of affairs within our own bodies. Instead, we believe we need external instruments and objective data to tell us how we feel. We have become increasingly disembodied, no longer at home or present within ourselves. At the precise moment we most need to reconnect with our internal knowing, we drift further away, inserting technology into our most intimate relationship.

I'll admit, I see the benefits of wearables. They have helped many of my patients improve their blood-sugar management and prioritize sleep; Vimal swears by his Oura Ring, and I occasionally wear one too. By objectively demonstrating the negative impact of things like alcohol and evening screen time on sleep quality, or how refined carbs spike blood sugar compared to fat- and protein-rich meals, wearables can motivate behavior change that might otherwise feel abstract or unnecessary. When I first started wearing my Oura Ring, I noticed that I would crawl into bed a bit earlier, spurred on by my eagerness to get a good sleep "score." Yet what we need even more than motivation is reconnection.

In this age of biohacking, self-help, and an endless pipeline of newfangled gadgets we're told we need, we can be tracking and optimizing our bodies endlessly without ever truly inhabiting those optimized bodies. What we actually need is to dust off the hotline to our internal proprioceptive awareness—our ability to feel our own state of being. In helping us optimize our health, wearables may inadvertently train us to distrust our own internal radar.

There's also the risk of a nocebo effect (the opposite of a placebo effect; where negative expectations actually worsen our symptoms) and the tendency toward obsessive tracking that can transform self-care into self-surveillance. This fixation on perfect metrics can backfire entirely, as my friend Jay discovered after months of chasing optimal sleep scores. "I'm off wearables," he texted me one day. "Because it created this counterproductive cycle of perfectionism around sleep. In chasing a perfect sleep score, I would get major sleep anxiety, and I started relying on sleep aids—which, ironically, worsened my sleep. Now I'm trying a new strategy: obsessing about sleep less so it can happen more naturally. And it's working."

My recommendation? Use wearables as useful feedback tools, but don't let them replace your innate somatic listening. Pay attention to the data, but also regularly check in with yourself independent of any device. How do you *feel* when you wake up? What does your energy tell you about last night's choices? Let technology serve your well-being rather than govern it. Part of clearing the static means reopening this vital line of communication—the one between you and your own body.

CULTURAL DISCONNECTION FROM BODIES

Our culture is disembodied, and this burden falls particularly heavily on women, who have been pitted against their physical bodies. Many of us move through an accelerated disconnection from our bodies during puberty. If we develop early, outpace the boys, or simply take on newly curvy shapes, we may develop the distorted belief that we're enormous, feeling oddly exposed—as though our bodies are betraying our desire to remain hidden and small.

Many women hear from the culture about how their bodies *should* look, about whether they are too thin or too fat, or otherwise not the desirable shape of the moment. Most of my patients in their thirties to sixties recall their mothers dieting and fretting about their weight. Each phase when our bodies naturally gain weight—puberty, college, motherhood, menopause—becomes a battle against our own flesh. Meanwhile, the sexualized female body—one that adheres to current standards of beauty and youthfulness—has remained front and center, holding the false promise of power for women. Beyond weight, we absorb countless messages that our natural bodies are somehow wrong—that our periods are shameful, our body hair unsightly, our normal bodily functions embarrassing or unladylike. We learn that our authentic physical selves need constant correction and management.

I say this with a content warning: the following section discusses sexual abuse and trauma. Perhaps the most pronounced severing between us and our bodies occurs anytime someone has been subjected to sexual abuse, which can cause a dissociative state so profound that in certain ways we leave our bodies, becoming numb to sensations and alienated from our needs. As one in nine girls in the United States is sexually assaulted before the age of eighteen, and over half of female-identifying people report experiencing sexual violence at some point in their lives, this is not a minor consideration. Given these statistics and the countless other ways our culture teaches women to mistrust and abandon our bodies, it's no wonder that so many of us arrive at adulthood feeling like strangers in our own skin.

But cultural conditioning isn't the only force driving us from our bodies. Sometimes the systems designed to heal us can create additional static.

"WHAT DO YOU HAVE?"

Even our medical system—meant to heal us—sometimes creates more distance between us and our innate capacity for well-being. This traces back to perverse incentives, a mismatch between the golden age of medicine and the epidemics of chronic illness that we see today, and the systemic sexism woven into the fiber of healthcare.

Consider as an analogy: my daughter is learning Spanish using the app Duolingo. One oft-heard criticism of Duolingo is that, in designing their user experience, they optimized for stickiness and engagement rather than for learning. At the end of the day, Duolingo is not a public school teacher—it's a publicly traded company with shareholders in a competitive ed-tech market. We would be naïve to think it held any goal higher than user engagement and shareholder value. Theoretically, engagement over time creates learning. That said, I'm not sure my daughter is learning much Spanish, but she is indeed addicted to the streaks, points, and crowns. Very clever, Duolingo.

Modern medicine operates with similarly misaligned incentives. Ever since healthcare in the United States began shifting to a business model in the 1970s—especially after the Health Maintenance Organization (HMO) Act of 1973 spurred the rise of managed care—conflicts of interest have become embedded in virtually every clinical decision. Is the system designed to optimize for health? To benevolently look after the well-being of the population? Or, like Duolingo, is it optimized for engagement, stickiness, and shareholder value?

I have immense appreciation for the individual nurses, techs, and practitioners working within medicine, and for the heroics of modern interventions that can rescue us from dire circumstances. At the same time, we need to see medicine for what it so often is: a business. And we need to understand how this business model drives a wedge between us and our internal navigation system.

The central question in allopathic medicine is: What do you have? Doctors and patients alike yearn for a diagnosis—that magic label that promises to make sense of suffering. To physicians, a diagnosis implies a treatment protocol, a way to feel effective. To patients, it offers validation, a name for their experience, the (often false) promise of relief or even a cure, or at least something concrete to research and understand.

This model once served us brilliantly. In the golden era when antibiotics were first introduced, a patient would present with symptoms, receive a diagnosis ("Your culture shows strep"), then take a prescribed treatment (penicillin), and be cured. The system worked with elegant simplicity: diagnosis led to treatment, which led to cure.

We've been chasing that clarity ever since.

But the chronic illnesses of modern life rarely follow this neat pattern. Many of today's epidemics—autoimmune conditions, digestive issues, mental illness, and the vagaries of chronic Lyme disease, long COVID, chronic fatigue, and fibromyalgia—don't yield to this linear thinking. Being delivered a diagnosis like fibromyalgia may validate a patient's experience and give them something to tell their workplace when they need accommodation. But that label says very little about how to help the patient find genuine relief.

Consider the typical medical response to fibromyalgia: "Well, you could try Cymbalta for the pain, or Neurontin for the nerve symptoms, or Flexeril for the muscle tension." The list grows longer not because we have many good options but because none of them address the root cause. We're grasping at symptoms while the underlying imbalance remains unexplored.

This is where functional medicine offers a different question: not "What do you have?" but "What's going on?" This approach investigates the *root cause* of illness—whether that's chronic inflammation, dysbiosis (imbalance of gut flora), intestinal permeability, insulin resistance and dysglycemia (poorly regulated blood sugar), mitochondrial dysfunction, micronutrient deficiency, toxic load, central nervous system sensitization, autonomic dysregulation, or unresolved trauma. And as I've discovered in my practice, illness of any sort is often due to a combination of physical and psychospiritual factors, all interweaving to create the tapestry of symptoms we call disease. When we focus exclusively on diagnosis—on the what-do-you-have—our diagnoses create identities. This runs the risk of pitting someone against their pathologized body. When we instead focus on the question of what's going on, we reacquaint ourselves with the body and honor its mechanisms for adaptation and communication.

But the problems with modern medicine go beyond diagnostic approaches. There is also the gender bias that is embedded in the system. American healthcare was designed around male bodies and male patterns of illness, with universal health coverage only starting at age sixty-five. This structure made sense for men, who historically could expect few health needs until retirement age—but it ignores women's need for consistent care throughout our reproductive lives.

And this erasure of women is baked into the science itself. For decades, medical research excluded women from clinical trials, especially during the drug development boom of the 1980s and '90s. The rationale was that fluctuating hormones made women "too complicated" to study, so male bodies became the default test subject. As a result, drugs were developed, dosed, and approved based on male physiology. Women, with different hormonal cycles, average body weights, metabolic rates, and even liver function, were left to navigate side effects and adverse reactions in a system that never studied how our bodies respond. In fact, the researchers were right: our fluctuating hormones *do indeed* make drugs behave differently in our bodies. All the more reason that it would be *good to know* the specifics of this before we release these medications onto the market. We're essentially conducting a massive, uncontrolled experiment on half the population.

Meanwhile, when a woman presents to the ER with so-called atypical heart attack symptoms—fatigue, nausea, pain in the jaw or back—she faces a medical system that calls her experience atypical simply because it differs from male presentations, not because it is any less common. Never mind that heart disease is the leading killer of women, or that women account for 41 percent of heart attacks but nearly *half* of fatal ones. In other words, a woman's heart attack is more likely to be fatal, perhaps because our symptoms are overlooked and our care delayed. The system hasn't been built to hear us or see us clearly.

The statistics grow even more dire when we consider race. In 2021, the maternal mortality rate for non-Hispanic Black women was 69.9 deaths per hundred thousand live births—2.6 times higher than the rate for non-Hispanic white women. These abhorrent numbers reflect a system that systematically discounts Black women's pain and requests for care, with devastating consequences.

Our healthcare system, which is laced with misogyny, requires enormous self-advocacy from women who just want to receive basic care. Before I had stepped into my own witchy power, I would crumple the moment a practitioner made me feel high-maintenance or difficult. All of this creates static in our ability to trust our own bodily wisdom—we learn to doubt our symptoms, disconnect from our bodies, and defer to external authority. The cost of this constant self-advocacy, this perpetual battle to be heard, creates its own form of *dis*-ease. The very stress of navigating the system, forever fighting to have our symptoms taken seriously, can create physical imbalance that further clouds our inner knowing. We need to be witches—connected to our power and knowing—simply to survive our own medical system.

THE BODY WHISPERER

Another aspect of health that conventional medicine largely overlooks is the mind-body connection. I witnessed this connection firsthand in my work with Kira, whose story illuminates how the psychospiritual becomes the material.

For a decade, Kira shuttled back and forth caring for her father as he slowly declined from congestive heart failure and dementia. Her father, once her rock, was progressively losing his ability to recognize her, though the severity of his symptoms would wax and wane unpredictably. These years of perpetual uncertainty left Kira in what therapists call ambiguous grief—a state of suspension where she was both anticipating future loss and mourning what was already gone. She could neither fully enjoy her father nor grieve or find closure. Her body held this tension, this inability to either fully exhale or take a deep new breath.

When her father did pass, Kira struggled to properly mourn. A psychology postdoc who had devoted her career to understanding others' emotional worlds, she ironically struggled to inhabit her own. She prided herself on emotional control, on being the person everyone came to for support. She stayed busy, intellectualizing her experience rather than feeling it. In our sessions, she would deflect questions about grief. I would prompt her to reflect on the loss, and she would respond with rehearsed therapy speak ("I'm just processing it at my own pace" or "I know grief isn't linear"), but I could tell she wasn't actually accessing her feelings. The deeper waters of loss remained undisturbed, but not unfelt—to borrow from the title of Bessel van der Kolk's bestseller about healing trauma, her body was "keeping the score."

On the one-year anniversary of her father's death, during a particularly stressful period at work, Kira contracted what seemed to be a simple cold. But weeks passed, and rather than resolving, her symptoms intensified. She developed what doctors eventually diagnosed as cryptogenic organizing pneumonia—an autoimmune condition in which the immune system attacks lung tissue long after any initial infection has cleared. From a purely physiological perspective, the location made sense: a virus had caused damage to the lungs, and now an overactive immune response was stuck in a loop of attempts at repair.

But in Chinese medicine—a system that has long recognized the intimate connection between emotions and physical health—the lungs are known as "the seat of grief." Kira's body, unable to process her loss through tears and expression, had manifested her stuck grief in the very organ traditional wisdom associates with mourning.

In a particularly poignant session, we arrived together at a profound realization: the body will always find a way to speak what we cannot say.

Kira's healing required a multifaceted approach. We used anti-inflammatory herbs to address the physical imbalance, and I referred her for regular acupuncture sessions to address the energetic imbalance. But more importantly, she needed to finally give herself permission to grieve—to open the floodgates of years of un-cried tears. Only when she stopped seeing her tears as weakness and began to see them as medicine did her breathing begin to ease.

This experience epitomizes what I've come to understand about illness: it exists at the intersection of the physical and the spiritual. Every diagnosis has its material basis in inflammation, imbalance, infection, or injury. But the way these manifest—which organs become involved, what symptoms arise, how the body responds—often carries deeper significance. Our bodies are not simple mechanical systems; they are storytellers. They hold meaning and they carry messages, attempting to bring our awareness to what needs attention.

Hippocrates revolutionized medicine by proposing that diseases have natural, empirical causes, rather than a supernatural basis. This shift laid the foundation for modern medicine. Before Hippocrates, illness was understood as divine punishment—an act of the gods visited upon mortals. Many would say, "Thank goodness that today we know better." But do we? Perhaps today we simply hold different assumptions. In casting out the psychospiritual basis for disease in favor of evidence-based ways of knowing, we may have lost some truth along the way. Illness can have both material and psychospiritual roots. So often, our symptoms tell a story.

THE BODY FINDING ITS VOICE

The modern epidemic of autoimmunity adds another layer to our understanding of meaning held in the body.

In the United States, approximately 13 percent of women are affected by autoimmune disorders (compared to about 7 percent of men), and this raises the question: Why have our bodies turned against themselves? The epidemic of autoimmune disorders is multifactorial: genes and modern insults to gut health and the immune system are central factors, but perhaps there is also a role for the ways we're disavowing pieces of ourselves. If we're not navigating life from a place of integration, where all parts of ourselves are welcome, our bodies have a tendency to call us out on that. This came into stark relief with my colleague Noor, a woman in her thirties with autoimmune thyroid disease.

Noor was the oldest daughter of Pakistani immigrants who had come to America with almost nothing, working tirelessly to build a stable life for their three children. Throughout her childhood, Noor learned to fit a certain mold to gain her parents' approval. When she began dating in high school or admitted to being at parties where others were drinking, her parents would explode in anger. From Noor's assimilated perspective, this punishment felt disproportionate to the crime. After all, she was by far the most straightlaced kid among her peers. But through her parents' cultural lens, these actions could damage her marriage prospects and their family's future for generations. Raised with the concept of *izzat* (family honor), they came by their views honestly, just as Noor, raised in a Pennsylvania suburb, came by hers.

So Noor became a master of composure. When asked about her interests, she had a perfect script: "I love science, cooking with my mom, and spending time with family." These weren't lies, exactly, but they were carefully curated truths, selected to win approval rather than express the whole of her interests.

What she didn't mention was her secret passion: poetry. She loved the works of Faiz Ahmed Faiz and other poets writing in Urdu, the language of her ancestors, whose words connected her to her heritage in ways her parents might have celebrated, had poetry not seemed like a diversion from the practical path to success they envisioned for her. In stolen moments between chemistry homework and lab internships, Noor would pour over her poetry journals, sometimes writing in English, sometimes experimenting with the Urdu her grandmother had taught her. Poetry was her refuge, her truth teller, her way of processing the growing divide between her outer and inner worlds. But as academic pressures ramped up, she was cracking open her poetry journals less and less.

During her freshman year at the University of Chicago, as Noor dutifully pursued premed requirements, her body began sending signals. First came the fatigue, then brain fog, constipation, dry skin, and perpetually cold hands and feet. The campus health center did some simple blood work and diagnosed her with Hashimoto's thyroiditis—an autoimmune condition where the immune system attacks the thyroid gland. She accepted the diagnosis and the prescribed medication with the same quiet compliance she brought to all aspects of her life.

But everything shifted when she met Kabir at Emory med school. Warm and jovial, goofy and fearlessly himself, Kabir saw past Noor's careful performance to glimpse the artist within. While he admired her discipline and intelligence, he also recognized how she used these qualities as armor. In their daily interactions, he would gently challenge her reflexive "I'm fine" responses, creating space for her to voice her actual feelings. Most importantly, he encouraged her poetry, seeing it as more than a hobby to be squeezed between "real" responsibilities.

"Kabir helped me find my voice," Noor would later say to me. The phrase was telling. The throat chakra—known as *vishuddha* in Sanskrit—is considered the energetic seat of self-expression, our capacity to speak our truth. Curiously, the thyroid gland, the target of Noor's autoimmune condition, sits precisely at the throat chakra. While conventional medicine might view this as mere anatomical coincidence, I've observed a striking pattern in my practice: autoimmune thyroid conditions often appear in women who have, for various reasons, learned to silence their authentic voice.

A connection between emotion and physical illness is supported by the evidence. The science reveals that autoimmune disease risk increases significantly with higher ACE (adverse childhood experience) scores and chronic stress. While researchers might explain this through the impacts of cortisol on immune function, I believe it points to a more poignant truth: our bodies manifest what our psyches cannot process.

Early childhood trauma can create emotional patterns—lack of basic trust and safety, internalized self-loathing, despair, unconscious shame—that can eventually surface as physical symptoms. When our communication is blocked, when we swallow our words, the body finds other ways to speak. In autoimmune conditions like Hashimoto's, the immune system quite literally points an arrow at the very tissues that overlay our ability to voice our truth in the world.

Yes, Hashimoto's has material causes—genetics, inflammation, environmental triggers, perhaps even molecular mimicry between gluten and thyroid transglutaminase. But what conventional medicine often overlooks is the question of why the immune system chooses this particular target. While science focuses on the how, integrative approaches allow us to also ask why. Consider the emerging field of psychoneuroimmunology, which explores the interactions between mental states and immune system behavior. Psychoneuroimmunologic research increasingly supports connections between emotional patterns and immune function. The rising prevalence of thyroid conditions among women—particularly those who've experienced significant stress or trauma—suggests something beyond random chance. When swallowed truth or internalized self-betrayal manifests alongside physical disease, we begin to see through the illusory separation between body and spirit that has characterized Western medicine for centuries.

My own health journey of inflammation and digestive issues forced me to reflect on the patterns of illness throughout my maternal line. I come from a lineage of what I would call suppressed witches—women who by necessity had to abandon their gifts of intuition and magic. Interestingly, this maternal line is also plagued with autoimmune conditions. While this is anecdotal and limited to the few women of my family, it has me wondering if we see higher rates of autoimmune disorders in those who have buried their magical nature.

When Noor pushed her poetry aside, she was suppressing the channel by which source wanted to express itself through her. Poetry was her soul's language and her offering to the world. When we deny our art—our magic—that energy doesn't disappear. Instead, it stagnates within us, perhaps provoking our immune system to draw attention to the problem—a physical manifestation of suppressed gifts.

Through her relationship with Kabir and her own inner work, Noor gradually began to integrate her different selves. "For so long, I thought I had to choose between medicine and poetry, between honoring my parents' sacrifices and making my art," she told me. "But over time I came to see that both could coexist."

Today, she's a physician who leads a narrative medicine program, teaching medical students how to help patients find and express their voices and tell their stories of illness. The impact ripples outward in concentric circles: from Noor to her students to the patients, all of them finding their voice. Noor's poetry has been published in medical journals alongside her research. While she couldn't reverse the thyroid damage, her condition stabilized as she stepped into fuller self-expression. And through her work, she is leading the way for others to honor their own truth, creating a bridge between the scientific and expressive aspects of healing.

BODY LANGUAGE

Many Eastern traditions—from traditional Chinese medicine (TCM) to Ayurveda and yoga philosophy—offer frameworks for understanding how emotions are stored in and expressed through the body. These systems map emotional and energetic states onto organs and other body parts.

While different schools offer varying interpretations, I find value in all of them. Here are some of the body-emotion relationships that inform my work with patients:

- **Lungs:** seat of grief and loss; associated with letting go (TCM)

- **Eyes:** called "the openings of the liver" in TCM; related to vision, clarity, and frustration
- **Kidneys:** fear, life force, and ancestral energy; associated with willpower, bones, hearing, and sexual vitality (*jing* in TCM, *ojas* in Ayurveda)
- **Heart:** center of joy, love, and consciousness (*shen, hridaya*); linked to passion and emotional openness
- **Liver:** stores unexpressed anger and resentment; central to smooth energy flow; tied to planning, decision-making, flexibility, and life direction (*qi* flow, *ranjaka pitta*)
- **Large intestine:** associated with discernment and emotional release; the ability to let go of what no longer serves (*apana vayu* in yoga philosophy)
- **Spleen/pancreas:** related to worry, overthinking, and a tendency to give too much rather than nourishing the self (TCM); governs physical and emotional nourishment
- **Hips:** in yoga philosophy, a storehouse for unprocessed emotion, particularly suppressed grief, trauma, or fear
- **Throat:** associated with expression and truth telling (*vishuddha* chakra); tension may reflect unspoken emotions or stifled communication
- **Stomach:** digestion of life experiences (*agni* in Ayurveda); often tied to anxiety or difficulty assimilating life events
- **Bladder:** stores fear (TCM), especially around control and survival
- **Lower back:** often tied to financial worry, questions of security, or feeling unsupported
- **Shoulders:** symbolic of burden, responsibility, and emotional load ("carrying the weight of the world")
- **Neck:** often holds stubbornness, rigidity, inflexibility, or tension from difficult people and situations
- **Jaw:** related to unexpressed words, suppressed anger, or need for control
- **Hands:** linked to agency, connection, and the ability to give and receive

These associations aren't diagnostic tools but ways to explore deeper meaning behind symptoms and leverage the body-mind connection for healing. I offer them as an opening inquiry—much like a tarot reading might spark self-reflection rather than predict the future.

If these connections feel helpful, wonderful. If they feel blaming or shaming, please discard them entirely. Kate Bowler, writing about her own chronic illness in *Everything Happens for a Reason: And Other Lies I've Loved,* describes how well-meaning helpers would take "spiritual inventories, paging through [her] life and taking out events one by one for examination," searching for the spiritual root of her suffering. As she observes, "In a spiritual world in which healing is a divine right, illness is a symptom of unconfessed sin—a symptom of a lack of forgiveness, unfaithfulness, unexamined attitudes, or careless words. A suffering believer is a puzzle to be solved." This kind of spiritual detective work can quickly become another form of self-blame. There's no need to use these mind-body connections as evidence of your own failings or hidden darkness. Sometimes our bodies simply break down, or as Bowler wisely notes, sometimes "the math doesn't math." Your healing journey is entirely your own, and it need not include finding meaning in every symptom or struggle.

LANDING BACK IN THE BODY

Olivia's gut wisdom. Kira's grieving lungs. Noor's silenced expression. Our bodies are telling stories.

Like a radio that's been slowly detuned, we have lost some of our natural ability to interpret life's subtle frequencies. Modern medicine, while miraculous in crisis, too often teaches us to put a sticker over the check-engine light rather than look under the hood. And we miss our bodies' whispered missives along the way.

In Madeline Miller's *Circe*, the ancient witch reflects on developing her gifts: "Little by little, I began to listen better: to the sap moving in the plants, to the blood in my veins. I learned to understand my own intention, to prune and to add, to feel where the power gathered and speak the right words to draw it to its height." This is embodiment—the patient, dedicated practice of learning to hear the subtle language of our bodies.

Fortunately, our bodies haven't forgotten how to tune in. From the neurological network of the gut to the way our self-expression seems to originate from source itself, we carry sophisticated instruments for accessing wisdom. When we clear these channels—through rest, nourishment, movement, grieving, or simply paying attention—we often find our intuition floods back with surprising strength. Physical healing begins to look a lot like spiritual revelation.

HOW TO HEAR WHAT YOUR BODY IS TELLING YOU

Our bodies are sophisticated receivers that never stop picking up information from the environment. Yet there are ways to turn up the volume on those intuitive hits and clear the static that's been drowning them out.

Create Space for Reception

- **Strategic silence:** When you'd normally fill quiet moments with podcasts or audiobooks, try leaving space instead. Do the dishes in silence or with instrumental music that won't compete for your attention. This mental downtime lets your brain defragment—closing unnecessary tabs and clearing bandwidth for new information to flow through. Think of it as creating space between thoughts for something new to emerge.
- **Walking without digital distractions:** Take walks without your phone, especially in nature. The left-right-left-right rhythm of

walking engages bilateral sensory-motor patterns that echo one of the mechanisms used in EMDR (eye-movement desensitization and reprocessing), a trauma therapy that uses rhythmic left-right stimulation to help the brain process unresolved emotions and memories. When you sync your body with the sensory gestalt of nature—feeling the ground beneath your feet, hearing the wind and the birds—you're creating ideal conditions for those radio signals to break through the static of daily life.

Tune Your Antenna

- **Ritual:** Any ritual that feels meaningful to you—lighting a candle, burning sage, lying on your bed with your hands on your abdomen, or simply pausing to ask for guidance—acts as a signal to your unconscious that you're ready to receive. Think of it as tuning your internal radio to the right frequency. The ritual doesn't need to be elaborate; it just needs to mark the transition from everyday awareness to receptive listening.
- **Proprioceptive awareness:** Notice physical sensations without immediately analyzing them. That activation in your chest when you think about a decision, the tension in your shoulders around certain people, how the quality of your breath tracks with the nature of your thoughts, and the way your body expands or contracts in different environments—these are all part of your body's communication system.
- **Living in sync:** Your body operates best when aligned with natural cycles such as morning sunlight, darkness after sunset, sleeping on a consistent schedule, and space between meals. For those who menstruate, this also includes embracing the natural ebb and flow of energy throughout the month.

Remember, the body is already picking up on these signals—the work is to simply tune in. And once we've learned to hear these signals, we also need to learn to trust what we hear.

Our body is the instrument with which we hear our intuition. Every salient sensation, every inexplicable knowing that rises from our depths is part of our magical inheritance. Our bodies are radio towers through which the mysteries of life are transmitted. Connecting to the spirit realm doesn't require us to transcend our physical nature—it asks us to sink more fully into it.

Chapter 6

BOTTLING IT UP OR LETTING IT FLOW: HOW TO UNBLOCK THE PSYCHE

> Problems that remain persistently insoluble should always be suspected as questions asked in the wrong way.
>
> —ALAN WATTS, *The Book: On the Taboo Against Knowing Who You Are*

Now we turn our attention to the topic that has been top of my mind since I chose my medical specialty in 2006: mental health.

We can think of healing from mental illness as climbing a mountain. The summit—where you're finally stable, energetic, and hopeful, with the resilience to meet life as it unfolds—is the goal. For decades, psychiatry has offered two well-marked trails up that mountain: medication and psychotherapy. And for some people, these paths get them all the way to the top. When that happens, it's cause for celebration.

But many of my patients arrive at my office after years of trying different medication regimens, cycling through therapists, exploring various therapeutic modalities—and they're still stuck partway up the mountain. They've hit a dead end, sometimes repeatedly. At some point, a dangerous thought takes hold: *Meds and therapy are supposed to help. They're not helping me. So I must be beyond repair.*

Here's what I know to be true: you are not stuck, and the situation is not hopeless. Those well-worn trails are simply not the right path for everyone. And the good news is: there are other ways up this mountain—paths that conventional psychiatry rarely discusses or explores. I call this approach "bushwhacking psychiatry." Instead of insisting you follow the marked trails that aren't working, we find the combination of routes that actually gets you to the summit.

This chapter is about those alternative paths. When we expand our view beyond symptom management and look at the root causes—inflammation, gut health, hormones, movement, trauma, circadian rhythms, and yes, even spiritual connection—people who once felt hopeless finally find relief.

WIRED THIS WAY

"I'll save you the trouble of having to figure out what medication to prescribe," Alicia announced within the first few minutes of our appointment. With her oversized earrings and bright pink lipstick, Alicia had a bold way about her. She continued, "My mom is on Effexor. My sister takes Effexor. My aunt takes Effexor. I honestly don't even know why I need a psychiatrist. I literally know Effexor is going to be right for me."

A struggling actor and waitress, Alicia had been dealing with depression and anxiety for years, but she told me that she hadn't had the time or energy to address it. Now that it had "reached a breaking point," we were here sitting across from each other—she on the couch, I in my leather recliner—surrounded by books and plants. Alicia went on to utter those same words I've heard countless times before:

"Depression and anxiety run in my family. It's just how we're wired."

I took a deep breath, because I realized that my unconventional approach to mental health would be a tough pill for Alicia to swallow.

As a child, Alicia observed her mom panicking frequently. When Alicia was learning to ride a bike, or heading out for a school field trip, or when she simply tripped and scraped her knee, her mom (a survivor of trauma) would gasp and fret. Even as a young child, Alicia had the sense that it was her responsibility to help calm her mom down rather than the other way around.

Alicia had always been exquisitely sensitive. As a kid, if she saw another kid crying, or if she saw a dog limping, or even if she was just walking past the lobster tank at her local diner, her heart ached in such a powerful way she almost couldn't bear it. As she got older, she realized that she was different—she could read the energy of a room, she could sense her mother's mood from down the hall, and she felt as though she had a sixth sense that helped her understand what made people tick. In therapy we refer to this as compensatory metacognition (an adaptive ability to infer others' thoughts and feelings). But Alicia's maternal grandmother, who was from Puerto Rico, had her own term. She used to call Alicia *brujita,* Spanish for "little witch."

Decades later, Alicia came to me with depression, endometriosis, rosacea, and prediabetes. "I've had enough of being so sensitive in such a loud world." She was ready for Effexor. But I suspected there was more to the story of her depression and anxiety than a serotonin imbalance.

While Alicia saw her depression as an inherited trait—a genetic destiny—I saw a genetic predisposition combined with environmental influences. While she had been taught to believe that mental health issues are the result of low serotonin—a simple chemical imbalance that should be addressed with a pill—I see them as polyfactorial states of imbalance with multiple possible root causes. While she saw depression and anxiety as disorders, I see these as *symptoms.* These symptoms tell us something is wrong, but they don't tell us *what* is wrong. They are the beginning of the inquiry, not the final verdict.

When a patient of mine meets criteria for depression or anxiety, this begins a process of reconnaissance to figure out what the root causes of *their* depression and anxiety are. It can be anything from inflammation to a micronutrient deficiency; sometimes it's a medication side effect, or even sleep apnea causing chronic sleep deprivation; often there's unresolved trauma, or social issues and psychological weathering; and quite frequently, a lack of community is playing a role. A lot of this can appear to run in families. While genes run in families, so do behaviors, lifestyle, eating habits, gut bacteria, socioeconomic stressors, and traumas. Not to mention intuitive gifts.

Not too long ago, up until the mid-twentieth century, mental illness was seen as a moral failing or weakness. We told people to "buck up" and "pull yourself up by your bootstraps." This attitude toward mental illness was shaming, uninformed, and wholly unhelpful. In time, we graduated to the disease model of mental health, suggesting that states like depression are biological diseases—no different from diabetes or heart disease.

With this evolution, instead of seeing depression as shameful and the result of weak character, the disease model swung all the way to the other end of the spectrum, positing that our mental health is our genetic fate—completely out of our hands. This new paradigm saved us from moral shaming. But it left us in a different pinch.

The 1980s and 1990s—the latter dubbed the "decade of the brain"—marked a turning point. In the search for an objective basis for the so-called disease of depression, researchers fixed their gaze on a particular neurotransmitter called serotonin. The serotonin model tells us that mental health issues like depression are the result of a hereditary serotonin imbalance. This explanation takes away the blame, which is lovely, but it can lead us to see ourselves as fundamentally broken—bad genes, bad luck. Of course, this comes with the promise that we can be fixed with a pill. But all too often, our limited menu of offerings—medication and psychotherapy—overlooks the root of the problem and fails to bring people enduring relief.

Another thing I've observed in my practice: it is often the most intuitive, sensitive souls who end up in the psychiatrist's office. The empaths. The witches. The ones who can sense what others are feeling, who can read the energy of a room, who feel the world's pain as their own. They are the canaries in the coal mine of modern life, the first to signal when something is wrong in our collective psyche. Their depression reflects the ways that modern life poisons their sensitive systems. Yet, instead of recognizing their sensitivity as a gift and supporting it properly, we pathologize it and attempt to medicate it away.

WHAT IS SEROTONIN?

Serotonin is a neurotransmitter—a chemical messenger that helps brain cells communicate. While it's found in brain regions associated with mood, most of your serotonin actually lives in your gut, with smaller amounts in blood platelets that help with clotting.

Despite decades of depression research and pharmaceutical marketing focused on serotonin, and a suite of about eighteen FDA-approved medications that target serotonin levels, here's what the science actually shows: serotonin is not synonymous with happiness. An umbrella review of all available evidence found no causal link between serotonin levels and depression. This doesn't mean medications are never effective, but it does mean the "chemical imbalance" story is far too simple.

My suspicion? If serotonin is involved in mood disorders, it's likely a *downstream* effect—meaning that serotonin signaling changes as a *result* of other upstream causes like sleep deprivation, inflammation, hormonal shifts, sedentariness, and trauma, rather than being the fundamental cause of depression itself. The real story of mood is far more complex than a single neurotransmitter deficiency. This reframing completely changes how we approach treatment—instead of targeting neurotransmitters with medications, we address the root causes that are disrupting those neurotransmitters in the first place.

A NEW UNDERSTANDING

For decades, the disease model of mental health served an important purpose: it removed blame and shame from those suffering. But focusing exclusively on genes and brain chemistry as the root cause of mental illness ultimately became one of the *least* hopeful narratives we could tell, leading people who are not helped by meds to despair. And, thankfully, this narrative is not wholly accurate.

Mental health issues were never a genetic chemical *destiny.* Genes were only ever a predisposition, not our fate. Our symptoms are not a sign of our brokenness; they serve a function. Symptoms like depressed mood and anxious thoughts are the body's way of communicating that there is either a state of physical imbalance, an unresolved trauma, or an unmet psychospiritual need. And for the most part, we can do something about it.

We are ready for a new understanding of mental health. It's time for a "growth mindset" reframe, where mental illnesses are not fixed, genetic traits, and we are not helpless—we have agency and influence over how we feel.

This understanding allows us to shift our thoughts from *What's wrong with me?* to *What is my anxiety telling me?* And once we understand what these symptoms are communicating, we can leverage that information to find relief.

FALSE MOODS

Clinical psychologist and author Julia Ross first coined the term "false mood"—a negative mood state that is artificially induced by physical imbalance, such as a nutritional deficiency, rather than being a true reflection of our life circumstances. While we do indeed have our "real moods"—when something happens, such as a loss, a divorce, a fight with a friend, a stressor at work, or a global atrocity—we have a tendency to believe that *all* states of unhappiness are so-called real moods, when in fact these states are often caused by physical imbalance.

A false mood arises when some state of physical imbalance in the body generates a neurochemical change. The cause might be anything from a blood-sugar crash to a hangover. Subjectively, we experience that neurochemical change as states like sadness, anger, or anxiety. In these moments, our minds—the consummate meaning-makers that they are—tell us a story to make sense of our mood. We might think, *I know why I'm anxious right now. It's because of that thing going on in the news*. And there may be truth to these stories. But these explanations are not identifying the *real* cause of our mood at that moment. The story our mind tells us is a retrofitted justification—our mind is simply attempting to make sense of what the body is feeling. We think our morose mood is some deep and inherent quality about ourselves, or an inevitable response to what's going on around us. But we fail to appreciate that, so much of the time, the mood stems from something physical—and completely avoidable. Maybe we're underslept because we were up late doomscrolling. Maybe we're overcaffeinated or hungover. Maybe we're underweight—we might think we look good, while our body is worried about starvation. We think that our angst is rooted in seeing the world as it is—that the world is as bleak as our mood state would suggest—when in fact, we're seeing the world as *we* are. Often, we're just experiencing an avoidable mood state caused by a blood-sugar crash and sitting for eight hours. Many of us are seeing the world through the distorted lens of physical imbalance.

It's worth noting that certain psychiatric medications themselves—what we take to attempt to mend our moods—can also create false moods. A common but underappreciated source of this is something called interdose withdrawal—when the body experiences withdrawal between doses. This can show up as anxiety, panic, irritability, or a hopeless outlook that colors how we see the world. If you're on a psychiatric medication and your mood changes right around the time that you're due for your next dose (e.g., perhaps you take your Lexapro in the morning, and you wake up anxious), consider the possibility that interdose withdrawal is impacting your mood.

Subacute withdrawal is a related phenomenon. Even after you've completely stopped taking certain psychiatric medications—like benzodiazepines and SSRIs—your body may continue experiencing withdrawal symptoms for months. Most people are advised to taper off these medications over the course of weeks or maybe a few months, but that is generally too rapid. The result of tapering too fast is that you may feel anxious, depressed, or physically unwell long after your last dose. This prolonged withdrawal can create mood symptoms that feel psychological (and are often misattributed to relapse) but are actually your brain chemistry readjusting.

Mental health is, at its core, physical health. What we often mistake as fundamental truths about ourselves—our anxieties, our despair—may actually be false moods triggered by physical dysregulation. When we understand this, we realize that much of our psychological suffering isn't inevitable or intrinsic to who we are. We think it's an indication that we're seeing the world *more* clearly than those around us, but instead it's often an indication that our physical imbalance is tainting everything we see. That is not to say things aren't heavy, but that we can be clear and intact as we take on the wrongs of the world. By addressing root causes in the physical body, we can free ourselves from unnecessary mental anguish.

States of physical imbalance not only masquerade as mental health issues, they also muddy the mental waters. For the witchy woman, the sensitive soul, clearing these false moods becomes especially critical. When our physiology is pinballing around from hangovers to medication withdrawal, the waters around our navigation system are murky and rough. Those choppy waters can feel like fear, and we confuse that with a deeper truth. When we are attempting to access our intuition, we need the waters to be calm, still, and clear. Only then are we in good communication with our inner compass.

AVOIDABLE MOODS VS. PURPOSEFUL MOODS

Avoidable Moods

Negative emotional states caused by underlying physical imbalance such as:

- Blood-sugar dips
- Sleep deprivation
- Digestive issues
- Inflammation
- The effects of alcohol
- The effects of caffeine

- The effects of food coloring and preservatives
- Dehydration
- Hormonal imbalance
- Sedentariness

Avoidable moods should be addressed at the level of the body in order to eliminate unnecessary suffering.

Purposeful Moods

Authentic emotional responses that serve as inner guidance, signaling when something in our lives needs attention.

- What remains after we've cleared up avoidable moods.
- The question is no longer "How can I stop feeling this mood?" and becomes "What is this mood telling me?"
    - This is our inner compass, nudging us to pay attention to something.
    - These moods often pertain to something being out of alignment in our personal lives, communities, or the world at large.
    - They can also be centered on themes of impermanence, uncertainty, control, and the inherent fragility of walking this earth in a human body.

Purposeful moods are not something to fix; they're something to listen to and honor.

PURPOSEFUL MOODS

Beyond our false moods lie our true moods—what we might call purposeful moods. These aren't distorted moods from imbalanced physiology; they are our inner compass speaking up. When we viscerally connect to what's out of alignment—whether in our personal lives, our communities, or the world at large—we feel off. That's our inner guidance system functioning exactly as it should. Society is quick to ask, "Why are you being so sensitive?" and we often turn that judgment inward, wondering, *What's wrong with me?* But feeling deeply connected to the world's suffering isn't a flaw—it's evidence of an intact heart and a finely tuned antenna. This sensitivity isn't something to pathologize; it's something to nurture, listen to, and heed.

After my first meeting with Alicia, we took a multifaceted approach to her mental health that drew upon her false and true moods. I knew from the rosacea rash on her face that she likely had intestinal permeability (when contents of the gut leak into the bloodstream) and systemic inflammation (a widespread immune response throughout the body). Her prediabetes told me that she was insulin resistant and dysglycemic, which I suspected was a central contributor to her anxiety. Her endometriosis clued me in to the fact that she was not only inflamed and hormonally imbalanced but likely carrying trauma in her lower abdomen and pelvis.

We took steps to heal her gut (probiotics, fermented foods, bone broth, beta-glucan, colostrum, Squatty Potty), reduce inflammation (decreased ultraprocessed foods, increased turmeric, ginger, fish, and fresh fruits in her diet), and stabilize her blood sugar (more protein and healthy fats, less added sugars and refined carbohydrates). As her hemoglobin A1c slowly improved and her rosacea lessened, her anxiety decreased and her panic attacks stopped. It turned out, much of her anxiety was based in the physical body. This life-altering suffering was an avoidable mood all along.

For her endometriosis, in addition to reducing endocrine disruptors (perfumes, plastic tea bags and food containers, conventional cleaning and personal care products, scented candles), addressing inflammation, and referring her to an integrative gynecologist, I assigned Alicia homework to lie on her bed, placing her hands on her lower abdomen, and dialogue with her body about what it was carrying—what stories it had to tell her. This was a powerful practice for Alicia that transported her to childhood memories, experiences in past relationships, and the sorrow that her maternal line had endured over the ages. She felt the presence of her maternal grandmother in the room while she wept and journaled about the experience.

With the combination of all these interventions, her endometriosis symptoms gradually improved. Although Alicia's depression lessened considerably, there was still a remaining knot of uneasiness that she carried despite all the changes she made.

"It is no measure of health to be well-adjusted to a profoundly sick society"—a sentiment often attributed to philosopher Jiddu Krishnamurti, though the exact phrasing may not be his. If we grant that our society is unwell, then the people who are diagnosed as mentally ill may in fact be the ones responding correctly to it. Are they broken, or are they having an appropriate reaction to a pathogenic world? The people most likely to *feel* the sickness of our society are the witches. They are the artists sensing how we have lost our way and alchemizing it on behalf of the rest of us. What we sometimes regard as a genetic curse may actually be a spiritual gift. For Alicia, after eliminating the unnecessary suffering of her false moods, our goal was not to suppress or solve this residual sense of unease; it was to get better at listening to it and honoring what it had to say. That sensitivity—the same one that made her tear up at the lobster tank as a child—wasn't a disorder to be diagnosed and medicated away. It was a vital part of her witchcraft.

CLEARING

In my experience, as we become more in touch with our witchiness, our hearts open and our antennae grow particularly sensitive. This is something to embrace, but it is also something that demands great care, as we live in a loud world.

If you have a highly sensitive antenna, you are taking on a lot of other people's baggage. If you find yourself feeling foggy, ungrounded, depleted, or anxious, it can be helpful to do some clearing and grounding practices to help **discharge unwanted energy:**

- Spend time in nature.
- Touch the earth with bare feet.
- Spend time unplugged and away from electronics.

- Set limits around news.
- Pause and do some deep diaphragmatic breathing.
- Dance.
- Shake. (Put on rhythmic drum music, close your eyes, and let yourself move and shake in whatever way feels good.)
- Set an intention: write down or speak aloud phrases like "I am only allowing in what is for my highest good."
- Try a smudging ritual (e.g., burning palo santo or sage)—an Indigenous practice from the Americas, traditionally used to cleanse energy and space.

If you have an open heart, you are likely feeling the hurts of the world deeply. That is a beautiful quality—we need you. But we don't want this sensitivity to deplete you. If you are one of our designated feelers, you may need to give yourself plentiful time, space, and permission to **move through emotions.** Here's my best advice for that:

- Journal.
- Schedule regular therapy.
- If you have a tendency to give too much, learn to notice your energetic limits, and take responsibility for setting boundaries *before* you become burned-out or resentful.
- Give yourself permission to cry.

While all these practices help clear our channel, tears remain our most potent medicine—something I was reminded of when I recently connected with my friend De'Ara.

TEARS ARE THE MEDICINE

"I'm just trying to hold it all in," De'Ara told me over the phone, her voice quivering. I was walking into my apartment after school drop-off. It was the one-year anniversary of her father's death. I was a few years further along the parental-loss path, so we'd made a plan to connect on this significant day.

Something happens when De'Ara and I come together, whether that's over coffee or at a conference. Her father seems to hover over our connection. On this phone call, I felt his presence. *He's right there,* I thought. Two things came through to me strongly: *Wow, he loves her,* and *God, he's cool.* I could sense his thoughts, and I felt like he and I were feeling the same way. I spoke on behalf of both of us.

"Why hold it all in?" I asked. "I think you need a good cry." And with that, I could sense the imperceptible shift—the release had occurred. The quality of De'Ara's breathing changed. Her voice gradually took on the nasal tone that comes with the rush of salt water and mucus. In time, words yielded to the guttural, pure expression of emotion.

How did we come by this cultural goal of suppressing our tears? When we start to tear up, we tamp it down, as if we're trying to hold in a sneeze. But why is that even the goal? Whether it's generations of misguided messaging about what it means to be strong or simply the fact that it's difficult to tolerate this level of vulnerability, our emotion-phobic culture has us all armored against our own feelings.

We need to cry more. We need to cry bigger. We need to get comfortable letting it hit us at inconvenient times, letting it be messy and blubbery and snotty and complete.

As the Isak Dinesen saying goes, "The cure for anything is salt water—sweat, tears, or the sea." That could pretty much be the whole mental health chapter right there. The urge to cry is the body, in its infinite wisdom, giving us a much-needed opportunity for release.

Tears were never the weakness; they were always the medicine.

I stood and held the phone while De'Ara had a full, complete cry. Most people think they're done crying way too early. Those moments when they're able to catch their breath—ha! Don't be fooled—those are false peaks. Those are actually the moments when, if you are lucky and skillful enough to catch the wave, you can take a heaving ride back down into the cry—reaching the kind of depth of tears where you momentarily stop breathing, where your face freezes in a timeless grimace, where something poignant is gathering in your jaw and your chest. When done correctly, crying goes on for an awkward length of time. I tend to think a big cry is complete only once a person lets out a medicinal sigh.

Crying softens us. You can think of emotions as energy in motion. When we're holding it all in rather than letting our sadness out, where does that energy go? I believe it gets lodged in the body, producing a coating of unfelt grief that then hardens around our hearts. Holding anything in requires effort and strain. Picture the way our pelvic floor clenches when we have to pee but we instead hold it in. This effortful forcing and energetic guarding has an effect on our hearts. The effort is muscular, but it is also energetic. Grief and sadness are like a heart with a full bladder—it cannot relax until it has had a good cry.

THE SCIENCE BEHIND A GOOD CRY

There's biochemistry behind the healing power of tears. Research shows that emotional tears have a different chemical composition than reflex tears (the kind of tears you shed when you're cutting an onion). Emotional tears contain stress hormones including cortisol, ACTH, prolactin, and leucine-enkephalin—essentially, the very chemicals our bodies produce during emotional distress.

When we cry, we're physically shedding these stress chemicals from our system. This is what researchers call "completing the stress cycle"—allowing our nervous system to move through the full arc of activation and resolution, rather than staying stuck in a stress response. By crying we're disburdening ourselves of these hormones and returning our bodies to their biochemical baseline.

This helps explain why we often feel lighter and more at peace after a good cry. We haven't just gotten it out emotionally—we've cleared our system of the stress chemicals that were keeping us activated. In this way, tears become one of our body's most elegant mechanisms for self-regulation.

This is where our mental health becomes inextricably linked with our capacity to grieve. When we suppress our tears and "hold it all in," we're creating internal pressure that will eventually need release. That unexpressed grief doesn't simply disappear; it transforms into other manifestations of distress. I've seen it countless times in my practice: the depression or utter lack of vitality that settles in after months of "staying strong"; the anger that emerges when we've pushed down too much emotion, and every topic feels like a live wire; the irritability that comes from carrying an invisible backpack of unexpressed pain.

Softening our hearts through free-flowing tears does nothing less than change everything. It allows us to forgive more easily (forgive others, but also forgive ourselves). We find it easier to love, easier to enjoy, and easier to hold compassion for others' differences. When our hearts are soft, they are pliable and elastic—they can expand to contain more love. But when we resist this softening, when we suppress our grief, the effects ripple beyond our individual mental state and begin to affect those around us.

In fact, I suspect that unmetabolized grief is a contributor to the ways our culture is hyperpolarized and brittle. Our mental fragility, our anger, our inability to tolerate one another's differences—so much of this can be traced back to our hardened hearts, which itself can be traced back to uncried tears. Many of us are walking around with a backlog of unexpressed emotion pressing on our chests at all times. It makes it harder to let new love in, harder to meet others with compassion, harder to access magic. This emotional armor might feel like protection, but it's actually a barrier to our joy.

As witches, we also need to recognize that tears help connect us to spirit. When we are standing in this material world and our lost loved ones are hovering in the spirit realm, we become like dried watercolor paint next to paper—yearning to merge but too rigid to connect. We are the paint stuck inside its plastic palette, unable to flow. The water of our tears becomes the necessary ingredient, allowing us to finally bleed onto the paper in a beautiful meld, bridging the gap between our world and theirs. Some of my most vivid visitations with the spirit realm have occurred in the midst of my deepest cries.

As I stayed on the line while De'Ara moved through her grief that day, I could feel more of her defenses melt away with each tear. By the end of our call, her tone had changed—not just from the congestion caused by crying, but from a subtler shift. She had allowed herself to feel fully, to let the tears do their healing work. This is the kind of mental health intervention that no medication can replicate: the simple, potent medicine of allowing ourselves to release and transform through our tears.

For the sensitive souls, the empaths, the witches among us, this ability to process grief fully becomes even more crucial. Our heightened sensitivity means we feel everything more deeply—both joy and sorrow. When we try to suppress that depth of feeling, we might think we are being strong or simply dampening our pain, but we are often muting our magic. Our tears are a vital part of our connection to the unseen.

BLUNTING VERSUS PURGING

When I check in on my patients after they've started an antidepressant (which I do prescribe from time to time), one theme that has come up over and over is that, once the medication has taken effect, they cry less. My patients (and the people in their lives: their roommates, partners, friends, and family) generally see this as a sign of progress. Interestingly, some patients even find they *can't* cry while medicated. I recall one patient who had lost his dad while he was on an SSRI, and he reflected, "I don't know what this means about me, but the tears just don't come."

One of the ways that conventional psychiatric medications work, to the extent they do, is by blunting strong emotions—by narrowing our emotional range. The lows are less low. The tears are tamped down. And this is something we perceive as health.

But psychedelic medicines, such as psilocybin, ketamine, and ayahuasca, come at mental health in an entirely different way. They are purgative, meaning they elicit a catharsis. Through somatic release (releasing stored bodily tension through motions like shaking, stomping, dancing, yawning) and sometimes even physical purging (like sweating, vomiting, diarrhea), we are able to move through our stuck emotions and bring them to resolution. Vomiting, sweating, and diarrhea . . . I know, I'm really selling it. But it's important to keep in mind that with each somatic and physical purge, we are releasing stale emotions and lightening our load.

Another important feature of psychedelic work is the degree to which these medicines aid and abet the flow of tears. In my experience, psychedelics help us get better at crying. If we usually cry at a volume of six or seven on a ten-point scale, psychedelics push it to eleven.

The summer that my mom died, I let my tears flow freely and cried several times a day. Pregnant, overwhelmed, and mentally whiplashed by the suddenness of this loss, I would slump to the floor in primal wails of despair. I was not holding back any tears.

Then, a few years after my mom's passing, an unexpected door opened: the chance to work with a particularly potent psychedelic medicine called ayahuasca. The opportunity arose during a casual catch-up with a friend who mentioned she was heading to Brazil for this work. The moment she spoke of it, something deep within me *knew* I would go with her, even as my rational mind was focused on my chronically overbooked schedule. When I checked my calendar, the exact dates she was going were uncharacteristically empty. Within days, I was standing in line at the Brazilian embassy for a visa, and soon after, I was on an overnight flight to São Paulo.

At that point, after nearly four years of reflection, talking, journaling, and free-flowing tears, I thought I had properly grieved my mom's death. Ayahuasca showed me that, indeed, I had only just begun. The depths to which I touched grief in the ayahuasca ceremonies was beyond my previous conception. That week in the Amazon opened up new ways for me to process emotions, and to support my patients and the people around me through theirs. I now try to help my patients cry fully, coaxing them past those false peaks, and letting them ride the wave into complete release.

I learned another lesson about emotional release from my dear friend Kate. A few years ago, when her daughter was only three, she was *in it*—deep in the trenches of early motherhood, struggling to keep her head above water. Her days were long, exhausting, overstimulating, isolating. What's more, bearing witness to her daughter's struggles was stirring up painful memories from her own childhood. When Kate was growing up, her mom would fail to attune to her emotions. On days when Kate would come home from school feeling sad about ornery teachers or challenging friendships, her mom's response was emotionally flat, focused on problem-solving rather than the comfort and validation that Kate was seeking. In retrospect, Kate realized that her mom seemed to have undiagnosed neurodivergence, and her nervous system was likely frazzled by the sensory overload of parenthood. (I can relate.) Kate has told me, "My mom did such a good job as a mother in so many ways, but the emotional piece was just not within her capability. As a deeply feeling kid, I was often left alone with my big emotions. My mom was not capable of meeting me in those moments." Kate came away from her childhood with the belief that her emotions were too much for another person to handle, and that she was alone in her sadness.

Then one stormy evening we sat in a (legal) psychedelic ceremony together. Kate was having a hard go of it. While the rest of us were having brushes with divine ecstasy, she was hunched over, nauseous, headachy, and feeling, once again, alone in her sadness.

A few hours into the ceremony, one of my favorite songs came on—a cover of the Sufjan Stevens song "Chicago" by a group called the Staves. Kate was reaching a fever pitch of her nausea, and I placed a bowl in front of her, in case she was about to throw up. The singers, in three-part harmony, repeat the phrase "I've made a lot of mistakes," over and over again. I sat next to Kate, my hand on her back, while another friend of ours sat across from her, holding her hands tight. While the energy of the song was building, we started singing along. "I've made a lot of mistakes, I've made a lot of mistakes . . ." We started crying. We continued singing, our voices bleary from tears.

With each repetition, the meaning of the words was dissolving. I've made mistakes, you've made mistakes, we've made mistakes, and we sing on behalf of others who have made mistakes. It felt like a confession and an absolution and a pure plea to the heavens all at once. The song reached its climax, and Kate let loose over the bowl. This was going to be a big one.

Except nothing came out. Her mouth opened broadly, her body heaved involuntarily, and a rush of moaning, tears, and energy poured forth. This went on for multiple undulations, though still no material content came out. Wave after wave ushered forth, accompanied by loud guttural cries. To an outside observer, this might have looked like dry heaving. But we knew it to be energetic purging.

The song landed on its final chord, and Kate's release began to abate. After a few aftershocks, she sat upright, breathless, her face sopping wet from tears. Her nausea had resolved. Her breathing slowed, and there was that medicinal sigh.

Kate's ceremony shifted after that—out of challenge and shadow and into a gentler experience of light. And her life shifted after that night. She released into that bowl years of pent-up heartache from missed cues and lack of attunement. What was once fraught—the feeling that her sadness was too much for those around her to bear—was now transformed into a felt experience of being held by community through her sadness. We moved through those emotions with her, our hands on her back, our voices, blurred by tears, enveloping her. Our little coven showed her that, no matter how big it was, we could handle her energy. She was no longer alone in her sadness.

This night was pivotal in Kate's life. It was as though she walked through a portal. On the other side, she was newly opened to her innate gifts of intuition, and she expanded into her magic. After this, Kate became aware of a latent passion for healing work. She began to study Reiki, relishing every minute of her training. And, as it turned out, she has an incredible gift for this work. She can read energy, she can listen to guidance from source, and she can use her grounded presence and deep attunement in service of healing others. It's as though the un-shed tears had been a block to this expansion.

☾ ☾ ☾

Our conventional meds create blunting, while psychedelics facilitate purging. Where antidepressants tamp down our tears, psychedelics elicit them. *Not* crying can look like health, but I think we've got it backwards. I don't directly prescribe or facilitate psychedelics in my practice, and I don't believe they're the right choice for all people or all circumstances. But it is my suspicion that psych meds can at times create the *appearance* of healing, while psychedelics help us accomplish the actual work of healing.

It is the sensitive, intuitive, witchy women who will be the most symptomatic in our poisonous world. As they move through the initiations of female life—adolescence, child-rearing, perimenopause—they are the most likely to end up walking out of a psychiatrist's office with a prescription. And indeed, women are more than twice as likely as men to take antidepressants. While I never want to deprive someone of the care they need (and at times I find medications to be a necessary bridge), I sometimes wonder if we are too quick to medicate away these mechanisms that our bodies use to move energy. Perhaps witchy women need something else entirely. Those tears, that sensitivity, the circle of support around us as we move through our raw emotions, may actually be a portal into our deepened, magical selves. In the words of a patient of mine, medications can create safety with a lowercase *s*. But moving through these emotions and emerging on the other side in our wholeness is a lifelong prescription for Safety with a capital *S*.

WHEN THE WATERS GROW STILL

Rather than seeing our mental health symptoms as inevitable genetic suffering, we need to see them as information. When symptoms signal physical imbalance, we recalibrate our physiology. When they reveal misalignment in the world around us, we receive this wisdom, alchemize it, and respond through our art and actions.

For too long, we've been told that our tears are a sign of weakness, and our big feelings mean we are too sensitive. We got it wrong. Our tears soften our hearts and open portals to the spirit realm. Our sensitivities allow us to sense others' needs and know when something is amiss in our surroundings. Our deep feelings connect us to the pulse of life itself.

As witches, we must not pathologize these traits or "hold it all in." We can instead take a more embodied approach to mental health—addressing false moods and handing ourselves over to tears—so that the psyche is clear. Only then do the waters grow still. And in that stillness, we can finally hear our intuition, feel the current of our magic, and know, with unshakable certainty, that what we once thought was broken wiring was actually an exquisite antenna.

Chapter 7

THE HEAD AND THE HEART: TUNING TO LOVE IN OUR CONTENTIOUS WORLD

> love is the voice under all silences,
> the hope which has no opposite in fear.
>
> —E. E. CUMMINGS, "being to timelessness as it's to time"

Octavia is seated onstage under bright lights in her padded chair, draped in a black velvet dress. Her heart races as some stragglers are ushered into the dark concert hall. She practices slow diaphragmatic breathing to calm her nerves. But she knows how this always goes: her preperformance jitters crescendo, and then they resolve just before the music begins, when the orchestra tunes their instruments.

You know that moment: right before an orchestra starts playing, when a wave of mildly dissonant staccato notes fills the air. The instruments are all slightly out of sync, creating a low-level cacophony. But soon, each instrument arrives into tune, and the dissonance transforms into balance and readiness. Octavia's body responds in kind—her tension eases, her nerves settle. The harmony signals to her: it's time to begin. As the music starts, Octavia dissolves into pure sound. Her bow becomes an extension of her, drawing across the strings, adding her signature vibration to the air. She becomes one note in the symphony, inseparable from the whole.

Months after that performance, Octavia sits on my couch, her cello far away. It's a dreary March morning, and her eyes are clouded with uncertainty. She's grappling with a difficult decision about her relationship with a wounded, sometimes unkind partner. As I observe her constricted body and physical discomfort while she describes her relationship, I'm reminded of the way she speaks about playing music onstage. The harmony she feels in her body while performing is such a stark contrast to what I see before me. In her music, she's alive, expansive, in tune. But here, in this moment, I see the embodiment of dissonance—her body closed off, her energy frayed.

"Should I finally leave her, this time for real?" Octavia asks, her voice barely above a whisper. Octavia admits that she knows she needs to, but what's holding her back is fear. She goes silent for a moment, second-guessing herself.

Then, after a pause, "How can I tell the difference between intuition and fear?"

FEAR VERSUS INTUITION

Octavia's struggle reveals a challenge we all face: how to distinguish between the signal of fear and the certainty of intuition. In order to discern the difference, we must learn to *feel* the difference between intuition and fear in our bodies.

Fear and intuition each carry a distinct vibration. Fear is like an instrument out of tune. It's dissonant, creating strain and discomfort in the body, an inner tension that eats away at us. It's a contracted state—a knot, a feeling of blocked energy flow.

As Mory Fontanez, author of *Higher Self: Reclaiming the Power of Your Intuition*, shared during a retreat that I attended, "We live in a culture that conditions us to believe that fear is intelligence." The message is that fear equals preparedness, that "if you don't live in fear . . . something bad is going to happen to you." But this mindset not only detracts from our ability to enjoy our lives, it creates more contraction, more discord, ultimately blocking our ability to *hear* our embodied wisdom.

Intuition, on the other hand, is that feeling of resolution as an instrument comes into tune. It feels balanced, ready. As doula Fatima Khadijah says, "Your intuition speaks in statements, your anxiety speaks in questions. That's the difference." Or as Fontanez explains, intuition "drops in like a period at the end of a sentence. It's not draining—it's calming, centered, rooted, even exciting." It feels fundamentally different from fear. An intuitive hit can feel like ease and expansion in the body, even when the guidance involves something challenging, like pursuing an ambitious creative project or, in Octavia's case, ending a relationship. There's a feeling of rightness and harmony in the body, even when it asks us to step into discomfort.

Now, to Octavia's question, how do we know if what we're feeling is intuition or fear? It's tempting to believe that some fears are a form of intuition. But to determine whether a new concern is intuition, we need to understand our baseline. If your nervous system is dysregulated and you're operating from a baseline of stress, hypervigilance, or chronic anxiety, a feeling of uneasiness is not necessarily an intuitive signal. Under those conditions, it's difficult to separate the signal from the noise. To distinguish when fear is actually intuitive guidance, we need a regulated nervous system that allows us to feel the contrast—the shift from a calm baseline to an acute, meaningful alert. Just as Octavia tunes her cello before performing, we need to tune our own instrument—we must learn to recognize a feeling of neutrality. I know this can be a hard message to hear if you're struggling with anxiety, but it's also motivation to prioritize nervous system regulation. From a calm baseline, a sharp signal of fear is much more likely to be meaningful intuitive guidance rather than background static.

HOW TO TELL WHEN YOU'RE DYSREGULATED

Our bodies always know when we've fallen out of tune. Here are the signs:

Physical Signals

- **Your breath is a clue.** Regulated breathing is calm, deep, and slow. Dysregulated breathing is shallow, rapid, or held. Check in: Can you take a full, easy breath right now?

- **Your body feels contracted.** Notice tension in your jaw, shoulders, chest, or gut. Are you tapping your foot without realizing it? Fidgeting or picking at your skin or hair? Dysregulation creates physical tightness, while regulation feels open and easeful.

Mental and Emotional Signs

- **Seeing only dead ends:** When regulated, you can think resourcefully about solutions. When dysregulated, you feel trapped, or convinced there's no way forward.
- **Reacting vs. responding:** Dysregulation has you shooting from the hip, saying things you may come to regret. Regulation allows you to pause and choose how you want to respond.
- **Taking low blows:** When your words turn cruel or accusatory, you've lost the vibration of love. Regulated communication seeks to understand the other person's perspective.
- **Getting defensive:** If you feel the need to protect yourself from perceived attacks, your system has moved into fight mode. As writer and healer Ayesha Ophelia says, "Letting people be wrong about you is so peaceful."

The Backstory

- **"If it's hysterical, it's historical."** As the saying goes in therapy circles, when your emotional response feels disproportionate to what's actually happening, you've likely tripped over an old wound. Sometimes these are preverbal memories from early childhood that you can't consciously access, but your body remembers. Returning to regulation often requires compassionate attention to these younger parts of yourself.
- **Levels of consciousness:** Psychologist David Hawkins mapped human consciousness on a scale from low-vibration

states (shame, guilt, fear) through neutral states (courage, acceptance) to high-vibration states (love, joy, peace). When dysregulated, we operate from the lower levels. Finding the path back to harmony requires recognizing where we are and consciously choosing to move up the scale—back toward love.

THE HEART AS INSTRUMENT

Many of us were taught to operate exclusively from our heads. We learned early that rationality and intellect were the keys to success in this world, and this approach has served us in many ways. But it also left us disembodied and disconnected from our heart center, cutting us off from an entire realm of intelligence that operates through feeling rather than analysis. What the future demands—what our highest contribution as witches requires—cannot be accessed through mental processing alone. Our clearest intuition and our most vital calling come from the heart.

The heart is both organ and energy center—the part of us that generates compassion, loving-kindness, and what we simply call love. According to research by the HeartMath Institute, the heart generates the body's most powerful electromagnetic field, measurably stronger than the brain's electrical activity. When we drop from our chattering minds into our heart center, we access an intelligence that operates at a different frequency altogether. This is where we can tune to the vibration of love, where we can *feel* rather than *think* our way through life's complexities.

As my friend Roya Darling, a writer and spiritual teacher, explains, "The heart is also the gateway to the deepest truth we have access to: our oneness with all that is. When I speak of heart (source) frequency, I'm also referring to the remembering of unity—that we're not acting alone. The heart dissolves the illusion of separation and reminds us that all is within us (and is us). It shifts us out of 'me doing this' into 'this is moving through me, with the whole, for the highest good.'"

When we shift our center of gravity into the heart, we can physically sense the difference between actions that create harmony and those that generate discord. This embodied, heart-centered awareness becomes our guidance system for contributing to the world's healing rather than its division. In Roya's words, "It is our frequency that is our most powerful offering."

FINDING YOUR FREQUENCY

Just as a musician adjusts their instrument until the strings are in tune, we can learn to tune our actions to the vibration of love. Here's how:

Recognize Your Frequency

- **Feel the frequency of love.** Picture yourself cuddling with someone you love or sharing a deep belly laugh with a friend. Close your eyes, scan your body, and notice what this vibration feels like. This is your signature for love's frequency.
- **Notice when you're out of tune.** Think of a time when you were triggered—maybe you felt misunderstood or judged, or you found yourself judging others' behavior. Picture the physical shift: furrowed brow, tight jaw, tense shoulders, a feeling of activation or heat rising in the chest. We even move our eyes differently in this state. This contracted state creates a feeling of cacophony—this is what the body feels like when it's out of tune.
- **Tune back in.** When you catch yourself sliding out of tune, pause. Take three slow breaths. Ask, "What would love do here?" Choose words and actions that create harmony rather than dissonance in the body.

Daily Tuning Practices

- **Surround yourself with resonant sound.** Throughout history, cultures worldwide have used harmonious music to shift consciousness. Whether it's specific healing frequencies like 528 or 741 Hz (available through a simple Spotify search), a choir's sacred harmonies, an orchestra's complex symphony, or a shaman's icaros (healing songs used in plant medicine ceremonies), surrounding ourselves with resonant sound creates an environment conducive to alignment.
- **Create sound yourself.** Even more powerful is making music—singing in a choir or hosting a living room sing-along allows us to physically embody harmony. When you sing, your voice sends healing frequencies throughout your body, naturally regulating your nervous system through the vagus nerve.
- **Practice sensory hygiene.** Our nervous systems are exquisitely sensitive instruments, continuously reading and responding to our environment. When possible, turn away from media that induces unnecessary tension or fear. If your immediate surroundings are overstimulating, see what stimuli you can dial down by turning off devices, clearing visual clutter from your space, and dimming harsh lights. (And, though controversial, you may even benefit from switching out some LED lights for incandescent bulbs to avoid the subtle flickering that can stress a nervous system.)
- **Immerse yourself in nature.** Allow your system to synchronize with Earth's inherent rhythms—the inhale and exhale of waves, the rustle of leaves with the breeze, the ancient songs of birds moving with the seasons. Nature co-regulates our nervous systems, and it can instantly drop us out of our spinning minds and into our hearts.
- **Create ritual.** Light candles, make altars with meaningful objects, call in spirit. These practices help us create a resonant field where we can more easily realign with the heart's fre-

quency. Through consistent practice, we strengthen our ability to maintain this connection, even in challenging times.

- **Allow emotional fluidity**. When you have the urge to cry, let yourself weep. As we've discussed, tears release emotional tension stored in the body, preventing the crystallization of grief and fear in our tissues. Crying keeps our hearts energetically soft and pliable.
- **Notice relationships that create discord in your body**. When certain people consistently trigger tension, pause before reacting. Sometimes the path forward requires setting boundaries. Other times, it means examining your own reactivity and the stories you're telling yourself about their behavior. Both responses can be acts of love.
- **Practice radical compassion**. When tempted to see a person or a group of people as "other," soften your heart and choose the most generous interpretation. Choose love, over and over again.

Maintain Your Foundation

- **Prioritize rest**. This allows for a calm nervous system and mental clarity, which helps you avoid getting pulled into lower vibration states like division and piling on to chaos.
- **Stay courageous**. Roya points out that "cor" means heart in Latin; courage literally means acting from the heart. Living a heart-centered life—speaking the truth and doing the right thing, even when it's counter to cultural forces—is always an act of courage.
- **Operate from wholeness**. Take a brutally honest (yet compassionate) look at your own shadows. Address internal conflicts and bring them to resolution rather than acting from a place of inner conflict and fragmentation. As Roya writes, "The outer world is a mirror of the inner one. . . . This reality doesn't bend to how noble our 'side' appears. It responds to vibration. . . . Anchor oneness within you."

Timing Matters

- **Protect the bookends.** The first and last hours of the day are when we are most receptive to programming. Even amid the chaos of daily life—packing lunches, racing to work, managing bedtime routines—carve out moments for quiet reflection, spiritual connection, or nature communion rather than inviting in the discordant frequencies of news and screens. Where you put your attention influences your vibration, and the bookends of the day have the most impact on your overall attunement.

As Roya explains, "The heart is where we awaken the consciousness of one—that we are interconnected, that everything we create affects the whole." When we are tuned to love, our actions naturally align with our highest form of magic. When we practice daily tuning, we can quickly recognize when we've strayed from our path and fallen out of key by the dissonance we feel. When we move through the world from our hearts rather than our heads, we become instruments of peace.

STAYING IN TUNE IN A DISCORDANT WORLD

The world is getting weirder, and this is not slowing down anytime soon. As the world around us deviates ever further from what we once took for granted as normal, it's easy to get pulled into a vibration of fear. That fear then engenders distrust, division, and separation, which only further reinforces the idea that we have good reason to fear. What we need in moments of heaviness is to return home to our hearts—placing our hands on our chests, breathing deeply, and consciously choosing the frequency of love over that of fear.

Our increasing separation from one another mirrors what some theoretical physicists predict: that the universe will ultimately end in "heat death." That is, as space expands exponentially, molecules will drift so far apart that chemical bonds can no longer form, leaving only cold, isolated particles in an empty void. We may be witnessing the microcosmic, social version of this phenomenon: isolated in car-dependent suburbs, absorbed in screens rather than gathering in community spaces, siphoned off into warring echo chambers, we're drifting further from warm, meaningful human connection.

Our already-polarized culture emerged from the pandemic even more fractured. In patriarchal systems, broad-scale trauma triggers fight/flight/freeze responses, pushing us into defensive postures and knee-jerk reactions. And that's exactly what we see at family gatherings, in workplace conflicts, and in the comments sections on social media. When we're scared, we contract, huddle with our tribe, and strike out against those we see as "other." This digs the grooves of division even deeper. Are we experiencing the first taste of heat death?

A system that is more balanced—more yin, more witchy—handles trauma differently. It tends and befriends. It prioritizes taking care of one another. Instead of further polarization, it meets crisis with genuine openness and compassion, providing a calm foundation for collective response.

As witches, can we play a role in keeping the universe connected? By dropping from our heads into our hearts, we emit love's frequency and restore the bonds that hold our world together. This heart-centered awareness is how we practice good magic: not from a disembodied, intellectual place but from the warm, sensing center that can feel whether our actions serve love or feed separation.

Like Octavia learning to recognize the harmony she feels in her body when playing music, we can learn to discern when our lives are in tune with love's frequency. When she finally made the decision to leave her relationship, it wasn't from a place of fear or anger, but from the same embodied knowing that guided her bow across the strings. Her body knew—with the readiness of an orchestra in tune. In moving through our lives from the heart instead of the head, we become agents of connection rather than division, helping to heal our fractured world.

Indeed, the true nature of reality is that isolation is the illusion and interconnection is the wild but demonstrable truth.

Our culture wants us dissociated, but a witch is embodied so that she can hear the call of her intuition.

SECOND PRACTICE: PRESENCE

Our Culture Pushes Us Toward Distraction. A Witch Comes Into Presence.

As we reclaim our embodied wisdom, we begin to gather great power. This is the moment when our witchcraft becomes potent—and potentially dangerous. We are no longer operating from the neck up, disconnected from our bodies' intelligence. Instead, we are awake, aware, and increasingly attuned to the subtle energies that move through us. This awakening comes with responsibility: How do we ensure that our growing power serves the light? How do we use our magic for good?

Having recognized the cultural forces that have kept us disconnected—the ways we've been conditioned to doubt our intuition and live dissociated from our bodies—we're ready to turn toward presence. This is where we clear away all the distortions, gather our energy, and wield it consciously, allowing our magic to flow in service of good.

Presence is the ability to be fully awake and aware in the present moment, anchored in ourselves, with what I call "the lights on." Our culture systematically works against this state, driving us toward distraction. This happens through algorithms that bait us into tribalism and endless scrolling, through engineered foods that override our satiety, and through fearmongering that dysregulates the nervous system. These forces make us vulnerable to manipulation, and they disconnect us from the inner compass that could guide us toward right action. When we're distracted, we become easy targets for those who would use our energy for their own ends. We risk unconsciously perpetuating the very patterns of harm we claim to oppose.

Presence is our protection and our power. It allows us to maintain sovereignty over our own energy, catching the subtle signals that alert us when something is trying to hijack our life force. It enables us to act with integrity, noticing the moment we begin to stray from our values—when we slip into manipulating others instead of communicating directly, or when we retreat into victim stories rather than claiming our agency. As we step into our full witchy power, presence becomes the difference between being a force for healing in the world and inadvertently adding to its chaos.

Chapter 8

KEEPING THE LIGHTS ON: RECLAIMING SOVEREIGNTY

The most common way people give up their power is by thinking they don't have any.

—Attributed to ALICE WALKER

Growing up, when my family would go on vacation we would set our lights on a timer—a hollow attempt to suggest someone was home. We believed that, as long as a light flicked on behind drawn curtains every evening at 6 P.M. on the dot, any potential burglars would surely be deterred.

A present person is like a house full of life. The lights are genuinely on. There's tending and awareness. Presence means being home in our own bodies—there's someone alert and awake behind our eyes. And what burglar would dare approach a home so clearly occupied?

But when we're not truly "home" in our bodies—when we're disconnected, distracted, numb, or dissociated—we become like an empty house with timer lights. Or worse: completely dark, unoccupied, abandoned. We become vulnerable. And there are many aspects of modern life that take us away from home—from addictive substances and cheap dopamine hits to manufactured outrage and fear.

As we step into our magical power, we must acknowledge a reality: not everyone uses their influence consciously or ethically. Some people operate from co-dependency and manipulation, others from greed or unconscious wounding that they project onto the world. There are bad actors out there. We don't want to *be* one of them, and we don't want to leave our doors unlocked *to* them. If we want to practice good magic—power that heals rather than harms—we need to follow two essential tenets.

First is sovereignty: taking full ownership of our energy, our choices, and our responses—refusing to give our power away or to be unconsciously influenced by others. Sovereignty means staying home in our bodies with the lights on, so no one gets to occupy our house but us.

Second is integrity: ensuring our actions align with our deepest values. This requires honest self-examination of our true motivations, ensuring we don't become the burglar of other people's homes.

Presence is how we keep the lights on—how we stay conscious and aligned with our highest good. It's our protection against becoming someone who misuses power or falling under the influence of those who do.

As witches, we are powerful, and this comes with tremendous responsibility: we must ensure this power serves the light rather than our own narrow interests. We are not here to cast hexes on enemies or manipulate outcomes for personal gain—we are here to help shift the world's vibration from fear to love.

SOVEREIGNTY

Our modern world teems with forces seeking to extract our energy—whether through our money, our attention, our beliefs, or our labor. These energy vampires operate through our food system, our media landscape, and our socially sanctioned addictions. Their success depends on keeping us disconnected from our power and hooked on their offerings.

Women today face an urgent imperative: to reclaim our sovereignty—our ability to make choices free from coercion, influence, or manipulation. But before we can reclaim our power, we must first recognize what binds us. Our soft addictions—to phones, food, distraction, consumerism, and fear—are more than just bad habits; they leave our doors unlocked and taint our magic.

THE ATTENTION ECONOMY: FEAR AS CONTROL

Gemma kept her phone face up beside her during our therapy sessions, eyes darting to each notification. During our conversations about her anxiety and insomnia, she reflexively checked X whenever I glanced down at my notes. As a journalist and social justice activist, she insisted that staying current with the public conversation was a necessary precondition to doing her job well.

But I was beginning to observe: by keeping her strung out and anxious, Gemma's incessant phone use seemed to be eroding rather than supporting her work. Any new cause felt like it required her immediate attention, even though this meant that whatever she'd been focused on previously would fall away. By jumping between causes, trying to be every kind of activist, she diluted her impact. She told me she felt demoralized in her work, like she was "screaming into the void."

When I suggested getting to bed earlier to address her insomnia, she returned the following week with a familiar refrain: "It didn't work. When my head hits the pillow, my mind is racing. Though I'm exhausted all day, I feel wired at night."

Here's what most of us living in the twenty-first century need to understand: when we're tethered to our phones in the evening, we can no longer rely on the sensation of *tiredness* to cue us for sleep. Melatonin is the hormone that makes us feel sleepy, but the blue light from our screens suppresses melatonin release. If we're looking at screens, we've lost that cue. Meanwhile, our phones are engineered specifically to keep us engaged. Unlike a book with chapters, which signals to us every so often, *Here's a good opportunity to close the book and go to bed*, social media platforms are designed without natural stopping cues. They call it "endless scroll" because these apps are intended to keep us scrolling indefinitely. Furthermore, our phones bathe us in fear. On that proverbial savannah of human evolution, sleep was a vulnerable state; we were lying unconscious in the dark, exposed to predators. Because of this, we need to feel some semblance of safety in order to fall asleep. But algorithms favor doomscrolling and "if it bleeds, it leads." So, in our modern landscape, our phones make us feel surrounded by danger—a surefire way to keep us wide-awake.

We are living in what's called the attention economy. That is, our attention has become the commodity being traded. Tech companies have mastered behavioral psychology, understanding that nothing captures attention quite like fear and outrage. While advertisers once relied on "sex sells," tech developers have discovered an even more potent truth: fear sells better.

The cost of this manipulation extends far beyond lost sleep. When we're constantly triggered into states of fear and hypervigilance, a certain kind of "intuition" ramps up—a reactive fight-or-flight instinct, tuned for survival, that is scanning for threats. But in this heightened state, we lose access to a deeper intuitive knowing, one that harmonizes our reactive instincts with our slower knowings. When fear overtakes us, our sophisticated cerebral structures—like the prefrontal cortex that enables delayed gratification and restraint—take a back seat. Our amygdala—the brain's primary threat detection center—takes control, shifting us from higher-order thinking to more reactive, survival-driven functions. This compromises executive function as well as empathy and big-picture thinking, making us more likely to prioritize self-preservation over collective well-being. We can't hear the guidance of our deeper truths when we're scanning for threats. Or, worse, we hear our fearful thoughts and mistake them for intuition.

When we feel overwhelmed by the world's wrongs, our first instinct might be to stay up late doomscrolling. But, as Gemma was learning the hard way, we don't change the world through exhaustion. What's more, whatever indignation we already feel about our stance only gets amplified by the rallying cries of our own echo chamber. The resulting self-righteous outrage is not a great strategy for changing minds. Gemma would mention, "I don't understand how anybody can be okay with what's happening in the world right now. Like, how can they post about their kid's birthday party at a time like this?" The trouble is, to Gemma, every day was "a time like this." In the words of poet and activist Andrea Gibson, "No one owes the world their misery. . . . Every activist I have ever known who believed they owed the world their unhappiness has burned out." Gemma was living proof of this burnout cycle—her constant vigilance wasn't changing the world—it was depleting her capacity to show up for it.

Not to mention, with the global connectivity made possible by the internet and social media, we are now aware of every crisis across the planet. Certainly, this is more than our human brains evolved to handle. If we are to have any positive influence, it will be through the power of mutual understanding. In order to face our differences with softness and compassion, we must first turn toward ourselves with genuine openness about our inner conflicts and blind spots. This doesn't tend to happen if we are allowing ourselves to be swept up in the current of an algorithm. Instead, we double down on our hatred toward the other, and our actions end up fueling the fires of separation rather than creating a ripple effect of peace. As Gibson suggests, "If we put our attention on the world's beauty, we will have far more strength and stamina to show up to the world's pain."

At its core, this is a question of sovereignty. This is about reclaiming our ability to make choices free from coercion and manipulation, to stay connected to our own inner knowing rather than being carried along by external forces. As Roya Darling explains, "The way out isn't bypassing anger. It's presence. It's pausing. It's becoming the observer. Only from presence can we discern what is actually moving us and choose not to unconsciously recycle the same energy we claim to oppose. Practicing presence is not passive. It is the most radical choice we can make."

When we're distracted—chasing a cortisol hit rather than being present—we become easy targets for manipulation. Presence allows us to sense the contraction in the chest when doomscrolling and notice the hungry quality of clickbait headlines. These signals are our early warning system against forces that seek to extract our energy. Remember, when the product is free, you're the product. Without sovereignty over our attention, we cannot access our deeper wisdom or create meaningful change. We risk being influenced by outside forces, mistaking their agenda for our own truth.

HOW TO RESTORE SLEEP

Our circadian rhythm is cued primarily by light—a system that was foolproof for most of human history. Morning light supports a rise in cortisol, keeping us alert. After sunset, darkness signals melatonin production, making us sleepy. But evolution didn't anticipate the plot twist of artificial light. With electricity and screens, we now stay wired long after nightfall. The solution: give your body the cues it evolved to recognize.

Restore Natural Light Cues

- **Take a circadian walk**. Get actual sunshine into your actual eyeballs as early as possible—not through sunglasses, a car windshield, or a window, but the real thing. This tells your brain it's morning and starts the internal clock that programs sleepiness at night.
- **Dim lights after sunset**. Rather than keeping lights blazing, start dimming them in the evening to simulate sunset conditions.
- **Wear blue-blocking glasses at night**. Block blue-spectrum light in the evening to protect your brain's ability to secrete melatonin, even in our artificially lit world.

Create Sleep-Supporting Habits

- **Keep your phone out of the bedroom**. Set up your charger elsewhere to avoid scrolling before bed, which floods your eyes with blue light and triggers danger signals. Read a paper book and use an old-school alarm clock instead. If you need to be able to hear your phone ring overnight, keep it within earshot but not arm's reach.
- **Earlier bedtime**: Aim for approximately three hours after sunset to "catch the wave" when your cortisol is low and your body is perfectly tired. This helps you avoid getting overtired

(when cortisol kicks in with a second wind of energy). In my experience, any hours of sleep we clock between 9 P.M. and 12 A.M. are especially restful. An earlier bedtime generally ensures better quality sleep.

Support Sleep Biochemically

- **Supplement with magnesium glycinate.** This is my first-line sleep support. It helps with sleep, headaches, menstrual cramps, anxiety, and digestion—and most of us are deficient.
- **If you're perimenopausal/postmenopausal, consider hormones.** As progesterone levels drop, sleep becomes dicey and especially prone to middle-of-the-night wake-ups. Early perimenopause: consider vitex (chasteberry) to help regulate prolactin and gently normalize progesterone levels. Later stages: discuss progesterone replacement with your doctor.

Don't Overthink Sleep

Between wearables, cooling pads, and biohacking culture, we can become obsessive about the quest for perfect sleep. But sleep is fundamentally a state of surrender—it works best when we don't fixate on it. Once you believe you're a bad sleeper and begin to dread sleepless nights, this activated state becomes a self-fulfilling prophecy. Follow the steps above to support healthy circadian rhythm, then let go. Remember: your body knows how to sleep, and it wants to sleep. Give it what it needs and then let it do its thing.

For Gemma, fear and distraction were disconnecting her from her power. The path out required three interconnected shifts: establishing sovereignty over her attention, restoring her sleep, and connecting to her intuition. Her constant vigilance, drowning in late-night blue light and fear-based content, was damaging both her rest and her inner guidance. Ironically, staying "informed" was making her less effective.

We started small. First, Gemma would no longer bring her phone into the bedroom. She set up her charger in the living room and kissed her phone goodnight by 9:30 P.M. In its place, she would read something life-affirming that had nothing to do with current events. (She came to particularly enjoy meditative musings by Vietnamese Zen Buddhist monk Thich Nhat Hanh.) This single boundary allowed her natural tiredness to return.

Once rested, she could take the next step: beginning each day with five minutes of meditation before checking her phone. During these quiet moments, she started receiving clear "downloads" about where to direct her energy for maximum impact. Rather than dispersing herself across every online cause, she started organizing on a local level. She focused on education in nearby underserved communities. Within months, she helped establish an after-school program that now serves hundreds of students. Finally, her impact felt tangible.

As author and spiritual teacher Byron Katie observes, "The world is your perception of it. Inside and outside always match—they are reflections of each other. The world is the mirror image of your mind." In time, Gemma also did some inner work, recognizing that her judgment of others—those people online and in her community who she felt weren't fighting for justice hard enough, or in the right way—was really projection. She had parts of herself that she didn't wholly accept, and unconsciously, it felt safer to direct that judgment outward than to take an honest but compassionate look at the tender parts of herself that carried shame. She had also been a "parentified" child (a child forced to take on adult responsibilities and care for parents instead of being cared for), so she carried a background story that the people around her were irresponsible, incompetent, and letting her down. She came to realize she envied friends and family members who were thriving while she struggled. In her mind, the only way someone could be thriving was if they were selfish capitalists—not fighting for marginalized populations or fully feeling the world's heaviness. But as she began integrating the parts of herself she had disavowed, meeting herself with radical acceptance, and getting better sleep while unplugging from the news, she started thriving too. She still held the full gravity of all the wrongs of the world, but she felt more tolerant of those around her, and she realized her own joy was also a form of activism.

BE STILL, AND KNOW

We all know we "should" meditate—we've heard it countless times. But let me make a fresh case for why: Have you ever tried to communicate with someone who's distracted? I encounter this daily with my husband and daughter, their faces in phones or books while I attempt conversation. "Are you even listening?" I ask, knowing they're not. Eventually, I stop trying. What's the point?

Now imagine this: What if *source* is trying to communicate with *you*? I believe we have a shared to-do list with the divine. Spirit is trying to transmit guidance, assign us tasks, show us our next steps. But we're constantly distracted. When we remain perpetually unavailable, the divine, like a frustrated partner, eventually stops trying.

However, when we show up for a few minutes of silence each day, dropping into pure awareness, we demonstrate our availability to receive. I no longer think of meditation as "trying to clear my mind." Instead, it's my *listening time*—my daily check-in with source.

This practice becomes especially crucial in the face of assaults on our sovereignty. Meditation creates a pause between stimulus and response, helping us resist the dopamine-driven pulls of our social media feeds and addictive substances. In that pause, we learn to distinguish authentic desires from manufactured cravings, real concerns from fear-driven content. Most importantly, it restores our connection to intuition, so often drowned out by the cacophony of modern life. The attention economy uses cortisol to drive engagement, keeping us trapped in fear-based thinking. By reclaiming sovereignty over our attention through meditation, we create the calm, receptive state where intuition flourishes.

But meditation is just one piece of the puzzle. To fully reclaim our sovereignty, we must understand the broader forces working to separate us from presence.

THE VOID AND ITS FILLERS

Lucy postponed therapy for years, claiming she couldn't afford it despite her successful PR career. The real reason emerged slowly: her money vanished into designer clothes and luxury handbags, leaving her drowning in credit card debt.

"I need to dress for the job I want, not the job I have, right?" she'd say with an air of playful self-awareness. Upon deeper excavation, she admitted that she liked the way people looked at her when she walked into a room "looking expensive." It made her feel like she was important, like she was *somebody*. As the middle child of two overwhelmed parents, she felt invisible in her childhood home—her needs coming last, her achievements overlooked. She yearned to be distinguished and noticed, even if it bankrupted her. Lucy's spending wasn't just about status. Growing up in a household living paycheck to paycheck, under the constant threat of financial hardship, she carried deep scarcity trauma. Accumulating stuff made her *feel* rich even if it was, ironically, making her broke. She also pointed out that, when work was stressful, dating was discouraging, and her friends were too busy with their lives to hang out, shopping was the one thing that reliably gave her a "jolt of dopamine."

The common denominator of our soft addictions—to phones, distraction, consumption, and food—is our longing to fill a void. That void stems from multiple sources: childhood trauma, disrupted attachment, the withdrawal effects of these addictive substances themselves (what I consider to be the most underappreciated factor), and our severed connections to community and nature. For some, this emptiness manifests as addiction to sex and love; for others, drugs, alcohol, or compulsive shopping. But what I've observed in my patients' and my own journey through depression and binge eating is that disconnection from source—our sense of meaning, our relationship with the deeper mysteries of existence—creates a particularly deep hole.

When we're held by community, our bodies have their needs met, and we're connected to source, we are content—but we're terrible customers. When we are whole, we have no hole to fill. Smart businesses recognize the threat of this spiritual self-sufficiency, and they work furiously to erode it. Our economy depends on our disconnection from magic.

I sometimes wonder if the engineers of early capitalism understood that community and spirituality left people feeling far too connected and content to ever fall prey to consumerism. As Don Draper famously says in *Mad Men*, "What you call love was invented by guys like me to sell nylons." By creating a false sense of separation from one another and the divine, by suggesting that the universe was senseless, early capitalists created a spiritual void we attempt to fill with endless consumption.

They say, "America runs on Dunkin'," but our modern economy actually runs on disconnection. When we perceive this world to be random, material, and cold, when we are estranged from community, nature, service, and source, we carry around a black hole of unmet needs. That's where advertisers step in to finish the sentence for us, reminding us that we're unsafe, unlovable, not enough, and fundamentally broken. But fear not! For three easy payments of $29.99, we can be saved. This hooks us into a cycle of spending, accumulating debt, working tirelessly to dig our way out, and then feeling so burned-out that we need to spend more money just to buy back any shred of joy. We become cogs in whatever corporate wheel we find ourselves in, never quite reaching the finish line. Meanwhile, we're overworked, unfulfilled, and so bereft of contentment that we keep the consumerist fires burning through desperate purchases of shoes and gadgets. We might be miserable (and in debt), but we're good customers and loyal employees.

The system reinforces this trap through tactics like planned obsolescence—products deliberately designed to fail, forcing regular replacements. Our phones mysteriously slow down just as new models launch. These aren't glitches but features of a system that requires our perpetual consumption.

Lucy's transformation began unexpectedly. One Sunday morning, nursing a hangover and wandering her neighborhood in search of greasy food, she heard beautiful harmonies drifting from what looked like a converted warehouse—a nondescript building she'd walked past countless times without ever noticing. Drawn by the sound, she peered through the open doors and discovered a cavernous room filled with folding chairs arranged in a wide semicircle. Some forty voices blended together as a community choir worked through their repertoire. She'd stumbled on their weekly rehearsal, when they prepared for free performances around the city. She decided to join.

Week after week, she found herself choosing choir rehearsals over high-end boutiques. Inside that simple space, Lucy found something shopping had never provided: genuine community and the experience of transcendence. She made real relationships, free of pretense. When she tuned in to presence, she noticed that choir rehearsals created an enduring source of contentment—completely distinct from the dopamine roller coaster that she had previously associated with pleasure. Gradually, her compulsion to shop eased. The void was filled not through accumulation but through connection.

FOOD SOVEREIGNTY

Cheryl came to me struggling with an eating disorder that reflected our culture's distorted relationship with food. She'd grown up in a chaotic household that offered only fast food and ultraprocessed snacks, and as an adult she swung to the opposite extreme. She would start the day with an oat milk matcha latte ("to rev up my metabolism"), make a smoothie for lunch, snack on seaweed and rice cakes throughout the day ("to stave off cravings"), and typically have "a huge salad" for dinner. She saw "eating clean" as her exit ramp from being overweight. Yet, at all times, Cheryl was starving. She felt like she was in a battle with her body—it wanted one thing (to eat) and she wanted another (to be thin).

Years of restriction left her undernourished and obsessed with food. When she finally gave in to her cravings, the pendulum swung hard. In feverish binges, she would devour family-size bags of her childhood comfort foods—Cool Ranch Doritos, Oreos, Sour Patch Kids. As her weight rebounded, she sat in my office, devastated: "I feel like I've lost all control."

This pattern—restriction followed by binge eating—is actually a predictable response to our modern, engineered food.

While our attention and consumption patterns are vulnerable to manipulation, perhaps no relationship is more fundamental to our sovereignty than our relationship with food. Our bodies are the vessels through which we experience life, receive intuition, and channel magic. The state of our physical health can either clear or block our intuitive channels. And here too, powerful forces work to keep us away from home.

Many of the most dominant companies achieved their success largely by figuring out how to addict the human brain. Whether we're talking about caffeine, tobacco, alcohol, sugar, ultraprocessed foods, certain medications, social media, video games, or porn, these industries exploit our neuroscience, stringing us out on reward and relief pathways involving dopamine, GABA (a calming neurotransmitter), and opioid signaling while engineering states of withdrawal and craving. In the process, they build lifelong loyal customers. Meanwhile, we, the law-abiding citizens—simply consuming what is affordable, pleasurable, often socially condoned, and sometimes even prescribed by doctors—find ourselves in a state of physiologic dependence. We wake up in caffeine withdrawal and end the day with sugar and alcohol cravings. We can't sleep without Ambien or relax without Xanax. We twitch when we can't check our phones. We struggle to have satisfying physical intimacy because our reward circuitry has been recalibrated to the extremes of pornography. We have little capacity to be still with our own thoughts and emotions because we are acclimated to being in a state of constant distraction.

If you feel on edge without wine or need benzos to simply exist, are you free? We are not sovereign in our relationship to addictive substances. In fact, we credit them with solving the very withdrawal they create. When loved ones encourage us to drink less or set boundaries with the phone, we snarl at them. It's no accident that we never think to blame the addictive substance. As author and recovery advocate Holly Whitaker argues in her groundbreaking book *Quit Like a Woman*, our culture (shaped by the alcohol industry) deliberately places the emphasis on an *individual* being an alcoholic, rather than acknowledging that alcohol is an inherently addictive substance.

The processed-food industry is an exemplar of stolen sovereignty, and it sets us up to fail. Cheryl's seemingly opposite extremes—orthorexic restriction (obsessive "clean" eating) and unbridled overeating—share a common root: the fact that ultraprocessed foods are engineered to be hyperpalatable. In other words, food has become a drug. This is the original source of the swinging pendulum. When foods are drugs, they create a state of out-of-control eating, which pushes people into a desperate attempt to regain control by way of restriction. This, in turn, begets food obsession and overeating.

While the wellness movement began as a radical act of reclamation—taking our health into our own hands—in many cases it has morphed into a sublimated eating disorder. In trying to eat "clean" and be well, many find themselves hungry, depleted, and obsessed with food until they finally break. When they do, the processed-food industry stands ready with open arms: "Welcome back. Treat yourself. You deserve it." Like addicts returning to their dealer, these starving wellness refugees collapse into the welcoming embrace of Big Food, gorging on engineered foods that hit their bliss point like a drug. The relief is fleeting—soon they're back in the cycle of withdrawal and cravings. We flee the abusive relationship of diet culture, only to fall into another. Meanwhile, our intuitive connection to hunger, satiety, and what our bodies truly need grows increasingly confused.

While Cheryl was blaming herself for a lack of willpower, willpower never had anything to do with her situation. Her satiety signals were distorted by design. Many of our most popular food companies were acquired in the 1980s by big tobacco firms, which brought their expertise in creating addictive products to the food industry, manufacturing drug-like foods to keep us coming back for more. Though tobacco companies have since divested from the food industry, their legacy lives on in the ultraprocessed foods that dominate our grocery store shelves.

Through millennia of human evolution, food cravings were based on bodily intelligence about what nourished us and what our bodies were missing. Our cravings guided us toward the foods that met our moment-to-moment nutritional needs. Even the way children are drawn to brightly colored foods is a remnant of an evolutionary adaptation—in nature, vibrant colors indicate the presence of nutrients and antioxidants. Today, artificial food coloring exploits this inbuilt mechanism, leading us to reach for nutritionally empty foods that merely mimic the visual signals of nourishment.

When the only foods that were available to us were real foods, our system of cravings was foolproof. Our appetites could be trusted. And when we had enough of what our bodies needed, we felt full. Unfortunately, this system has been commandeered by the processed food industry, which engineers foods to be not only something that we crave like drugs (even when the foods are nutritionally bankrupt) but something that overrides satiety. All the while, though these foods are caloric, they fail to satisfy any of our real nutritional needs. This leaves our bodies with a feeling of never having enough, driving us to continue to consume. The industry can then sell more products. They win. But sovereignty loses.

This rift with our body extends beyond food—it represents a fundamental break in the present, embodied relationship that allows us to navigate life intuitively. When we can't trust our appetite, how can we trust our other bodily signals? Indeed, numb, addicted people make better customers. When we're away with the lights off, burglars can enter—our bodies, our pocketbooks. The path out is presence—learning to check in with ourselves and discern what truly serves us.

Cheryl's appetite had been hijacked, turning what should have been a harmonious relationship with her body into an internal war. As we worked together to rebuild her natural cravings and satiety signals, Cheryl had a revelation: "I feel like I'm in couples therapy with my body." That metaphor captured it perfectly—she was learning to trust her body again, rather than fight it. As she and her body gradually became allies instead of adversaries, she discovered that the real battle wasn't with her appetite or willpower—it was with an industry scheming to override her body's wisdom.

We are in a dizzying moment of contradictory messages about food: plant based versus carnivore, whether or not to eat the yolk, and apparently there's never enough protein. It can make us want to give up altogether. When we feel overwhelmed, it can be helpful to come back to the simplest and most important dietary compass: eat real food and avoid fake food. Do this whenever possible, and when it's not possible, don't overthink it.

CHOOSE YOUR HARD

When we're manipulated by systems designed to keep us dependent and lacking agency in our choices, we often feel trapped between impossible options. Meet Reneé, who came to me because she was struggling with psoriasis, prediabetes, and depression while raising children with their own health challenges. The entire household relied on ultra-processed foods. The kids were inflamed, with eczema and recurrent ear infections. Their diet put them on a roller coaster of sugar highs and food-coloring-induced hyperactivity, followed by a crash every evening. Renée, who took immune-suppressing drugs for her psoriasis, was on her third bout of strep that winter, which made her already-difficult daily life feel nearly impossible. She and her wife decompressed from the stress with several glasses of wine every evening.

When I mentioned that diet and lifestyle changes could help her situation, she shot me a death stare. "I'm in survival mode," she said. "I can barely make it through the day, let alone start packing organic bento boxes for everyone's lunch."

Looking back, I realize there was a subtle dynamic at play in our brief time together. I sensed that what Reneé really wanted to hear was: "You didn't do anything wrong." She was seeking absolution—not just from guilt about the past, but from responsibility for the future. She was already drowning, so the idea of being responsible felt untenable. In fact, what she yearned for, even more than being told she wasn't to blame, was being told: "Don't worry, there's nothing you need to do differently."

This is understandable. We want relief, but we want it to be easy. We want to take a pill. We want to wave our fists in the air and blame broken systems—and they are indeed broken—without having to look toward solutions that require effort from us. As Byron Katie reminds us, "As long as you think that the cause of your problem is 'out there'—as long as you think that anyone or anything else is responsible for your suffering—the situation is hopeless. It means that you are forever in the role of the victim, that you're suffering in paradise."

As Reneé's psychiatrist, it was tempting to tell her what she wanted to hear. She would have felt validated and supported. She would have liked me, and she might have even stayed in treatment. But I knew that while such absolution might bring fleeting relief, it wouldn't touch her real suffering. For that, she would need to assume agency and take action.

The uncomfortable truth is that lasting relief often lives on the other side of effort—the effort of changing habits when we're already depleted. Of taking responsibility, even when we feel overwhelmed. Even when it's unfair. Of fighting for what little shred of empowerment we have, even in systems of oppression. The game is rigged—it's true. And yet, we still shouldn't give up the fight.

Our culture increasingly wants to be coddled rather than empowered. "You're enough." "It's not your fault." "Treat yourself." But sovereignty means something different. It means recognizing that we are the authors of our own lives, for better and sometimes for worse. It means understanding that, while we may not have caused our problems, we do have agency in addressing them. The most fulfilling version of our lives doesn't come from being absolved of responsibility—it comes from choosing to take it on.

This is what we call "choose your hard." Yes, changing eating habits is difficult. Believe me, I know—I live this daily. But you know what else is hard? Depression, recurrent strep, and getting the call from the school nurse that your child has *yet another* ear infection. Of course, neither Reneé's primary care doctor nor her rheumatologist connected the dots that her immune-modulating medications, designed to *literally suppress* the immune system, were contributing to her recurrent strep infections. Addressing her psoriasis at the root could have caused a chain reaction of health improvements.

Beyond physical health, screen time presents another version of this choose-your-hard dilemma. Whenever the chaos of parenthood felt unbearable, Renée would understandably hand her kids their iPads—her only reprieve from the constant demands. But the temporary peace inevitably gave way to a household of dysregulation, screen-time battles, and meltdowns that left everyone more fractured than before.

The truth is, we're not choosing between hard and easy—we're choosing between different kinds of hard: the temporary challenge of changing habits, which leads to better health and greater ease, versus the relentless grind of dysregulation and chronic illness. Hard now or *harder* later.

Reneé never came back for a second appointment. In those early days of my practice, I was clumsy at building rapport and generating buy-in before dropping the suggestion of lifestyle changes. But if she had continued working with me, I would have encouraged her to eat real food and avoid fake food. I would have helped her understand how ultraprocessed foods are engineered to be highly palatable (i.e., addictive), and that this is part of why change feels so hard. I would have reassured her that, even though our cultural idea of healthy food looks like deprivation (think chia-seed pudding and piles of raw kale), my idea of healthy food is actually delicious (red meat, healthy fats, starchy tubers, full-fat dairy, and fresh fruits). We would have worked on practical steps: how to grocery shop, bulk cook, and stock her freezer with ready-to-go meals. I suspect we could have improved her psoriasis, recurrent strep, and mental health, all by addressing her underlying state of inflammation and insulin resistance.

Over time, we would have worked together on how shifts in mental clarity and physical stability create the foundation for accessing intuitive gifts. She might have stepped into a place of sovereignty and agency, rather than feeling victimized by her circumstances. She might have come out as a witch, with a deep sense of wholeness and power from within, empowered and strong enough to craft a life that feels good.

A witchy woman is unlikely to be swayed by marketing that preys on insecurity. A witchy woman is present enough to know when to put down the phone. A witchy woman is hard to addict. This makes her highly inconvenient to those who profit from manipulation, and inherently threatening to any system that requires compliance and conformity.

The journey of reclaiming our sovereignty begins with recognizing the systems that have separated us from our power—whether it's algorithms that hijack our attention or foods that override our satiety. Either way, they dim the lights in our homes. True agency emerges when we can see these systems clearly and make conscious choices about how to engage with them. Sometimes this means choosing a different kind of hard.

Without sovereignty, our intuition remains clouded by the noise of external influences, and our magic can be distorted. But when we reclaim our presence, we are a house with the lights blazing—impenetrable to robbers.

FILLING THE VOID

Once we recognize how modern forces work to separate us from our power, we can begin reclaiming it. The path to sovereignty isn't about total abstinence from modern conveniences. Rather, it's about conscious choice and clear seeing. It's about recognizing manipulation so we can choose differently:

1. Reclaim Your Attention

- Set firm boundaries around technology.
- Practice distinguishing between real and manufactured fears.
- Learn to recognize when algorithms are trying to bait you with outrage and fear.

2. Couples Therapy with Your Body

- Return to real, nutrient-dense foods when possible.
- Rebuild your natural hunger and satiety signals by eating satiating protein and fat and avoiding hyperpalatable foods.
- Remember that the body was always your ally.

3. Remember Your Innate Wholeness

- Connect with community.
- Be of service.
- Spend time in nature.
- Cultivate a connection to something sacred.

When we begin reclaiming sovereignty, we often discover that the void these addictions promised to fill wasn't real to begin with. Our intuitive gifts and magical nature are powerful, yet we navigate a world designed to exploit our vulnerabilities. We need our sovereignty to keep these powers true and in service of good. We need to be a house with the lights on—fully present in our bodies. Then we can be the witchy women we truly are: self-possessed and impossible to control.

Chapter 9

INTEGRITY: HOW TO PRACTICE GOOD MAGIC

> I was always ashamed to take. So I gave. It was not a virtue. It was a disguise.
>
> —ANAÏS NIN, *The Diary of Anaïs Nin*

I recently attended a wedding where something striking emerged during the toasts. As friends and family praised the bride—a dear friend I'll call Amina—a pattern repeated: "She always puts everyone else's needs above her own." Each speaker meant this as the highest compliment, and the room nodded in warm agreement.

Indeed, Amina is an incredible human being. But as I listened to all the toasts, I wondered: Why is this our metric for feminine goodness? When we celebrate women primarily for their self-sacrifice, we send a powerful message about what matters. Having wants and needs, or simply feeling worthy, gets cast as somehow villainous. The memo is clear: a good woman is a selfless woman.

This conditioning is built into the fabric of women's lives. We learn that the path to approval lies through modest self-sacrifice with a smile. Our own desires take a distant back seat to everyone else's needs. Yet this feminine ideal of perpetual selflessness comes at a steep cost—we lose connection with our wants, we feel unworthy of asking for what we need, and in time we may find ourselves burned-out and resentful.

For witches, the cost of this is especially grave. Magic amplifies whatever energy we bring to it, which means we carry profound responsibility for how we wield that power. Being good witches means using our magic in service of the light rather than for ill. This requires meticulous integrity: we must know our values and intentions, and ensure our actions align with those deeper truths, even when no one is watching.

This kind of integrity demands present-moment awareness. When we act from unconscious motives—when we tell ourselves we're being helpful while actually creating a sense of obligation for others to reciprocate, or when we think we're being generous while we're actually seeking recognition, or even when we're self-sacrificing in a way that generates burnout—our bodies always know. They'll tighten in telltale ways: our throat will pinch when we're expressing something untrue, we'll feel a flutter of activation in our chest, or our facial muscles will constrict in ways that belie our performance. Our physical sensations become the detector of misalignment. To stay in integrity, we must be so deeply attuned to our bodies' murmurings that we catch ourselves the moment we stray from our authentic intentions and values. This moment of noticing is presence in action. We don't need to be able to clear our minds in meditation; we just need to be committed to strengthening this muscle of present-moment awareness. This is how we keep ourselves honest. Our presence becomes our most reliable guide for wielding magical power responsibly.

Staying in integrity requires understanding ourselves deeply—including our shadows. Three major obstacles to integrity impact women in particular: the trap of selflessness, the prison of likability, and the shadow of manipulation. There is no blame or shame here. None of these patterns make us bad people. Rather, these are historically adaptive strategies we've developed to survive in a world not designed for our flourishing. But when they go unexamined, they can pull us out of integrity, causing us to unconsciously use our power for ill. By bringing these patterns into awareness, we can transform them and step into our power with clear intention.

THE TRAP OF SELFLESSNESS

Consider Danica, who came to me with burnout and a strained marriage. To give me a better sense of her marital frustration, she described a recent holiday party she and her husband hosted.

As soon as the doorbell started ringing, Danica found herself running between kitchen and living room, hanging coats, taking drink orders, clearing tables, and wrangling kids. At one point, she glanced toward the sofa and saw her husband, Ivan, sitting comfortably, drinking a cocktail and engrossed in conversation. She had yet to sit down or eat a bite of food. Her blood boiled with resentment.

"He never once offered to help me in the kitchen. He sees me running around, and here he is, relaxing and enjoying himself. I mean, how selfish can someone be? It's shameful," she told me, shaking her head.

This scene illuminates several crucial dynamics about women's relationship with selflessness. On the surface, we see the familiar imbalance of labor—Danica was hyperfunctioning and managing all aspects of hosting while Ivan, blissfully unaware, enjoyed the party. But beneath this lies a more complex web of co-dependency and unhealthy self-denial.

Danica's body had been sending clear signals all evening: the tightness in her neck and shoulders as she rushed between tasks, feeling as though she was carrying the weight of the world; the hollow sensation in her stomach from not eating; the rising heat of resentment as she watched Ivan relax. But years of conditioning had taught her to override these somatic messages in service of being "good." Her body knew she needed rest, nourishment, and support, but her mind insisted she keep performing the role of giver, martyr, and perfect hostess.

While Danica railed against Ivan's selfishness, it actually served as a useful foil—his relaxation allowed her to see herself as *good* by comparison. Her sense of goodness became contingent on his selfishness, creating a toxic but stable dynamic where she was embittered and exhausted, but also virtuous. She had entered what therapists call the "drama triangle," a dynamic where people cycle through the roles of savior, victim, and villain. For Danica to maintain her identity as good, she needed to frame herself as either savior or victim—and by extension, frame others as villains.

Later that night, after the guests left, Danica stormed around the house, slamming doors and giving Ivan the silent treatment. When he eventually confronted her, she lost it, screaming at him in front of their children. "I'm not proud of that," she admitted quietly. Multiple factors had converged: she'd spent the evening collecting grievances against Ivan while trapped in the victim mindset, and in her constant motion between tasks, she'd never stopped to eat any of the beautiful food she had prepared. By night's end, her blood sugar was crashing and she was running on fumes. Danica spent the rest of the weekend exhausted and depressed, unable to budge from the couch, even when her daughter made bids to connect. The irony wasn't lost on her: in trying to be perfectly selfless, she ended up being less able to give to her family than if she'd simply tended to her needs along the way.

Part of Danica's work involved looking at her unexamined stories. When we pause to ask, "What story am I telling myself right now?" we often discover that our narratives are more about preserving our identity than reflecting reality. Rather than reflexively casting Ivan as selfish and herself as his victim, Danica began to explore. "The story I'm telling myself is that . . . Ivan is self-absorbed. He thinks he can leave me to do all the work. And he doesn't appreciate my efforts." Upon further reflection, Danica acknowledged that Ivan wasn't aware that he was doing anything wrong; enjoying the party felt to him like the right thing to be doing. This simple reframe helps us separate facts from the meaning we've assigned to them, often revealing that others' behavior has little to do with us at all.

As author and teacher Geneen Roth observes, "The distance between being happy and being miserable is made of the lies we tell ourselves." Danica's suffering wasn't directly caused by Ivan's behavior—it was largely caused by the stories she told herself about what his behavior meant and what she was worthy of demanding.

As Elise Loehnen and Courtney Smith discuss in their book *Choosing Wholeness over Goodness*, resentment often masks an uncomfortable truth: we resent in others what we secretly wish we could do ourselves. Ivan felt free to relax and enjoy the party, while Danica's conditioning (that being selfless and self-sacrificing is synonymous with being good) made that unthinkable. Her resentment wasn't really about his behavior—it was about the permission he gave himself that she couldn't give to herself.

Danica, like many, has a backlog of resentment from the broader context of gender dynamics in household labor. The nearly unavoidable imbalance of mental load and emotional labor that falls on women in heterosexual relationships creates fertile ground for resentment. Add to this the phenomenon of weaponized incompetence—where partners leverage perceived inability to avoid certain tasks.

Danica mused on this with exasperation. "It's about so much more than dividing the tasks fairly. It's the extra work of being the manager in the first place. Why must I 'make a list'? Why can't Ivan recognize what needs to be done and just do it?" she wondered aloud.

While society slowly works toward redistributing mental load, we must find a balance between acknowledging this systemic unfairness while refusing to let our resentment trap us in a cycle of martyrdom that ultimately serves no one.

When we consistently deny our own needs in service of others, those needs don't disappear—they just transform into larger, more unwieldy forms of neediness. What begins as a simple need for rest might evolve into debilitating exhaustion. A need for acknowledgment, when chronically unmet, can morph into attention-seeking behavior, histrionics, or emotional volatility. If we habitually pour from an empty cup, our bodies eventually step in to advocate on our behalf, often through complete shutdown or illness. The cruel irony is that these amplified needs often make us *more* dependent on others, not less.

This pattern has an even more insidious underbelly: using "selfless" service to create obligation. Any act of self-sacrifice that is engineered to make others feel indebted isn't truly selfless—it's an indirect attempt to get our own needs met, which is arguably self*ish*. Not to mention, it often breeds resentment from others. If we were clear-eyed about those consequences, would we still do it? Who truly wants to be resented? And when others fail to meet these unspoken expectations of reciprocity, we feel disappointed and bitter.

The antidote isn't to swing to pure self-interest but to find sustainable balance. This requires challenging the false dichotomy between selfishness and selflessness. We support our integrity by being generous while also being honest about our needs and limitations. At its core, unchecked selflessness is fundamentally disconnected from the body. Our bodies have energetic limits, and they will send signals to communicate when we're approaching depletion. But in our rush to maintain our selfless image, we override these warnings and push past our capacity.

And I want to give Danica grace here—her reliance on selflessness was an adaptation to a world that punishes women for having wants and needs. Unable to ask directly, she learned to create obligation through self-sacrifice—an unsustainable strategy, but an understandable one.

As witches seeking to maintain integrity, we must learn to listen for our bodies' limits and honor them. Being present becomes essential for recognizing when we're overstretched, often in service of preserving an idea of ourselves rather than genuine care for others. When we surpass our bodies' limits, we end up drained—unable to stand in our power or practice good magic. From this depleted state, we risk acting out in ways that don't reflect our highest values or most mature behavior. Like Danica, we might resort to lashing out, passive aggression, the silent treatment, or withdrawal. To protect our ability to act with integrity, we must remain intact, striking the right balance between generosity and prioritizing our own needs.

The path forward for Danica and so many of us requires some fundamental shifts: we must put down the sword of martyrdom and learn to speak our needs directly. Can we ask explicitly for what we want instead of manipulating the situation to get it? Can we genuinely root for others to succeed at meeting our needs, rather than unconsciously hoping they'll fail so we can feel virtuous by comparison? This means trading the familiar safety of passive aggression and victim mentality for the uncomfortable courage of clear communication. When we make our needs explicit ("I need help with dinner prep") rather than silently martyring ourselves, we create opportunities for genuine partnership rather than cycles of burnout and resentment.

THE FALSE SAFETY OF SELF-CRITICISM

Over time, we began to unpack the roots of Danica's patterns. In our early sessions, she had presented a simple narrative: "I had a wonderful childhood. My parents were loving and supportive. No complaints." But I've been at this work long enough to know that the story is never quite so simple. The more layered truth always precipitates out of solution with time.

And it did. In one session, Danica revealed that she had felt compelled to attend law school to secure her parents' approval. She observed how her parents treated her brother—how his behavioral issues frustrated them and threatened his bond with them. Danica knew she never wanted to be the object of their scorn in the same way. She also suspected that her parents were at their breaking point and couldn't handle any more strain. So she shaped her behavior in ways that would ensure that she was never the problem in the household. Childhood tantrums? Teenage rebellion? There was no space for that. Over time came a revelation: the entire structure of Danica's personality revolved around being a people pleaser. Her worth, she realized, depended entirely on others' approval. As long as people described her as selfless and nice, she felt safe.

And there wasn't a single person in Danica's life who wouldn't describe her as exactly that. Except, of course, Danica herself. Her inner voice was viciously cruel. She described herself as a failure, and on her bad days, she felt like she was in the way. Though she'd gone to law school, she had been adrift in an unsatisfying career for the past fifteen years.

Having a critical inner voice often feels like a socially safe choice. How can others judge or hurt us when we're way ahead of them on that? There's a perverse safety in self-loathing—it protects us from the pain of others' rejection by being the first to reject ourselves. When I brought up the topic of self-love, Danica got noticeably uncomfortable. In her mind, it wasn't that she struggled to accept herself; she actually disapproved of the very notion. She didn't see it as the goal. In her words, that would be "conceited, like Ivan," and she preferred to remain "humble."

As women, we learn that self-deprecation makes us more "relatable," that downplaying our achievements keeps us from being labeled as arrogant. The inner critic becomes a kind of social insurance policy, ensuring we never shine so bright as to threaten the group's cohesion. But this critical inner voice isn't our higher self speaking—our higher self is never cruel.

That cruel voice, in contrast, is socially learned—an echo of wounded generations before us who carried their own damaged relationships with self-worth. Do we want to add another link to that chain? Or do we want to break the cycle?

Like many of us, Danica unconsciously believed that self-criticism made her a better person—as though diminishing herself somehow elevated others. The opposite is true: genuine care for others flows from a foundation of self-kindness. When we make a show of modesty, we don't lift others up; we merely signal that everyone should dim their light to maintain harmony. True generosity flows from knowing our own worth and encouraging others to claim theirs.

This work demands a complete reimagining of humility. True humility isn't about making ourselves small; it's about rightsizing our place in the world, being neither inflated *nor* diminished. In Danica's case, the lack of self-worth manifested in a destructive cycle. Needing to be liked and feeling unworthy of getting her needs met, she chose martyrdom. Her unchecked selflessness then led to resentment. She bottled up her feelings—maintaining her image of selfless victim—until she erupted, as she did the night of the party. After these outbursts, terrified of losing relationships, she retreated into even more extreme, selfless caretaking, perpetuating the pattern.

When we disconnect from our needs in pursuit of "goodness," we also taint our power. Our authentic truth gets buried under layers of accommodation, and this relentless self-denial seeds deep feelings of unworthiness, as well as resentment toward others for having what we deny ourselves. This toxic resentment pulls us out of integrity, causing us to act from unconscious wounds rather than conscious intention. When our magic flows from this place of unmet needs and suppressed anger, it serves our shadow rather than our light.

THE PRISON OF LIKABILITY

> *My seventeen-year-old son, Chase, and his friends are in the family room watching a movie. . . . The boys are draped all over the couch. The girls have arranged themselves in tiny, tidy roly-poly piles on the floor. My young daughters are perched at the feet of the older girls, quietly worshiping. My son looks over at me and half smiles. "Hi, Mom." I need an excuse to be there, so I ask, "Anybody hungry?" What comes next seems to unfold in slow motion. Every single boy keeps his eyes on the TV and says, "YES!" The girls are silent at first. Then each girl diverts her eyes from the television screen and scans the faces of the other girls. Each looks to a friend's face to discover if she herself is hungry. They are polling. They are researching. They are gathering consensus, permission, or denial. Somehow the collective silently appoints a French-braided, freckle-nosed spokesgirl. She looks away from the faces of her friends and over at me. She smiles politely and says, "We're fine, thank you."*
>
> —GLENNON DOYLE, *Untamed*

As Glennon Doyle observes, "The boys looked inside themselves. The girls looked outside themselves. We forgot how to know when we learned how to please."

This external scanning creates a particular kind of disembodiment. When our attention is perpetually focused outward—reading faces, gauging reactions, calibrating our responses—we lose touch with our own somatic experience. We might say yes to plans while our body contracts with exhaustion, or laugh at jokes that make our stomach turn, all in service of maintaining social harmony. Each time we over-ride the body's murmurs, we weaken our proprioceptive signal, until we become strangers to our own internal experience—radio receivers tuned to everyone's frequencies but our own.

Our drive for pleasing is more than social conditioning. Research in evolutionary psychology suggests that for women throughout history, being liked wasn't just a nice-to-have—it may have been connected to survival. Some studies examining early human societies propose that ostracized women, whose well-being and that of their offspring often depended on social bonds for mutual aid, protection, and child-rearing support, could have faced greater risks than men. Modern research indicates that our bodies still carry this ancient imprint: social rejection activates neural pathways similar to those involved in physical pain, and this response is notably stronger in women.

I recognize this viscerally whenever I talk to my husband about a tense dynamic with female colleagues or friends. His well-meaning responses of "Just ignore it" or "You're probably overthinking this" miss the mark. And his casual shrug only highlights how differently we experience social rejection. What feels like minor workplace friction to him registers as a full-body threat for me. For women, social ruptures are processed as genuine danger because they actually do matter more. Evolutionarily, they may have been a matter of life and death.

Primate studies are particularly revealing. Among female primates, social sophistication is a form of reproductive fitness—it predicts offspring survival rates more accurately than dominance rank. That is, the most successful female primates aren't necessarily the strongest or most aggressive but those most adept at maintaining complex social bonds. They're the ones who can read the room and navigate group dynamics with finesse.

These biological imperatives shape countless daily interactions. We preface ideas with "I don't want to step on anyone's toes." We frantically text friends, "What are you wearing?" before events to avoid standing out. We deflect compliments and pepper conversations with self-deprecation, performing a carefully calibrated modesty that keeps us safely within the bounds of group acceptance. Watch a group of women at a restaurant deciding what to order. There's often an intricate dance of mutual accommodation: "What are you having?" "Oh, I'm fine with anything." "Should we share something?" No one wants to be the first to express a direct preference. This isn't mere politeness; it's an ancient survival strategy playing out over appetizers.

But what if we are, in fact, hungry?

These pressures reach their most destructive form on social media. Psychologist Jean Twenge's research, popularized by Jonathan Haidt in *The Anxious Generation*, shows that beginning around 2012—when smartphones and social media use among teens became ubiquitous—rates of depression, anxiety, self-harm, and suicide attempts among teenage girls skyrocketed—far beyond the increases seen in boys. Girls experienced a 52 percent increase in major depressive episodes from 2004 to 2017, compared to 36 percent for boys. Hospital admissions for self-harm among young girls (aged ten to fourteen) increased 189 percent from 2009 to 2015.

Why do these new technologies impact girls more severely than boys? The explanation lies partly in how these platforms create an environment where women's evolved social sensitivity—once adaptive in small tribal groups—becomes a liability. It's worth noting, girls aren't using social media more than boys, but they have migrated to visually driven, identity-forward platforms like Instagram and TikTok. These products amplify appearance comparison, peer evaluation, and constant self-presentation. Boys use them too, but many have shifted toward performance-based digital spaces like gaming, YouTube, and Discord, where status comes from skill, humor, or mastery rather than curated appearance.

The visually driven platforms that girls gravitate toward happen to map directly onto our hardwired imperative for social approval. For girls, social media creates a 24/7 performance of likability—every post and comment becomes a referendum on their social standing. Young girls have taken on the part-time job of managing their reputation across hundreds of digital connections. Meanwhile, relational aggression, which was once confined to the school day, has now moved into the amorphous twenty-four-hour online environment. Home is no longer a refuge, because the experience of exclusion and social cruelty follows girls into the sanctuary of their bedrooms. Our ancient social wiring, once a survival advantage, makes us uniquely vulnerable to the harms of social media.

These different mental health outcomes between girls and boys exposed to the same technology point to the conclusion that girls exist within a fundamentally different social reality. While social media strains boys' mental well-being, it devastates girls' mental health. The data reveals what we intuitively know: that, from adolescence onward, women navigate a prison of likability that simply doesn't constrain men in the same way.

Our primal drive for social acceptance shapes our professional lives as well. For Danica, it manifested in a depleting hypervigilance about others' perceptions. "I'm not just doing my job," she explained, "I'm doing my job while simultaneously watching myself do my job through everyone else's eyes." Indeed, studies show that women in leadership positions face what researchers call the likability penalty. A female CEO shows decisive leadership or displays confidence? She's attacked for her "cold" leadership style. The same behaviors that get men labeled as assertive get women branded as difficult. This creates a double bind: be assertive and face social penalties or prioritize likability and sacrifice effectiveness. For Danica, this constant external scanning created a particular kind of energy leak and exhaustion, setting her up for irritability and shutdown later.

And what happens to our integrity when we're constantly scanning outside ourselves for how to feel, what to want, what to need? The very strategies that once ensured our survival now disconnect us from our truth. Each time we suppress our genuine response in order to maintain harmony, we lose touch with our inner compass. After years of prioritizing others' comfort over our own knowing, that inner voice can go nearly silent.

Staying in integrity requires us to be firmly anchored in our own knowing, even when that knowing might make us temporarily less likable. Good magic requires learning to distinguish between genuine care for others and the self-abandonment that masquerades as virtue.

NEURODIVERGENCE AND LIKABILITY

The likability dynamic becomes even more complex when we consider autism. Most children pick up on subtle cues from caregivers—facial expressions, tone shifts, body language—that teach them which of their behaviors ensure attachment and which threaten it. Children quickly learn the social calculus: suppress authenticity when necessary to preserve connection. It's a reasonable trade-off when you consider that, throughout human history, attachment to caregivers translates to survival.

But autistic children are more prone to missing these subtle cues, failing to receive the full memo about how to perform for love. While this can create real challenges in forming secure attachments, it also preserves something increasingly rare: a more direct hotline to their authentic desires and aversions.

Many autistic adults observe allistic (non-autistic) social interactions with the detached fascination of an anthropologist, noting the intricate performance required in social settings—the rhetorical questions never meant to be answered, how we're expected to deflect compliments with practiced self-deprecation ("Oh, this old thing?"), the polite laughter, sympathetic brow furrowing, and hollow compliments. They see the complex choreography of connection building and recognize how much of it relies on small deceptions rather than a genuine translation of our inner state.

When neurodivergent people learn to "mask"—performing these social niceties, acting "normal"—it's often exhausting precisely because it requires translating between their native language and this foreign language of social performance. Every interaction requires conscious effort to decode facial expressions and deliver the expected social responses, a performance of normalcy that can leave them utterly depleted by day's end.

As someone who has come to recognize autistic traits in myself and across my family, I recognize this exhaustion intimately. Sometimes I mask, and at other times I find myself answering rhetorical questions with literal, concrete answers, and prioritizing truth over social comfort in ways that others can find jarring. I'm easily overwhelmed in loud, overstimulating environments, and I often miss social cues that others seem to navigate effortlessly. This loyalty to authenticity above likability, to truth above sensitivity to people's feelings, makes me disagreeable and resistant to groupthink in ways that sometimes create rifts in my relationships. But it also preserves something—my raw, unfiltered reactions, unscathed by social expectations.

I'm beginning to believe there's something here to be explored as it pertains to witchiness. Indeed, research suggests that neurodivergent cognition appears naturally less susceptible to groupthink and social conditioning. This same quality—an inability to simply go along with collective assumptions—has been essential to my work. It's what allowed me to forge an unconventional path in psychiatry, questioning established paradigms when they didn't serve my patients. And it's what drives this book—identifying the invisible matrix that influences our beliefs. I see my subtle, high-masking autistic traits as a type of professional assignment, and a form of clarity—a clear-eyed resistance to social conditioning that allows me to detect patterns in our culture.

And I think I'm not alone; there may be a significant subset of autistic women who share this natural resistance to collective thinking. Perhaps this is exactly the rebellious way of being that made witches a threat to power structures throughout time—a refusal to conform that comes naturally to neurodivergent folks.

There may be another basis for this overlap between neurodivergence and witchiness. Research suggests that autistic brains undergo less synaptic pruning during development, potentially preserving more neural pathways and creating heightened sensory sensitivity. In other words, autistic people may be perceiving subtle patterns and energetic information in their environment that others miss. There is also a documented correlation between autism and hypermobility conditions like Ehlers-Danlos Syndrome. Given that our connective tissue is rich with interoceptive nerve endings, I find myself wondering if part of how autistic people "listen" to the world happens at the level of the fascia. Or, as author and psychic medium Laura Lynne Jackson puts it, people with autism "have the ability to perceive the unseen energy that the brains of neurotypical people filter out." It might make us prone to sensory overload, but perhaps it can also manifest as stronger intuition and witchy knowing.

Clinical psychologist Dr. Kristina Kyser's exploration of neurodivergent cognition offers another lens into this connection. She describes how autistic people often have a "porous boundary between the self and the energetic field" around them, along with "differences in mirror neuron syncing" that make them "less likely to fall in line." As she notes, they "don't automatically fall into hierarchical social scripts or perform the emotional obedience" that is expected of us. Building on the synaptic-pruning research, Kyser theorizes that "the autistic brain retains more pathways, meaning it takes in more of the relational field instead of collapsing reality into a single linear channel." It's exactly this quality that allows for the kind of clear-eyed questioning and attuned receptivity that witchcraft requires.

When we're constantly wired to the group's preferences, we lose connection with our own wants and needs. We might find ourselves saying "No, thank you" to the snack we actually crave, echoing the girls who look to one another's faces instead of their own hunger. How can we access our inner compass when we're conditioned to look everywhere but inward?

Good witchcraft requires navigating a fundamental tension: staying connected to our inner knowing while remaining attuned to our relationships and the needs of others. Autistic women often have easier access to that inner hotline, while allistic folks tend to navigate relationships more intuitively. Perhaps neurotypical people could learn from the fierce loyalty to authenticity that comes more naturally to autistic people. Meanwhile, the neurodivergent among us might benefit from some of the social fluency that helps us attune to the needs and feelings of others. Both approaches have gifts to offer in this delicate balance between staying present to our truth and caring for others. But to be witches, we need both. Both impulses ultimately serve the same purpose: making our unique contribution to this world.

THE MODERN-DAY WITCH HUNT

The pressure to be likable takes on a whole new dimension in the age of cancel culture—one of our modern versions of witch hunts.

The pattern is predictable: A woman steps outside the narrow bounds of acceptable female behavior? Watch the media mob descend.

Look at Monica Lewinsky—a twenty-two-year-old intern scapegoated by a global media machine while the far more powerful man involved retained his status. Branded a seductress and made into a public punch line, she endured years of shame while Bill Clinton's career recovered swiftly. It took decades and a cultural reckoning for her to be rehumanized.

Or take Janet Jackson—after the infamous 2004 Super Bowl "wardrobe malfunction," she faced an industry-wide blacklisting while Justin Timberlake, who exposed her breast on live television, saw his career flourish. This asymmetric reputational harm reinforces our instinct to point fingers at the woman when something goes wrong.

Consider Martha Stewart—a demanding perfectionist who became one of the first female self-made billionaires. Her 2004 trial was widely dubbed a "bitch hunt."

And look at two Olympic athletes: Simone Biles, who withdrew from competition after experiencing "the twisties" (a dangerous loss of spatial awareness), and Lindsey Vonn, who competed through a fully torn ACL. Despite making opposite choices, both faced harsh criticism—Biles was called selfish for abandoning her team, Vonn was called selfish for taking a spot from a healthy athlete. The message is undeniable: we're damned if we do, damned if we don't.

"This is a well-oiled machine," activist and actress Jameela Jamil observes, "the one we use to destroy a strong woman, amplify her tiniest errors, paint her in the most off-putting and threatening light, in order to not only silence her, but to discourage others from speaking out too, for fear they too will be hunted and smeared." The effectiveness of this machine depends on a crucial element: our need to be liked. Reputational damage is a two-way contract: for it to work, the person being taken down needs to feel the pain. We punch where we know it will hurt. And it is women's very need for likability that makes us vulnerable.

What's telling is who we choose to cancel. It's rarely the most egregious offenders (often, powerful men). Rather, it's the women—those who still care enough to feel shame—who are brought down by criticism. A mob will only mobilize when it senses a reasonable chance of success. Deep-seated cultural misogyny provides reliable ammunition.

All it takes is identifying a woman who seems reachable. Perhaps she has an enviable life—her success guarantees an audience eager to witness her fall. Or perhaps she's visibly insecure, making her "cringey"—a perfect target precisely because her downfall will be messy and she'll likely apologize repeatedly, feeding our hunger for contrition. Our culture stands ready with popcorn, eager for the spectacle. Just as Shakespearean comedies require a scapegoat for resolution, our culture seeks women to bear our collective shadow. By projecting all our ugliest impulses onto one woman, we can banish her and feel virtuous again without examining our own shadows.

The cancel culture double standard is rooted in how we socialize girls and boys differently. As Elise Loehnen writes in *On Our Best Behavior*, "We have been trained for goodness. Men, meanwhile, have been trained for power," and that makes us incredibly susceptible to reputational harm. Loehnen also notes, "Around the same age that girls learn to say 'I don't know,' boys learn to say, 'I don't care.'" The ideal target of a mob takedown is the "I don't know" woman who will grovel appropriately, saying "I'm so sorry, I'm so bad"—effectively confirming, "I *do* care." These qualities—the need for approval and the tendency to grovel, both born of our biological need for belonging—make women perfect scapegoats. And once this ritual is complete, once we have designated one person as the source of our problems and successfully cast them out, society can return to its comfortable equilibrium.

This is precisely why the true sociopaths—the ones who wouldn't even break a sweat—remain untouchable. They "don't care," so our attempts at reputational damage don't leave a scratch. And when we do take men down, we do it differently. When men face criticism, it's usually for specific actions. When women face criticism, it often centers on their character and fundamental likability—they're difficult, unhinged, selfish, or entitled.

The cumulative effect is what we can call the likability tax—the extra energy women must spend managing perceptions just to achieve the same outcomes as men. This tax is both psychological (constant self-monitoring) and practical (the additional time spent softening emails, soothing egos, managing relationship friction, and overthinking interpersonal dynamics). As you might imagine, these constant adjustments disconnect us from our authentic truth. This is especially relevant anytime that truth happens to conflict with what makes us likable. The antidote isn't pretending we don't care. By embracing our witchiness, we connect to a deeply grounded knowing—we may still care, but more importantly, we *do* know.

GOSSIP

Even gossip, commonly maligned as a feminine vice, highlights the way likability is hard-wired into female social behavior. A fascinating metastudy reported in the *Journal of Experimental Social Psychology* reveals that we've developed sophisticated strategies for competing while maintaining an appearance of caring—because we face conflicting evolutionary pressures: we need to compete for mates and resources, and yet direct competition threatens the social bonds essential for that same success.

The researchers found that when women share negative information about other women *while* expressing concern ("I'm worried about Sarah; she's been acting so erratically lately"), it is effective at damaging the target's reputation while simultaneously protecting—or even enhancing—the gossiper's social standing. The study showed that women who delivered gossip with apparent concern were viewed as more trustworthy and desirable as both social and romantic partners compared to those who spread information maliciously.

This finding illuminates multiple layers of the female experience. First, it suggests that gossip, particularly when cloaked in concern, serves as an effective strategy in female competition. But more importantly, it exposes our culture's subtle misogyny around gossip itself. We've long disparaged gossip as a feminine character flaw, when in fact it appears to be an evolved social strategy—one that women have developed precisely because direct confrontation or competition can be detrimental.

Gossip also connects directly to witch hunts. Throughout history, women who could skillfully navigate social dynamics—gathering and sharing information through whisper networks—held a form of power that operated below the radar of formal authority. In patriarchal systems where that authority was reserved for men, these informal networks became women's domain of influence. The word "gossip" itself originally meant "godsibling," referring to godparents who were intimately involved in a family's sacred moments. Over time, Old English *godsibb* evolved into "gossip" and came to refer to female confidants. These were the women who attended births, deaths, and celebrations, and connected their communities. The village wisewoman, later labeled a witch, was frequently the keeper of community knowledge, wielding influence through her understanding of social undercurrents.

The study's greatest value may be in how it captures the impossible tightrope women must walk: We must compete (for mates, resources, social status) while never appearing competitive. We must advance our interests while maintaining an appearance of selfless concern for others. Even in moments of social aggression, we must come off as caring and considerate—a testament to how deeply the imperative to be liked is embedded in the female experience . . . and just how much effort and Oscar-worthy performance that sometimes requires.

So when my husband, consulting me about a work dynamic, tells me I'm "overthinking it," I'm aware that the situation is, in fact, *that complicated.*

When we shame women for gossiping, we're shaming them for having developed adaptive strategies. Rather than condemning gossip outright, we might ask: What does it reveal about the constraints within which women have been forced to operate? What does it tell us about the premium placed on female likability that even our competitive strategies must be draped in the language of care?

This isn't to suggest that gossip is harmless—certainly, when wielded as a weapon, it can cause pain and harm. But understanding gossip as an adaptive strategy rather than a vice allows us to examine it with more nuance and give women more grace. Perhaps most importantly, it invites us to imagine a world where women don't need to compete through indirect means. How nice would it be if we were able to be direct about our needs, desires, and ambitions without sacrificing our social standing?

When we operate through indirect means—even adaptive ones like concern-cloaked gossip—we split our inner knowing from our outer expression. This doesn't mean the goal is to eliminate gossip entirely. In my experience, the drive to gossip feels like a natural biological impulse—an instinctive way to form social alliances, vent, and hone cultural norms around behavior. Rather than shaming ourselves for this hardwired behavior or allowing others to judge our morality based on it, we can bring awareness to how we engage in it. The antidote to this split is presence. When we catch ourselves in the midst of gossip, we can pause, take a breath, and, with compassion for our very human tendencies, simply ask ourselves: "Am I in integrity right now? Is what I'm saying coming from love, or have I slipped out of compassion?" If we notice we've drifted out of alignment, we should be patient with ourselves—after all, we are hardwired for this behavior. But in that moment of awareness, we can also choose differently about what we want to say next.

Being a force for good magic requires alignment between our inner and outer selves, between our stated intentions and our actual motivations. This means becoming aware of when we're using tools like gossip. Only when we own our competitive instincts and needs can we choose how to express them with integrity.

THE SHADOW OF MANIPULATION

Consider the zebra's stripes. We might assume they evolved for camouflage, but black-and-white stripes hardly seem like an effective way to blend in with the savannah's tan-and-green palette. The truth is more fascinating: zebra stripes create "motion dazzle," a visual disruption that makes it hard for predators to track individual zebras or predict their movements. The stripes work specifically because they exploit limitations in predators' visual systems.

Women's patterns of manipulation function similarly. We have developed sophisticated strategies for wielding influence in a world that historically denied us direct power. Like zebra stripes, these strategies evolved not as simple camouflage but as complex adaptations that exploit perceptual blind spots. These forms of indirect influence operate largely outside conscious male awareness.

I witnessed this dynamic while counseling Mei and Eddie, a couple in their early forties, about their ongoing conflict over moving cities for Eddie's job. While he approached the situation in good faith, looking for an open-minded discussion of pros and cons, Mei employed increasingly indirect tactics. She began orchestrating elaborate scenarios to demonstrate why moving would be impossible—strategically making plans during house-hunting weekends, "discovering" their daughter's sudden passion for her current school's unique drama program, and staging emotion-laden phone calls about her mother's care needs within earshot of her husband. When I gently noted these manipulative patterns in session, she shot me a look of outrage, her expression seeming to ask, "Whose side are you on?" It recalled the old familiar feeling of being a "chill" pick-me girl and its impact on female friendships—the breaking down of an unspoken alliance I didn't realize we were expected to have. This moment epitomized how the system pits women against one another: we're caught between honesty and solidarity, forced to choose between professional integrity and female alliance. But even more striking, Eddie just blinked slowly and said, "Manipulative? What do you mean? I don't think Mei is manipulative; she's just dealing with legitimate concerns."

Eddie's reaction illustrated how manipulation often operates outside male awareness. This isn't because men are obtuse but because women have necessarily developed these indirect strategies *precisely because* they evade detection. In a world where women have been systematically denied direct power—where we are physically smaller, historically disenfranchised, and often economically dependent—we had to find alternative ways to get our basic needs met. Like the stripes that help zebras survive by exploiting limitations in their predators' visual system, over generations, women have cultivated sophisticated methods of influence that work specifically because they operate in others' blind spots.

Our tendency to manipulate is also connected to our need for likability. Directly asking for what we want risks being seen as looking out for our own interests—the very qualities that threaten our social standing. So we learn to get our needs met while maintaining our image as selfless, agreeable, and concerned about others. Anytime Mei would show up late to our sessions (which happened frequently), she would have an excuse that was related to caretaking and maternal goodness: "Sorry I'm late, I needed to feed the baby," or "I'll be there in ten, I had to walk the dog." Similarly, with their decision about Eddie's job, Mei couldn't simply say, "I don't want to move, and here's why." That would make her seem selfish or unsupportive of Eddie's career. Instead, she orchestrated circumstances that would lead him to the same conclusion while preserving her reputation as a caring wife and mother. The manipulation served a dual purpose: achieving her goals while keeping her likability intact.

THE MOTHER-IN-LAW EFFECT

The mother-in-law relationship, and our cultural cliché that a mother-in-law and a daughter-in-law are pitted against each other, reveals another layer of manipulation. Mei told me about a reunion trip she took with her college girlfriends. She said they stood around the kitchen island of an Airbnb for hours venting about their universally strained relationships with their mothers-in-law:

"Oh my god, my mother-in-law is so controlling."

"Mine is always demanding that we visit, and she plays the victim if we don't."

"Mine is certifiably crazy."

Are mothers-in-law fundamentally crazy, controlling, and bad? Or perhaps the pervasiveness of this difficult dynamic suggests something more systemic than individual personality failings. Consider the context: having spent decades in marriages where direct power was denied, trapped between exhaustion and the prison of likability, these mothers developed sophisticated strategies for getting their needs met through indirect means—often by creating emotional obligations in their children, particularly their sons. Because their sons had blind spots that concealed this manipulation, it worked. They built intricate systems of influence through guilt, obligation, and emotional currency. All in the name of getting their needs met in a world that wasn't designed for their thriving.

Throughout the past, women understood the stakes: be direct and face potential ostracism or even violence, or develop indirect ways of shaping their environment. When physical strength couldn't ensure survival, psychological sophistication became essential.

This legacy lives on. Even in contexts where direct power is now available, we still live in the prison of likability, and these ancient survival strategies activate automatically. Our manipulative tendencies generally operate below conscious awareness—that is, until we find ourselves on the other end of the dynamic.

Enter the daughter-in-law. Unlike the son, she isn't blind to these behaviors. (After all, it takes one to know one.) She threatens the mother-in-law's system in two ways: by creating a shift in the son's loyalty, and by potentially exposing long-standing patterns of manipulation. No wonder these relationships often become battlegrounds.

Rather than dismissing these mothers-in-law as "controlling," we might see them as mirrors—reflecting both our shared powerlessness and the creative strategies we've developed to survive it. The resulting tension may appear to be about clashing personalities, but it's really about shared survival strategies colliding. The mother-in-law's seemingly "crazy" behavior often stems from a desperate attempt to maintain her only proven system for getting her needs met. Meanwhile, the daughter-in-law feels resistance and tells herself she's setting boundaries around bad behavior. But, in truth, there's an underlying visceral rejection of tactics she recognizes from her own shadow. She might recoil at her mother-in-law's weaponized guilt while conveniently overlooking her own carefully placed *sighs* anytime she herself is displeased.

I want to emphasize: this isn't about judging our elders for their survival strategies. We can honor their resourcefulness while choosing new ways forward. For Mei, this meant learning to say directly, "I need us to spend Christmas at our house this year because hosting works better for our family," rather than maneuvering to engineer that outcome. As we heal these ancient wounds around needs, influence, and likability, we can finally communicate our needs with clarity and kindness.

Direct power has become available just in time, as our initiation into magic requires us to own this shadow and stand in full integrity. When we operate from unconscious patterns, we risk using our power irresponsibly, in service of our own hidden agendas rather than the collective good. Making these patterns conscious ensures that our actions align with our stated intentions. Only then can we wield power as a force for good rather than perpetuating the very dynamics we claim to reject.

THE SISTER WOUND

Growing up, my patient Jennifer was much more comfortable being friends with boys than with girls. She carried what I call a sister wound—a deep distrust of women rooted in early betrayals by other females, creating a protective hypervigilance she would bring into female relationships. She believed that the root of this was when the crew of popular girls turned against her in fifth grade, taking her down with vicious gossip and ostracization. But further digging revealed that her sister wound started much earlier—with her own sister, in fact.

When they were little, Jennifer and her older sister would misbehave together. But when their parents would find out, her sister would craftily frame the misbehavior as Jennifer's fault. Though Jennifer's blood would boil, at that age she lacked the vocabulary to articulate what felt so unjust about this situation. She only knew that something inside her twisted painfully each time her sister successfully manipulated their parents' perception, leaving Jennifer to shoulder the blame while her sister maintained her image of innocence.

This early betrayal planted seeds of distrust: Jennifer learned to keep her guard up in female friendships, always watching for the subtle knife of manipulation. She recognized in other women's behavior the same patterns she'd witnessed in her sister: the careful crafting of narratives, the strategic positioning of blame. Female friendship began to feel like navigating a minefield.

Only when she met Clara in a book club did Jennifer glimpse another possibility. Clara, a speech therapist from New Mexico, had done deep work to integrate her shadow and move with integrity. She neither manipulated nor tolerated manipulation, meeting life's challenges with healthy confrontation and clear boundaries. Over time, Jennifer made friends with several women like Clara who had processed their unconscious tendencies and chose to move differently in the world.

Women cannot walk this path of witchcraft alone, so finding a way to feel safe in female friendship is imperative. We need the examples of others who have done their shadow work: women who can show up authentically and share generously, without strings attached.

For me, there's profound resonance in the image of witches gathered in a circle around a fire. Though patriarchal forces cast these gatherings as sinister, they actually represent women supporting one another and maintaining safety through collective power. Whether we're talking about literal covens or simply book clubs and group chats, we need our witches' circles. But for these circles of female friendship to feel truly safe—whether around an actual fire or a kitchen table—each woman must confront her own manipulation patterns, heal her sister wound, and commit to moving through the world with transparency and integrity. Only then can we create the circles of safety and trust that our magic requires.

METICULOUS INTEGRITY

Integrity requires facing our shadows with courage. These patterns—unchecked selflessness, manipulation, and our drive for likability—served as brilliant survival strategies when direct power was denied to us. Today they disconnect us from our true intentions and poison our integrity. To wield our power responsibly, we must compassionately integrate these shadows.

First, we must recognize how selflessness becomes martyrdom. As Danica discovered, constant self-denial leads not to service but to resentment and collapse. Our own cup must be full for our generosity to flow sustainably. Second, we must examine how our need for likability compromises our authenticity. Constant external scanning disconnects us from our inner compass. Integrity requires trusting our present, embodied knowing, even when it makes us temporarily less likable. Third, we must transform our manipulation patterns. While these strategies once ensured our survival, we now have access to direct power. We can give ourselves grace anytime these tendencies arise and then use presence to consciously choose a new way forward.

Most crucially, we must become crystal clear on our intentions. When we're unconscious of our motivations, we muddy the channels through which our power flows. Magic amplifies whatever energy we bring to it. If we're unclear about our true intentions, if we're operating from unconscious neediness or unexamined wounds, our magic will reflect that confusion. This is where we can go astray: when our intentions don't align with our deepest values of compassion and service.

True integrity isn't just a mental commitment to doing the right thing—it's a full-body alignment where our values, intentions, and actions flow as one coherent self. When we're fully present in our physical experience, we can feel the difference between good-faith compromises and masterminding a situation. From a place of steady presence, our power flows clear and strong, untainted by hidden motives.

As we more fully occupy this identity of witch, we'll increasingly see that our thoughts and actions shape reality. This comes with responsibility, because each action and interaction ripples out with force. This is how we practice good magic: by ensuring our power serves our deepest values rather than our unconscious wounds.

We're ready to step into our power—not as "good" or "wicked" witches but as whole women who hold both light and shadow. We choose, countless times per day, to be in service of the light.

Our culture pushes us toward distraction, but a witch comes into presence so that she can stay in integrity and use her power in service of good.

THIRD PRACTICE: VALUING YIN

Our Culture Is Imbalanced Toward Yang. A Witch Values the Yin.

Beyond privileging the rational over the intuitive, there is another way that our culture biases toward straight lines over spirals. We live in a culture with its foot stuck on the gas pedal. Yang energy represents the active, doing, outward-flowing force—think productivity and achievement. Yin energy embodies the resting, being, inward-flowing force—receptivity, reflection, and regeneration. The Taoist philosophers would not have seen these forces hierarchically—both were considered essential, eternally dancing in dynamic equilibrium. But our modern world has become yang dominant: we value action over rest, doing over being, and we've structured society around masculine solar rhythms that demand consistency every day, rather than lunar rhythms that ebb and flow over the course of a month.

This imbalance is particularly problematic for women, because the female experience is inherently cyclical. The menstrual cycle is a perfect illustration of this yin-yang balance—the follicular phase brings yang energy (confidence, productivity) while the luteal phase calls for yin (introspection, rest). Even our life phases—from puberty to menopause—mirror these same rhythms of expansion and contraction.

Yet our culture pushes us to maintain yang energy throughout every phase, and it throws us off balance. The third practice is to fly in the face of our cultural obsession with yang and finally embrace the yin. We've been conditioned to see yin qualities as weakness or indulgence, when in truth, the yin is where the magic happens.

Chapter 10

CHASING ENDLESS SUMMER

Beware the barrenness of a busy life.

—SOCRATES, quoted in Plutarch, *Moralia*

Serina came to me during an uncharacteristic rough patch in her life. On paper, she had optimized everything. Her schedule ran like precision clockwork: predawn workouts, cold plunges that made her feel invincible, ten-hour days conquering the tech world, evenings packed with networking and friends. She tracked her macros, monitored her heart rate variability, and until recently, had even engineered her menstrual cycle down to four predictable bleeds a year through the miracle of Seasonique (an extended-cycle birth control pill that reduces periods to four times a year). A life perfectly calibrated for maximum output.

But that carefully constructed edifice was beginning to crack. Six months earlier, thirty-five and eager to start a family, she went off birth control. Now she was working with a roster of specialists, one of whom had suggested she seek me out for extra support. Sitting in my office, her usual take-charge demeanor wavered as she described her mounting anxiety about the inability to get pregnant the way she thought she should: straightforwardly and efficiently. This made her feel lost and out of control. Her specialists had cleared her. Yet her body, for the first time in her adult life, wasn't responding to her precisely calculated inputs with the expected output.

"I'm doing everything right," she said, her voice tight with frustration. "I'm following all the protocols. My diet is cleaner than ever. My Oura Ring is tracking my cycle, and we're having sex *exactly* when I'm ovulating." She paused, foot unconsciously tapping. "But every month . . . nothing. Shouldn't I be pregnant by now?"

I watched her, noting the subtle signs her body was sending, even as her mind raced ahead with plans and strategies. The slight rigidity in her posture, as though she were perpetually poised to leap into the next task. The clinical precision with which she rattled off her hormone levels and cycle data. The way she spoke about her body as if it were a stubborn piece of technology that was glitching and needed debugging.

Month after month, her pregnancy tests came back negative, each one a tremendous devastation, made worse by her belief that she was somehow failing.

I was moved by Serina's conundrum. At some level, I knew it well myself. All the women I work with do. Not all of us are speeding through big-city careers, trying to conceive, or training like triathletes. Some are walking different paths entirely. Yet what binds us together is this conditioning to push—to override the quiet messages of our bodies and live at arm's length from the inconvenient truths they're telling us.

In Serina's case, her workup showed no overt hormone issues. I believed her obstacle was something harder to measure: her resistance to slowing down, to doing less. She refused to give her body the "padding" it needed to click into optimal fertility—more downtime, slower mornings, or the signal of safety that comes from more carbs and maybe some love handles. She was disconnected from the yin aspects of her being—the rest, receptivity, and softness that create fertile ground both literally and figuratively.

It wasn't her fault. Like many women, she had been shaped by a cultural consensus that a successful woman was strong, not soft—that she should move in efficient straight lines, not spirals or cycles. She relished the positive reinforcement the world provided: people were impressed by her accomplishments, girls envied her hard body, and she loved the way her husband, Craig, celebrated her at the gym when she would deadlift like a guy. ("You're a beast, Serina!") So she had tried to power through this fertility journey the way she did everything: directly and assertively. Until her body told her no.

Fertility is inherently witchy: it asks us to trust in forces beyond our control, to work with lunar rhythms and mysterious timing, and to surrender to the body's ancient wisdom about when conditions are right for new life. As licensed clinical social worker Judy Ford puts it, "Pregnancy is a process that invites you to surrender to the unseen force behind all life." Pregnancy is what I would call a peak-yin period of life—conceiving a child is the ultimate act of receiving, happening in a woman's deeply yin body part, the dark and fecund womb. But Serina was still hurtling through life in full yang glory. It was no wonder she got so tripped up in her journey.

During one of our meetings, I reflected on what would be the antidote to Serina's relentless drive. I thought of the passive and relaxing practice of yin yoga. Doing next to nothing for sixty minutes was the antithesis of Serina's MO of strength training and HIIT workouts—but I asked if she'd be open to trying it. She agreed, though her expression suggested she was already calculating how to maximize the return on investment of that hour.

At our next session Serina gave me her report. Entering the softly lit space, her inner critic fired up instantly. All that palo santo, and the way the silver-haired teacher held long, unwavering eye contact. But it was too late to back out, and she was soon lying on her yoga mat with a few blocks under her hips, warm blankets on her torso. There was nothing for her to *do*, nothing to fix. The teacher walked around, gently adjusting blocks to help each student's body open. As her spine softened and her pelvis relaxed, Serina felt herself well up with a poignant mix of what seemed like longing and release.

The next morning, when Craig tossed her the Apple Watch for their usual Saturday HIIT session, her body pulsed with an unfamiliar resistance. She let the watch fall to the floor. And for the first time in her adult life, instead of powering through, Serina stayed in bed with a cup of tea and the novel that had been gathering dust on her nightstand.

Craig muttered something about how she wasn't acting like herself. But this time it didn't send her sprinting to prove him wrong. Something had shifted in her that couldn't be forced back into place through sheer willpower.

I murmured gentle acknowledgment as she spoke, but inside I was cheering. The hurtling-forward, never-stopping, ever-driven Serina had, for the first time, allowed herself to slow down and surrender to the yin.

NATURE'S ESSENTIAL BALANCE

When I was a girl, I would scribble the monochrome yin-yang symbol on my notebook the way one might doodle flowers. There was something deeply satisfying about drawing that circle with my No. 2 pencil, fluidly putting down the sinuous line through the center, coloring in the black side with thick hatches. But it wasn't until much later, when I was studying acupuncture and Chinese medicine, that I would understand how my doodles represented the dual nature of reality.

I would come to learn that the yin-yang symbol captures a truth so fundamental it flows through every level of existence. Life moves in a perpetual interplay between opposing yet complementary forces. It's in the way day yields to night yields to day again; in summer's expansive energy flowing into autumn's gathering inward. It's in our bodies—the yang upper regions active and expressive, the yin lower regions quiet and generative.

Even if you haven't studied Taoist philosophy, you likely know the basics of the yin-yang symbol. As we've discussed, the white side, yang, represents the traditionally masculine-coded aspect of existence—that penetrative and active force associated with light, warmth, and assertiveness. The black side, yin, represents the feminine aspect—the receptive and yielding energy associated with darkness, coolness, and regeneration. Yin is the night to yang's day, the lunar to the solar. Each one waxes until it reaches the tipping point, then converts into the other. Even the yin moon contains this duality within itself—the full moon is yang relative to the new moon, which is yin.

This interplay between yin and yang maps metaphorically onto our discussion of the left and right hemispheres of the brain. The left hemisphere, with its focus on analysis and explicit knowledge, embodies yang energy—the realm of action, visibility, and certainty. The right hemisphere, with its grasp of implicit meaning and holistic understanding, carries yin qualities—the domain of receptivity, mystery, and intuitive wisdom. Just as nature requires both day and night, our minds need both kinds of knowing to be whole. Yin is the implicit that balances the explicit, the mystery that balances the known. And yes, yin equals witchy.

But our society has lost the balance. We value high productivity, maximum profit, and relentless drive above all. Yang dominates our modern lives. The yin aspects of life—rest, introspection—are often seen as unproductive or even a waste of time.

And this imbalance also manifests in how we treat the subtler ways of knowing. The qualities of sensing and intuitive knowing are sidelined, relegated to the shadows. Evidence-based arguments receive applause while intuitive hunches are dismissed as nonsense. The way our culture values yang over yin is a key piece of what conditioned us to disavow our mystical nature.

I'm not here to say we should dismiss the yang way of thought. Ever since the Enlightenment and the scientific method prompted us to put our hunches to the test, objective rationality and, in time, evidence-based medicine have helped us distinguish reliable facts from unfounded claims. But we forgot to value the yin *alongside* the yang. Yin has been denigrated in our culture, and this has left us not only imbalanced but disconnected from magic.

What captivated me about drawing the symbol was its elegant simplicity. Later I would understand the yin-yang as a template showing the Tao, the way of life. Each state generates itself from the other. From action comes rest. From growth and expansion (outward, yang) comes death and dissolution (inward, yin), which then fertilizes new growth (yang). This duality exists at grand cosmic levels and tiny cellular ones—our cells oscillate between oxidation and reduction every second, and even at the quantum level, electrons behave as both particle (concrete, measurable, yang) and wave (fluid, diffuse, yin). The teaching is clear: neither yang nor yin holds more importance—they exist in *dynamic equilibrium*, and we need both.

WHEN LUNAR RHYTHMS ARE FORCED TO LIVE BY SOLAR TIME

Serina's pattern of denying her body's needs is pervasive in modern women's lives, though we rarely discuss it openly. From our earliest years, we're taught to value our *doing* over *being*, our output over our inner experience. We learn to override the body's quiet pleas in favor of maintaining a consistent performance curve. Need to rest? Push through. Feeling introspective? Listen to a podcast to drown out the silence. Hearing the call to slow down and turn inward? There's a supplement for that.

One of society's most estranging forces is the pressure to live like machines—reliable, consistent, productive. This stands in direct opposition to our true nature, which is inherently cyclical and ever changing. We're constantly pushed to live against our natural rhythms rather than aligned with them. And this imbalance takes a unique toll on women's bodies.

We live in a world calibrated to men's rhythms. The male hormonal rhythm is solar, aligned with the straightforward twenty-four-hour cycle of the sun. Testosterone peaks in the early morning with the sunrise and gradually declines throughout the day—a rhythm that stays consistent, repeating in the same way every day of the month. This solar rhythm has become our cultural metronome for work, school, and the daily balance between effort and unwinding.

Meanwhile, reproductive-age women operate on a fundamentally different cycle—approximately twenty-eight days long, with estrogen building toward ovulation, then declining toward menstruation. For some of us, our cycles may even sync with the phases of the moon, with estrogen waxing toward the full moon and waning toward the new moon, creating a lunar rhythm.

Women's bodies call for the slow, deep, and cyclical, even though the modern world demands the fast, surface-level, and linear—feminine physiology is forced into a masculine-designed system. This leaves women caught in a square peg, round hole existence, trying to squeeze our lunar bodies into the demands of this solar world.

This expectation of consistency is pervasive: women are expected to maintain identical energy every day of the month, exercise at the same intensity regardless of cycle phase, and embrace wellness trends like cold plunging and intermittent fasting—approaches designed around male physiology that may affect women differently. We're asked to perform as if our hormonal landscape were as steady as a man's, ignoring the ebb and flow that defines our biology.

One result is hormone disruption. A woman's body is constantly assessing whether conditions are conducive to healthy reproduction. When we're depleted, our bodies wisely suppress fertility through complex hormonal cascades—an evolutionary safeguard. When we override our bodies' natural rhythms—pushing through fatigue, staying up late staring at screens—we force them to operate on what Dr. Azra Bertrand calls "clock time" (the rigid, external schedule dictated by society, work, and artificial light), rather than "organic time" (the body's innate biological rhythms, aligned with nature, day and night, and seasonal cycles). The result? Our delicate hormonal systems fall into dysregulation. And, like Serina, we struggle.

Traditional healers view the menstrual cycle as a window into our overall state of health—our sixth vital sign (after pulse, respiratory rate, temperature, blood pressure, and oxygen saturation). Our bodies urge us to live in organic time, but our rational minds, shaped by industrial capitalism, insist that's impossible. We believe we'll be left behind, that we haven't done enough. And so we choose clock time, to our detriment.

Even our modern calendar defies the body's natural inclinations. The Gregorian calendar, adopted in 1582, arbitrarily places the new year in the depths of winter. This timing has spawned a culture of aggressive self-improvement on January 1—exactly when nature calls for turning inward and resting. In the northern hemisphere, January is deep yin: a time when animals hibernate, when the earth lies dormant beneath frost, when the farmer rests, when our ancestors understood the need to slow down. Yet this is when we force ourselves into "new year, new you" exercise regimens and ambitious resolutions.

A more organic new year arrives with the spring equinox around March 21, when lengthening days and warming earth signal a time to stir from our winter rest and emerge from our caves. This is when animals birth their young, when seeds push through soil, when the natural world embarks on its genuine cycle of renewal. But we've become so disconnected from these rhythms that we barely notice the dissonance.

In earlier calendar systems—particularly those used by many pre-Roman and Indigenous cultures—the year was divided into thirteen months of twenty-eight days, totaling 364 days, with an extra "day out of time" added to account for the solar year. These months aligned with the lunar and menstrual cycles, reinforcing a natural connection between timekeeping, the moon, and the female body. But with the rise of the Roman Empire, this lunar-based calendar was replaced by the Julian calendar in 45 B.C.E., which imposed a twelve-month structure, aligned with the solar year. Later, Julius Caesar and Augustus Caesar renamed Quintilis and Sextilis as July and August, adjusting their lengths so both emperors' months had thirty-one days (because size does matter, I suppose). This disrupted the prior symmetry of month lengths and further untethered time from our menstrual cycles.

The move away from the cyclical, feminine rhythms of nature toward a linear, masculine order of empire was also a shift from thirteen to twelve months. The number thirteen, once considered sacred and revered in many goddess traditions as the number of lunar cycles per year, was vilified: Friday the 13th became a day associated with horror. We began pretending that buildings don't have a thirteenth floor and airplanes don't have a thirteenth row—a form of mainstream superstition we never think to question. A number once associated with the divine feminine became coded as unlucky, even cursed. It's hard not to see this as a kind of mythic misogyny—a quiet erasure of a worldview where time followed the womb, not the empire.

ALL YANG, NO YIN: A CULTURE OUT OF BALANCE

Look around our modern world and you'll see the ancient balance between yin and yang has tipped dangerously askew. Our culture worships yang. We've constructed our cities to blaze with artificial daylight around the clock, our schedules to run with mechanical precision regardless of season or phase of cycle. We celebrate the visible, measurable, evidence-based, and explicit while pushing the subtle and mysterious to the margins.

If we drew what the yin-yang symbol actually looks like for most women today, it would tell a different story than the symmetrical circles of my childhood notebooks. The bright, white yang would be bloated, leaving only a thin crescent of yin. This visual distortion mirrors our lopsided lived experience. Who among us actually feels that easeful flow between the outward and the inward? Ask most women and they'll tell you it's yang all the way. Yang gets the accolades, the attention, and the big bucks. Yang is what generates cities, empires, and societies (or so we think). Meanwhile, all that yin rest and reflection sounds cute, but who has time for it?

We see this yang bias in the jobs that command authority and in the income disparities between yang professions (like surgeons and engineers) and yin ones (like therapists and caretakers). Consider how we label disciplines: "hard" sciences versus "soft" ones. The language reveals our cultural bias: hard equals rigorous, valuable, serious; soft equals fuzzy, secondary, somehow less. We speak of "soft skills" with thinly veiled condescension, as if empathy were a consolation prize for those who aren't naturally good at math. It's even in the shape of things—magazine covers and city blocks show us that our society prefers hard bodies and angular skyscrapers over soft curves and rounded buildings.

The yang bias is explicitly coded into our healthcare system, assigning concrete dollar values to different types of medical care. Every patient interaction has a price tag attached through ICD-10 and CPT codes—the bureaucratic language of medical billing. A neurosurgeon removing a brain tumor might bill thousands of dollars per hour, while a physician spending that same hour counseling a diabetic patient about lifesaving dietary changes earns less than sixty dollars. This stark disparity reveals more than simple market forces at work. There's a pattern: the more a procedure *penetrates* or invades the body, the higher its monetary value. Conversely, the more *receptive* or preventative the care, the lower its compensation. These billing codes become an unexpected mirror of our culture's value system—one that prizes aggressive intervention over patient listening, invasive procedures over holding space for healing. Like the interplay of yin and yang, or even the fundamental design of human anatomy, our medical system has come to value the act of penetration far above the art of receiving.

Our denial of the value of yin keeps us in perpetual motion, even when we're running on fumes. Instead of blaming this yang-dominated overculture for our exhaustion, women blame *themselves* for not doing enough. I catch my patients in negative self-talk, berating themselves for being lazy or unproductive after surrendering to their quiet yin. The pressure to stay plugged in, charged up, with all the lights blazing becomes nearly irresistible, even when our bodies scream for powering down in the dark.

We are chasing endless summer, with its juicy, youthful vibes—what we might call a perpetual follicular phase, like Serina on Seasonique. We've lost our comfort with wintering, with leaves falling, with the necessary dissolution of the luteal phase, all its bleeding and sometimes teary letting go. Who wouldn't want to keep surfing that summer wave, even until exhaustion?

THE PRICE OF PERPETUAL YANG

As women, we may find ourselves overriding our natural tendencies to gain approval—striving for bodies that are tamed and managed, never messy. We fear the shame of spilling over the edges. Often, we seek solutions to our yang-induced fatigue through even *more* actions and purchases: the latest mushroom supplement or stimulant to push through brain fog and lack of focus—even when these symptoms stem from sleep deprivation and pervasive exhaustion. When we resist slowing down, the world stands ready to sell us the next biohack to optimize our lifestyle. But what works more easily for men—who are, biologically, more consistent and linear creatures—doesn't always work for women.

We end up contorting ourselves to fit into this system. Sure, we manage to succeed, because we are capable shape-shifters. But each instance of ignoring our inner pull toward yin exacts a heavy price. We end up not just physically out of balance but at odds with our innate knowledge.

If you're raised in the modern world, you enter adulthood already shaped by the understanding that the outward stuff of life—your actions and achievements, not to mention your outer identity and appearance—carries more value than the cultivation of your inner world. To put it simply: you learn early and often that your yang matters more than your yin.

The problem is, the yin is where the magic lies.

MISSED CONNECTIONS

As women, we are forever trying to prove to this patriarchal society that we are just as good as men. In a world of hustle, this means negating any features of our bodies that might slow us down. Yet this approach directly undermines the reclamation of our witchy nature. Connection to source can be a shy and quiet force. When we're running around in a yang scramble, that quiet wisdom is nowhere to be seen. We are too busy, too distracted, and our mental chatter is too loud to hear the subtle nudges of intuition.

While yang represents action—and of course we do need that on tap in our three-dimensional world—yin represents *connection*, essential to our well-being, and to our witchcraft. This includes connection to our bodies, to the people who we love, to our desires and the inner rumblings of what we want and need. Connection to our quiet, creative parts where beautifully irrational knowings arise. And connection to nature itself, whose cues guide us to live in sync with its ever-changing rhythms. Connection is essential for us to be able to feel our inner lives and drop into our witchy selves, but who has time or space for it? Everything conspires to keep us facing outward for answers and fixes, not turning inward to listen.

But how can we hear the whispers of intuition if we never get quiet enough to hear and feel ourselves? If we can't locate and touch the unnameable stuff inside, how will we detect it around us?

When we perpetually push through our bodies' messages, we silence the very channel through which our deepest knowing speaks. This is our internal navigation system—our body's ability to communicate what's right for us through physical sensations and embodied knowing. When we ignore these messages for too long, the communication lines atrophy. The severance begins with ignoring the body's needs and ends in disconnection from source.

The lost art of feminine knowing pulses beneath the surface of our lives, having weathered centuries of suppression and countless attempts to rationalize it away. It persists because it's a biological birthright, encoded in our very cells. We may never fully bridge the gap between our cyclical nature and our mechanical world, but we can begin to build back that yin crescent. When we create space to listen, when we learn to value the yin, we begin to hear not just our body's needs but the deeper stirrings of our witchy wisdom. It turns out, our greatest contribution doesn't depend on denying our bodies—it requires honoring them.

SEASON*S* OF THE WITCH

The path back to our witchiness lies in embracing what our culture resists most—the yin phases of life. And our menstrual cycles offer the perfect portal.

Consider how the menstrual cycle mirrors the seasons of the year. The high-energy follicular phase and ovulation, with their outward focus and drive, mirror nature's spring and summer. But it's often in the more inward luteal and bleeding phases—our body's autumn and winter—that our intuition speaks most clearly. Many of my patients report enhanced insight during these premenstrual days, a heightened ability to see through pretense and name uncomfortable truths. What we dismiss as PMS mood swings might actually be a temporary lifting of the filters we maintain to get along in society.

Pregnancy and the postpartum period offer another profound gateway to the yin. During pregnancy, a woman's brain actually changes, developing enhanced capacity for emotional attunement and nonverbal understanding. The postpartum period, with all those nocturnal hours spent honing our capacity for connection, can offer remarkable clarity—if we resist the yang pressure to "bounce back" and instead protect this sacred time. And if we struggle around motherhood, this too takes us into the unknown, sometimes through difficult initiations of loss. Even perimenopause, with its notorious sleep disruptions, can be understood differently: the middle-of-the-night wakings often bring important insights, as if the body knows it needs quiet hours to be heard.

Winter, too, calls us into this different way of sensing. As the natural world pulls back and goes dormant, our bodies crave more sleep, more stillness, more inward time. Fighting this and pushing to maintain summer-level energy year-round cuts us off from the quiet regeneration that winter naturally brings.

Nature provides the blueprint for the balance we seek—it already exists in every turning of the seasons, every cycle of the moon. We need only align ourselves with these yin-yang rhythms instead of fighting them. What might we discover if, instead of chasing endless summer, we turned toward the winter, the new moon, the yin?

NEEDY

I understand how Serina got to the place where she couldn't slow down. As different as we are, Serina and I both absorbed the same cultural message early on. We perceived how to get our needs reliably met—and moreover, what would help us win some power and respect: be rational, be reasonable, be strong, be yang. This orientation to life seemed the one and certain truth. And we didn't question it. Until life made us.

Perhaps one of the biggest barriers to embracing our yin nature is the fear of being seen as needy. That fear is what had me so intent in my teenage years on being perceived as low-maintenance. When Serina finally claimed her right to rest, her husband lobbed the accusation that she wasn't acting like herself. Serina's fear of seeming high-maintenance was partly why she had embraced her even-keeled birth control pill, which erased mood swings and menstrual inconvenience. It let her exist in an endless follicular phase, always "up" and bright, meeting the high expectations of her partner, her boss, and herself.

But let's look closer at this word "needy" and its negative connotation. From puberty onward, our bodies operate with greater complexity than male bodies. The female body *has more needs.* Full stop. During certain seasons—menstruation, pregnancy, postpartum—our bodies perform intricate biological symphonies. What we cast as high-maintenance is in fact the very foundation for the survival of the species.

You'd hardly know it, though. From our first period to our last, we're encouraged to manage, medicate, or simply make these needs disappear. We learn to silence what we're actually feeling in order to go with the grain. Rather than tuning in to our bodies, especially our most yin layers—e.g., the womb—we push awareness away. It starts young: Pop a Midol and power through school when cramps take you over. As careers advance, heavy bleeding that calls for a hot bath instead of a ten-hour shift can earn you a poor performance review—or worse. Postpartum, when you're overcome with massive hormonal shifts and healing from birth, the pressure mounts to return quickly to work and pre-pregnancy weight. Menopausal women face the same challenge: handling their insomnia and hot flashes without inconveniencing those around them. The genius of this system lies in how it teaches us to participate in our own numbing. We learn to take pride in pushing through our limitations.

Finding this balance between yin and yang is harder than ever. We live in a world of artificial light and endless notifications, where time is money and rest exists behind a paywall of outsourced tasks. Our bodies *are* needy, but without the support of community or extended family networks, stepping off the treadmill of constant productivity can feel dangerous. Who will catch us if we fall?

Though we can't fully escape modern constraints, that's not a reason to give up altogether. Small acts of rebellion are possible. Maybe it's blocking out time for a bath, or giving yourself permission to eat liberal amounts of chocolate in those days before your period. Maybe it's embracing the pull to hibernate in winter, even if it means missing some social connection around the holidays. Perhaps it's reclaiming pockets of peace or even joy amid life's pressures. It could be simply sitting in the dark for a few minutes—being with *what is*—before reaching for your phone.

☾ ☾ ☾

For Serina, embracing the yin meant approaching her fertility journey differently. She stopped obsessively tracking every metric and instead listened for her body's waxing and waning interest in different foods, physical activity, and intimacy. She followed her cravings for buttery mashed potatoes and slow mornings. She learned to trust the days when her energy pulled her inward, understanding that this too was an essential part of her cycle.

The transformation wasn't immediate or linear. There were days when the old programming reasserted itself—when the drive to push through and maintain perfect control felt irresistible. But gradually, the numbness that had protected her from being needy began to thaw, revealing a sophisticated internal guidance system.

Serina still works in tech, still enjoys movement and challenge, and still values excellence. But now she navigates these waters differently. Some days this means working intensely when she feels the surge of creative energy, other days it means surrendering to her need for quiet reflection. The same body that she once treated as a machine to be optimized has now become her most trusted advisor. She's discovering that her productivity actually improves when she honors her need for rest. And she's also coming to understand: productivity was never what mattered most.

The story is still unfolding for Serina, as it is for all of us learning to live differently in a world that demands constant yang energy. Her journey included an early miscarriage, a deeper reckoning with what truly mattered, and ultimately some significant life changes. She went on to become a stepmom with a new partner and, in time, conceived a child of her own. And along the way, she shifted—from treating her body as a piece of glitching technology to recognizing it as a source of wisdom, from pushing for perpetual yang to embracing the softness of yin.

Chapter 11

WELCOME TO THE WORLD OF WOMANHOOD: THE RITUALS AND CONVERSATIONS WE MISSED

Our bodies are beautiful, truly. Gorgeous inside and out. They are deserving of the good lotions, the good sex, the good words. They should be heeded like the safest, smartest, truest, most knowing source of wisdom possible, because they are.

—JEN HATMAKER, *Awake*

My initiation into womanhood was anything but ceremonious. One nondescript evening in the seventh grade, I noticed a rust-colored stain on my underwear. My whispered announcement to my mother—"I think I got my period"—was met with a flat "Well, welcome to the world of womanhood." The exasperation in her voice delivered a clear connotation: walking this world as a woman is a burden.

"Do we have any pads?" I stammered. No. She directed me to her medicine cabinet, where she kept tampons. I spent what felt like a lifetime locked alone in my parents' bathroom, making flailing attempts at mastering the art of inserting a tampon. I was triggered and overwhelmed, physically uncomfortable and emotionally isolated.

This moment could have been—should have been—marked with ritual and reverence, an honoring of the entry into the mysterious powers of womanhood. Instead, I got the perfect illustration of how we *do*, in fact, handle the trials of womanhood in our culture: alone, unsupported, and slightly ashamed.

I don't hold this against my mom. She was likely perimenopausal at the time, dealing with her own hormonal challenges. And I can only imagine how her first period was handled by her own mother (and her mother's mother before that). I'm guessing that many of you had your own version of this inadequate experience. But we have an opportunity to improve upon this rite of passage.

In many Indigenous cultures and ancient societies, menarche (the first period) was celebrated as a sacred threshold—elders would guide young women through this initiation into the matriarchal lineage.

But the shift toward secrecy and shame parallels the broader suppression of feminine wisdom that we see throughout all our cultural biases. Instead of ritual, many of us are met with squeamishness or silence. We learn to wear black pants and squirrel a tampon surreptitiously into our pocket before walking to the restroom. This cultural failure sets the tone for how we relate to our bodies: as messy and sometimes humiliating; as problems to be managed rather than vessels of wisdom.

THE PILL'S PROMISE

In spite of the brutal lake-effect weather that day, Hayley was giddy on her walk back to her dorm. She had just left the student health clinic with her first-ever prescription for birth control, hot in her mittened hand. This was the promise of so many good things to come: unprotected sex with her boyfriend, reliable contraception without the awkward pause to put on a condom (or the fear of the condom breaking), less period cramping, clearer skin, bigger boobs. And then there was an intangible benefit: she would feel like a sophisticated, sexually active, birth-control-taking, grown-ass woman. Jake, her boyfriend, was also stoked.

In many ways, sex did become smoother. But on a subtle level, things got weird. It started taking Hayley longer to reach orgasm. And she would notice that, even after foreplay, she wasn't getting wet. Jake must have noticed, because one day he brought lube over to her dorm room, which Hayley shooed away, noticing that she felt vaguely inadequate and insulted by that suggestion.

In time, she lost interest in sex altogether. But she continued to have sex most days, even when she wasn't in the mood, because she didn't want Jake to stop liking her.

Those college years and that transition onto the Pill was ancient history by the time a now twenty-nine-year-old Hayley began seeing me for depression. We started unpacking the chronology of her mental health history. I asked her when she first started feeling depressed, and Hayley launched into a story about college.

She described a confluence of school stress (she carried a heavy course load), drama with her roommates, rocky times with her boyfriend (and an eventual breakup that shattered her heart), weight gain that she found triggering (especially the part where she desperately needed a new wardrobe to fit her now bulging abdomen and thighs, but didn't have the money to buy new clothes on her tight student budget), the dreary Rochester winter, and perhaps a touch of homesickness. Whatever the combination of causes, midway through the year, Hayley started crying every day. She had low self-esteem, she felt ostracized by friends, and she was convinced that she was unattractive to men. In Hayley's words, she felt "fat, unlovable, and left out."

She had been in midterms when she first realized she needed help. She returned to her primary care doctor at the student health clinic, who promptly diagnosed her with depression and put her on Paxil. Hayley thought it was somewhat helpful. She stopped crying every day. She made it through college. She eventually saw a psychiatrist, who added Ativan for new anxiety symptoms, and Ambien for sleep.

Now, washing up to shore in my office ten years later, Hayley was wondering if we could optimize her medication regimen. I asked her about any other medications she takes.

"Sure, just Synthroid for my thyroid. That's it. . . . Oh, and birth control, if that counts as a medication."

Yes. It most certainly does.

"When did you start birth control?" I queried.

"Um, that would have been . . . like . . . the fall of my sophomore year of college."

"I see. Hayley, can you remind me again when in college you first started feeling depressed? When you first started crying every day?"

"Well, I think it was right around winter break of my sophomore year. I remember that transition back to school being really hard. The weather was getting me down. And I was actually pretty homesick."

"And you were never depressed before that? Not freshman year? Not in high school?"

"No, not really. I was always pretty upbeat, optimistic."

I was struck by the timing. Here was a twenty-nine-year-old woman sitting in front of me. According to her medical chart, she carried diagnoses of major depressive disorder, panic disorder, insomnia, and Hashimoto's thyroiditis. But I was starting to have the sinking suspicion that what she really had was medication side effects. She'd started the Pill in November, felt depressed by December, and the rest is history. That was ten years ago.

Hayley is not unusual, in that her entire psychiatric history began just after going on the Pill. We know from the medical literature that exogenous hormones can impact mood. Yet not a single psychiatrist, and not even the primary care doc who first prescribed Hayley the Pill, connected the dots. As I like to say, your brain and your hormones are talking to each other, even if your psychiatrist and your gynecologist are not.

Why is it not our first instinct to wonder about the physical body—for example, hormones—when someone is newly depressed? Most women have had the experience of their mood shifting alongside their hormones. (This is, after all, what we call PMS.) So the idea that *taking hormones* might *affect our mood* feels a bit like "Yeah, duh." Yet this commonsense truth was somehow denied by the medical establishment for decades. Women would complain about mood changes from the Pill, and they'd be met with a dismissive "There's no evidence for that."

Hayley was someone who didn't have a history of psychiatric problems. That is, until she started the Pill. And then after starting a medication that was *known to impact mood*, her doctors just accepted that, all of a sudden, she developed major depressive disorder a month later. They labeled her, they treated her, and they never stepped back to ask themselves: "Is this the inevitable expression of some inherent genetic trait for depression, or is this a medication side effect?"

Birth control was originally touted as the gateway to sexual freedom and female liberation. What we've come to understand over time tells a different story. The Pill is associated with increased rates of depression—women on hormonal contraceptives are 23 to 70 percent more likely to be diagnosed with depression within six months and 40 percent more likely to be prescribed an antidepressant. It can also reduce vaginal lubrication and decrease libido for some, sometimes even long after stopping the Pill. The Pill did end up being the key to sexual freedom—for men. It allowed condom-free sex without the risk of pregnancy. But for many women, it translated to depression and a dried-up sex drive.

PHEROMONES: THE INVISIBLE COMPASS

The Pill also impacts something more subtle than mood and libido, but equally profound: our pheromones—signaling chemicals that we detect through our scent organs and that still largely evade medical research. These chemical signals influence attraction in ways we're only beginning to understand.

A fascinating study (let's call it the sweaty T-shirt study) illuminates this connection. Researchers had men work out in T-shirts, which women later smelled to rate their attraction to each scent. The researchers also analyzed everyone's genetic profiles, specifically looking at something called HLA types—proteins that help our immune system distinguish between our own cells and foreign invaders.

Here's where it gets interesting: we're naturally attracted to people with different HLA types than our own, and for good reason. This genetic diversity helps prevent inherited diseases that are more common when closely related people mate, while also creating offspring with stronger immune systems. When parents have distinctly different HLA types, their children inherit a wider range of HLA proteins, making them better equipped to fight off various pathogens. Think of it as winning the immune system lottery.

But how do we know someone's genetic makeup just by meeting

them? We don't—consciously. Instead, this study suggests, we can detect these differences through smell, theoretically via pheromones (though the exact mechanisms are still being investigated). The results revealed that women who were not on the Pill were naturally attracted to the scent of men with the most different genes from their own. In other words, their bodies' innate wisdom was working perfectly. However, women on the Pill lost this ability—their attraction no longer tracked with genetic difference. Their chemical GPS was effectively disabled.

Today, countless women struggle to trust their own knowing, yet many physicians routinely disable one of nature's most ancient guidance systems without a second thought. When we alter how we perceive the chemical signals around us, what else are we changing? It's reasonable to wonder whether we're also disrupting our self-trust and our ability to chart a course through our lives.

I witnessed this through my patient Irina, who found herself suddenly unattracted to her husband after stopping birth control to start a family. The shift was dramatic and unexpected. She had met him while on the Pill, dated him while on the Pill, married him while on the Pill. Only when she stopped taking it did she realize her chemical attraction to him had been artificially altered. Beyond creating relationship strain, this revelation shook her trust in her own judgment. How many other subtle signals had she been missing? How many other aspects of her internal compass had been chemically muted?

I'm not here to tell you there's a perfect solution. While hormonal birth control can impact mood, libido, and pheromones, the alternatives have their own trade-offs. Condoms can fail. IUDs are a blessing for some women but can cause subtle health disruptions for others, from the severe cramps of the copper IUD to the spotting, bloating, and mood changes of the progesterone IUD. Every woman's circumstances require individual consideration. But given that depression often begins with the initiation of the Pill, and pheromones play an underappreciated role in our internal guidance system, physicians owe it to women like Hayley and Irina to discuss all options before resigning to the trade-offs of hormonal contraception. We can do better.

FERTILITY AWARENESS METHOD

My own journey to doing better began when a series of seemingly orchestrated events led me to get my copper IUD removed. When considering my remaining options, I found myself drawn to an alternative that would bring me *more* in tune with my cycle, rather than less. The method I landed on is called the fertility awareness method (FAM). It involves tracking your cycle through various data points, such as basal body temperature and cervical fluid, and recording this information on a menstrual cycle chart. The main downside is that it requires meticulous tracking in order to be effective, which is not always easy. The upside of this method is that it acquaints us intimately with our waxing and waning hormones, and it allows for a deepening of our relationship with our bodies—a relationship I wish I had established at age twelve rather than age thirty-four.

The good news is that the process of tracking is getting easier with the advent of "femtech" devices like wearable thermometers and home urine hormone tests. Katinka Locascio, an osteopathic manual practitioner and certified fertility awareness educator (FAE), observes that these technologies lend legitimacy and decrease the burden of tracking, but "ironically, they can come between a woman and her body or make her think she needs the tech and can't know her body on her own." Her recommendation? "Learn from a fertility awareness educator without the tech first, and then use the tech as a shortcut."

One aspect of FAM that gives people pause is that it necessitates a very physically intimate relationship with your own vulva, vagina, and cervix. I urge people to see this as a *feature* rather than a *bug*. Isn't it time for us to drop our discomfort and disgust with the female reproductive organs? Can we instead develop a familiarity and even reverence for this liminal space between spirit and the material world?

GETTING TO KNOW YOU

In an online group that I frequent, made up of one hundred mostly middle-aged moms, one woman vulnerably admitted that she's afraid to use a menstrual cup because "what if it gets lost up there?" Incredibly, several more women responded with plus-sign emojis, indicating they shared this fear. I was incredulous—but perhaps I shouldn't have been.

It's endemic that women are disconnected from their own genitalia. Between cultural squeamishness and anatomical reality (the vagina is yin—hidden in shadow—especially compared to the penis, which is yang and openly visible), many of us have grown up estranged from our most intimate geography. But we can change this. Here's how to begin:

Visual Exploration

- **Mirror work:** Use a small handheld mirror, or simply position yourself in front of a floor-length mirror. Take a good, long look at yourself. It can be helpful to have an anatomical illustration of the vulva nearby so you can orient yourself to the location of the clitoris, labia majora, labia minora, urethra, and vagina.
- **Notice if judgments or critical thoughts arise:** What if you shifted out of that learned mindset and instead approached your body from a stance of awe and appreciation? There is nothing wrong with you, but there is a lot that is unique about you. Can we discard our internalized misogyny and let that be a good thing?

Cycle Awareness

- **Track your cycle:** Choose one of the many cycle-tracking apps and use markers like basal body temperature, cervical fluid, libido, breast tenderness, and ovulation pain to track where you are in your cycle.

Internal Listening

- **Dialogue with your body:** Lie on your bed with hands on your belly. Close your eyes and simply listen. What is your body telling you today? What does it need? What does it know? This practice of internal dialogue can reveal underlying states that we rush past in our daily lives.
- **Explore your internal landscape:** Find a quiet, spacious time when you can slowly acquaint yourself with your vulva. Gently insert a clean finger into your vagina and explore the different textures and parameters of your anatomy. Find your cervix—the firm protrusion typically at the deepest part of the vagina. This exploration can become a self-pleasure practice if you choose, or it can simply be an act of self-discovery. Both approaches honor your right to know yourself fully.

THE EBB AND FLOW OF NATURAL CYCLES

One unexpected benefit of the fertility awareness method is that it makes a woman keenly aware of where she is in her cycle at any given moment. This helps with family planning and self-awareness, and allows us to sync our daily activities with the energetic quality of each phase. For me, learning to recognize my follicular phase, ovulation, and luteal phase was like putting on glasses for the first time and realizing everything had previously been blurry. I used to wonder why my libido or weight would vary; I would believe that my mood changes were random or related to the circumstances around me. I can now see that, so much of the time, it's simply tracking with my hormones. I wish I had put on these glasses decades earlier.

The way many of us currently handle our cycle is to see it as an inconvenience. We take pain meds to suppress the cramps, birth control to rein in the irregularities, and antidepressants to blunt the premenstrual dysphoria. Our period blood is seen as something to flush away immediately. And no matter how old we get, can we ever shake the shame of feminine hygiene products?

When we feel tired in the days before our period, we resent this lack of energy. Oftentimes we'll push through it, insisting on the spin class in spite of our body's reluctance. We squeeze ourselves into the mold of the masculine-oriented work world that demands that we show up for the job with the same energy every day of the month, rather than expecting the work world to accommodate our body's rhythms.

In forcing our cycling bodies into the straight lines of this world, we have severed a critical connection with ourselves. When we are human *doings* rather than human *beings*, seeing our value in terms of what we can produce, our lives are too frenzied and loud for us to hear the calls from within.

Take, for example, birth control pills like Serina's Seasonique or its cousin, Seasonale, which override the menstrual cycle so a woman only gets her period four times a year. From a yang-imbalanced perspective, this is a victory—fewer days of cramping and bleeding, no more inconvenience, no more energy or mood fluctuations. Now women can be hormonally consistent, day after day, just like a dude. Imagine the productivity! But from a perspective that values the rhythms of the body, this has drawbacks. Rather than allowing the yin luteal phase to perfectly balance out the yang follicular phase, we create a ratio of eighty-four yang days to only seven days of yin—a physiologic illustration of our cultural imbalance.

I realize that many women choose therapies like Seasonique because they find their menstrual cramps to be intolerable. While I don't want anyone suffering needlessly, I also want to gently point out that, although severe PMS is indeed *common*, it's not *normal*. It's a check-engine light from the body, alerting us to a state of underlying imbalance, such as inflammation, nutrient deficiencies, thyroid dysfunction, endometriosis, or uterine fibroids. Instead of understanding the imbalance at the root, we are trained to put a sticker over the check-engine light. We see these conditions as inevitable and genetic rather than recognizing that they're often solvable. Not to mention that, when we suppress the symptoms while doing nothing to correct the underlying issue, we are often exacerbating the root cause of our problems in the process.

Our bodies offer us the perfect template for relearning how to balance opposing forces. Instead of exerting dominance over our bodies, we would do well to take our cues from its energetic crests and troughs. The menstrual cycle is the ultimate illustration of yin and yang.

As you can see in the accompanying graphic, our cycle mirrors the moon's phases. Some scientists would caution against drawing biological conclusions here, but as a witchy doctor, I see a meaningful parallel. While science hasn't established a causal relationship, I find it compelling that our average twenty-eight-day cycle echoes the moon's monthly journey of waxing to the full moon, and then waning down to the new moon. Whether this alignment is symbolic, physiological, or both, it offers a framework for understanding the lunar yin-yang rhythm of the menstrual cycle.

A symbolic framework, not a claim of causation

The follicular phase, days one through fourteen of your cycle (day one is the first day of bleeding), is dominated by estrogen. The follicular phase can be thought of as the waxing moon. It brings the outward-facing energy our culture prizes—confidence, sociability, productivity. The follicular phase is a good time to say yes to social events and more intense exercise. This is the time when we're inclined toward all the things that our culture and our own inner monologue see as intrinsically positive. Things don't get on our nerves quite so easily, and, relatedly, we don't get on other people's nerves so much either. Our jeans fit us comfortably, and we are docile and flirty—just the way the world wants us. The follicular phase is the yang of our menstrual cycle, and it is thus a natural fit for our modern world.

Then, around day fourteen, we ovulate. We can think of this as the moment of maximal yang—the full moon of our cycle. Some women experience increased energy and higher libido. We typically have a different type of cervical fluid, which is essentially mother nature's lube. That fluid creates an optimal environment for sperm survival and helps transport them toward the egg. Ovulation (and the four days or so leading up to it) is when we're fertile. We feel our most attractive, and our sexual pleasure is heightened.

The moment of maximal yang is a tipping point into the beginning of yin. Here begins the luteal phase (days fourteen to twenty-eight of your cycle). Like the waning of the moon, this is a decrescendo—a converting of yang energy into yin—that lasts until we bleed on the dark nights of the new moon, which is maximal yin. This phase is dominated by the hormone progesterone, and the vibe is very different from the follicular phase. Gone are the days of feeling energized and outgoing. We're a little more tired and tender. This is the time for journaling instead of happy hour and for yoga instead of spin class. We may have made plans during our follicular phase, and now, when they come up on the calendar, we'd prefer to stay home and take an Epsom salt bath or watch reality TV. It can be harder to sleep, especially in the perimenopausal years. We might find ourselves wide-awake at 2 A.M., and no amount of sleep hygiene will help. We retain water, we can feel bloated, our breasts might become tender, we can get constipated, our libido can be lower, and we often don't feel our most sexual.

Our mood also shifts in the luteal phase. As we inch closer to bleeding, we might start to feel more irritable. Feeling annoyed by the sound of our partner chewing is a complaint I hear a lot. Our outlook on life can be biased toward pessimism—seeing our flaws, feeling insecure, and perhaps even feeling hopeless about certain difficult situations. Have you ever had the thought *Nobody likes me* or *I don't like anybody*? Next time you do, check your menstrual calendar to see if you're about to get your period.

When we're in our luteal phase, thoughtless action by a partner or the geopolitical wrongdoing that we were able to shrug off in our follicular phase now feels much more consequential. What felt like no big deal in the follicular phase now feels like an untenable injustice.

The luteal phase has the most cultural baggage—this is when the world tells us we're being irrational, or even bitchy. I see it differently. Our reproductive system is more than just a biological mechanism—it's an exquisite antenna, finely tuned to receive information from the invisible realm. And it's during the luteal phase, often dismissed as PMS, that I believe this antenna becomes most sensitive. Contrary to the prevailing narrative that a woman's emotional responses in the days before her period can be written off as overreacting, it's actually during the follicular phase that we have a distorted view—when we might gloss over the wrongs of the world. It's in the luteal phase that we're most in touch with the truth. We can access buried insights and deeply held convictions. It is not a time when we are *less reasonable*—it's a time when we have *less tolerance* for BS. What our culture labels as irritability is actually enhanced clarity—a temporary lifting of the rose-colored glasses that let us ignore life's harder truths.

We become energetically sensitive and intuitive during these weeks. I have even found that those 2 A.M. wake-ups play a role in the heightened attunement of the luteal phase, as I believe we have more direct access to the spirit realm in the middle of the night. The veil is thinner in this phase, and we want to leverage this to access deeper insights.

But in our hyper-yang world, we disown the deep feminine magic that resides in the luteal phase and in menstruation. The phases of ourselves we're taught to reject may in fact be some of our greatest sources of intuitive knowing and personal power. The luteal phase is maximal yin, and it's peak witch.

EAT THE MASHED POTATOES; TAKE THE NAP

So many of my patients experience some form of hormonal chaos. What I want women to know is that our bodies aren't broken—they're asking for alignment with their natural rhythms. This means embracing the ebb and flow of our energy throughout the month: channeling our outgoing energy during the follicular phase, then creating space for judgment-free, guilt-free rest during the luteal phase. It means honoring our body's needs during menstruation, whether that's taking salt baths, napping under blankets, or eating the foods our bodies crave.

These basic needs—rest, warmth, nourishment—have somehow taken on a connotation of laziness in our bodily disconnected, yang-dominated world. But our luteal cravings aren't character flaws; they're just yin expressions. They're essential counterbalances to our more active phases. When I was discussing the need to embrace the yin of our cycles with my friend Ingrid Fetell Lee, author of *Joyful*, she astutely pointed out that the idea of being gentle with ourselves during the luteal phase "is not to infantilize us"—we are strong and capable of handling what life throws at us. But the natural alternation between yin and yang ensures that our energy is restored before we begin another fertile cycle. Offering ourselves softness during the more tender phase of the month is a radical act of self-care in a culture that denies us our yin.

SACRED SEXUALITY

At the crossroads of body and intuition lies our sexuality, a powerful gateway to mystery, creativity, and our deepest yin wisdom. Yet this is also where many women carry emotional wounds and heavy armoring.

Somehow, we've arrived at a place where sexuality is cloaked in shame—taboo, forbidden, even deviant. What if sexuality is not depraved, but one of the most sacred aspects of being human? Our sexual energy connects us directly to the creative force of the universe. The womb—the liminal space where life takes shape—reminds us that sexuality is an act of creation, whether we're bringing forth new life or simply creating pleasure and connection. When sexual energy flows freely, our creative expression in all areas tends to flourish. When it's stagnant or suppressed, we often feel blocked in various arenas of our lives.

The cervix is the threshold between realms, a holy space where spirit becomes matter. Reclaiming it as a source of creative energy rather than shame is both personal and political. Every time we speak about our bodies with reverence instead of embarrassment and show up to intimate encounters with fierce self-respect, we help break centuries of conditioning that taught us to disconnect from these innermost places. When we heal our sexuality, we open up a channel for free-flowing intuition.

Coming into new relationship with our bodies—in all their messy, cyclical, sensitive glory—is precisely the medicine our times require. We need to feel what we've numbed and express what we've silenced. Sometimes this healing comes in unexpected ways, teaching us lessons we didn't know we needed to learn. My own journey with fertility awareness would prove to be one such teaching.

A DUD THAT WASN'T

Fourth of July weekend is a fulcrum in my life. My husband's birthday is July 2. And in 2014, one year into our marriage and at the beginning of my journey of opening to magic, we celebrated his birthday by having our first (legal) psychedelic experience. We kicked off the ceremony by drawing a card with a spiritual message (similar to tarot cards). We used our beloved Crystal Ally Cards deck by Naisha Ahsian, a trusted companion that has brought us uncanny guidance over the years. "The crystal cards don't lie," we say. On this verdant July morning, I had my hopes set on drawing a particularly resonant card for the occasion—perhaps Journey, Growth, or my aspirational favorite, Joy and Gratitude. I yearned for a card that would mirror the epic quest ahead, one that would speak to my inevitable transformation, the profound insights waiting to be discovered, and the possibility of pure ecstasy along the way. Instead, I pulled Cycles.

Cycles? I thought, deflated. The card, associated with moonstone and "the feminine," left me cold. Not for this chill girl. I read the passage in the accompanying guidebook with skepticism:

"Are you at the planting stage, when a seed is just being set? Or has the seed already grown into a young plant, which you are nurturing and helping to grow? Or are you at the harvest, when the fruit has come and is ready to be gathered? Perhaps you are moving into a fallow period, when you are resting and integrating what you have learned from the other cycles."

Lovely words, but they didn't resonate. As far as I was concerned, the card was a dud.

Yet the Crystal Cards don't lie. I had no idea just how prophetic this card would prove to be.

REAPING THE HARVEST

To my friends at home using the fertility awareness method (FAM) to avoid getting pregnant, please do as I say and not as I do. FAM is a side-effect-free way to plan or prevent pregnancy while strengthening your connection with your body. When done correctly, it's a beautiful and effective method.

When you take a cavalier approach, on the other hand, as I did in the winter of 2015, you can make certain Crystal Card prophecies come true. Six months after I pulled the Cycles card, I found myself frantically searching for a pregnancy test. Before I could find one, I drew a card from the deck for guidance. I pulled Child Within. *Gulp.* A few hours later, I learned I was unexpectedly pregnant. The cards don't lie, and the *cycles* of life—birth, death, and renewal—were unfolding in real time.

But even as I anticipated this harvest, I couldn't yet see that elsewhere in my maternal lineage, a different cycle was drawing to a close.

Six months after I pulled the Child Within card, my mom and I attended a family wedding. The bride's father (my mom's beloved cousin Dean) had died years earlier of cancer. Watching his daughter walk down the aisle without him, we all felt his loss acutely. The moment came when there would typically be a father-daughter dance. In an act of commemoration, the bride announced that, instead, there would be a mother-daughter dance. We cried as the bride and her mother embraced, moving around the floor to Dean's favorite song, tears streaming down their faces. Then they invited all other mother-daughter pairs to join them.

My mom and I made our way to the dance floor. By this point, I was six months pregnant with my daughter, so we joked that this was a mother-daughter-mother-daughter dance. It felt like a preview of the joy we would have bringing this new life into our family together. I had visions of afternoons spent sitting on the floor with my mom and baby, chatting over tummy time, listening to that anciently familiar sound of my mother's lyrical voice reading *Goodnight Moon.* I could tell that my mom saw me differently now that I was about to become a mother. There was something about this unexpected pregnancy that accelerated a long-overdue healing between us. On that dance floor, our tears had the salty taste of God in them. We experienced a new closeness that had eluded us in our relationship throughout my life.

That turned out to be the last time I saw my mom. The next morning, I waved goodbye to my parents as they continued along a road trip. (It was, strangely, the one time I didn't feel the need to perform my usual ritual of "Drive safely, see you later, I love you.") A few days later, my mom developed a blood clot in her leg, then a pulmonary embolism. On the platform, waiting to go up to the Seattle Space Needle, she collapsed.

It was July 2015—my husband's birthday, and the one-year anniversary of pulling the Cycles card. The prophecy of the card was now clear: The feminine life cycle is a dance of planting, harvesting, resting . . . and, as painful as it sometimes is, beginning again.

☾ ☾ ☾

Life moves in cycles, not straight lines. Our bodies hold intrinsic wisdom in their rhythms of creation and integration, just as nature moves through seasons of growth and dormancy. The card had taught me that loss, like birth, is simply another turn of the eternal wheel. When we resist these cycles, we muddy the very channels through which our intuition flows. But when we honor them—both the monthly rhythm of menstruation and the broader arc of a woman's life through seasons of seeding, fruiting, and lying fallow—we tap into ancient choreography.

The Cycles card wasn't a dud after all. It was an invitation to remember that between birth and death, we encounter the sacred dance between yin and yang—each generation in our maternal line moving through its own season.

My mother's season had ended just as my daughter's was beginning. In the space between, my body was heavy with loss and new life. The harvest and the field going fallow were happening simultaneously, and I had no choice but to surrender to both.

Chapter 12

MOTHERHOOD: A VULNERABLE INITIATION

> There really are places in the heart you don't even know exist until you love a child.
>
> —ANNE LAMOTT, *Operating Instructions*

Grieving, foggy, and aching, I was thrown into motherhood. This is another portal into witchiness that is woefully mishandled in our culture. I witnessed this in myself, and I see this in my patients as they navigate childbirth and matrescence (the process of becoming a mother). In my practice and in my life, I have been holding the vision of a new model: where these phases initiate us deeper into our magic.

THE BUSINESS OF BIRTH

"My doctor saved my baby's life" were Helen's words when she signed on to our first postnatal Zoom session. But as she shared her birth story, a more complex picture emerged—one that illuminated how our medical system can subtly undermine women's connection to their bodily wisdom.

Having read all the books about hypnobirthing (relaxation techniques and breathing exercises for birth), Helen had initially envisioned an unmedicated birth, trusting in her body's innate capacities. But just shy of thirty-eight weeks, her carefully crafted birth plan began to unravel in her obstetrician's office. Staring at her computer screen, the doctor sighed and delivered a cascade of risk factors:

"Well, as you know, this is a geriatric pregnancy [Helen was thirty-five], and you have gestational diabetes [though her blood-sugar readings would not have qualified as diabetic mere weeks earlier, before a recent guideline change], your blood pressure is measuring high [Helen had rushed to the appointment and always felt stress and unease at the doctor's office], and the baby is measuring small [of note, Helen and her partner are both petite and of East Asian descent]. I am recommending that we induce."

Helen felt a sudden clench in her stomach—like her body and baby were saying no to this. While she trusted her doctor, her gut instinct had always been to let labor happen on its own accord. The induction recommendation didn't align with her body's signals, but the medical authority of risk statistics and diagnostic codes began to override her internal compass.

Her doctor's recommendation wasn't without merit. Research supports induction in situations like Helen's. The ARRIVE trial, a landmark randomized controlled study, found that elective induction at thirty-nine weeks reduced cesarean rates and hypertensive complications without increasing adverse outcomes. For scenarios like gestational diabetes, maternal hypertension, or fetal growth concerns—Helen's risk profile—induction can indeed be lifesaving for both mother and baby. Yet Helen felt an undeniable hesitation.

Helen negotiated a short-term compromise—daily ultrasound monitoring instead of immediate induction. But this victory came with trade-offs. Instead of spending her final days of pregnancy nesting and resting, Helen found herself making daily treks from Queens to midtown Manhattan for screenings. At thirty-eight and a half weeks, with no new indication for induction but feeling worn down by the daily appointments, she and her partner checked in to the hospital to begin the induction process.

What followed was a series of interventions. First came the Cervidil to soften her cervix, which ended up causing ineffective contractions every twenty minutes. Not enough to start labor, but just enough to interrupt her last night of sleep before becoming a parent. Exhausted the next morning, she received Pitocin through an IV. Rather than the gradual build of natural labor that would have allowed her to find a rhythm with her breath and movement, the synthetic contractions crashed over her like a tidal wave. The meditative birth preparation she had practiced for months dissolved in the face of this zero-to-sixty, artificially induced active labor.

Soon she found herself asking for an epidural—a request she later described as both a resignation and a plea. Now she lay immobile on her back, legs numb, connected to finicky monitors, her birth ball deflating in the corner.

Hours passed without sufficient cervical dilation. The fetal heart rate began showing concerning patterns. "What does that mean?" Helen's partner asked.

"Fetal distress," the obstetrician responded definitively. The phrase sent a bolt of fear through the room, and when the doctor recommended an emergency C-section, Helen felt relieved for this potential salvation. This woman, with her years of training, would save Helen's baby from whatever dangers her body apparently posed.

Moments later, her baby boy was born weighing six pounds, seven ounces—perfectly healthy despite all the preceding drama. Helen would go on to tell friends and family how thankful she was that medical intervention had saved her son's life.

But had it?

This is where the story gets complicated. While modern obstetrics absolutely saves lives—and thank goodness we have access to induction and C-sections when truly needed—the current system has medicalized birth in ways that often *create* the very emergencies it then heroically resolves.

Consider how the hospital environment itself disrupts our body's natural capacity for birth. Women labor flat on their backs, though this position works against gravity, inhibits effective contractions, and reduces the size of the pelvic outlet. Movement—essential for easing labor and guiding the baby through the birth canal—becomes restricted by monitors, IVs, and epidural-induced immobility. Through no fault of the obstetrician, the clinical setting (bright lights, a parade of strangers) activates our fight-or-flight response, which inhibits the production of oxytocin—a key hormone driving uterine contractions. This triggers the fear-tension-pain cycle, a dynamic first articulated by Dr. Grantly Dick-Read in the 1940s, whereby fear creates muscle tension, which increases pain, which then deepens fear. By contrast, the parasympathetic nervous system—our rest-and-digest state of relaxation, which is in short supply in a medical setting—reduces pain, promotes oxytocin release, and facilitates labor progression.

The perverse incentives of our medical system amplify these issues. A scheduled C-section allows an obstetrician to deliver more babies in less time, with less liability exposure, during convenient business hours. While C-sections can be lifesaving, they comprise about 32 percent of U.S. births in recent years—likely far higher than medically necessary, especially when we compare this to the lower C-section rates in countries like the Netherlands and Sweden, which have *better* birth outcomes than we have in the United States. However, these comparisons aren't entirely equivalent—those countries also have universal healthcare, lower obesity rates, greater economic stability, different cultural attitudes toward risk, and better integration between midwifery and obstetric care.

While C-sections do indeed reduce certain short-term risks that could result in adverse outcomes, they also increase longer-term risks like asthma, allergies, altered gut flora, and autoimmune conditions that unfold over decades. By the time that baby grows up to be a three-year-old with eczema, then a six-year-old with asthma, and finally a twenty-five-year-old diagnosed with celiac disease, nobody is connecting those dots back to their C-section birth, and nobody is knocking on the obstetrician's door with a lawsuit. C-sections also carry significant maternal risks that extend beyond the immediate recovery period—adhesions that can cause chronic digestive and pelvic floor issues, increased risk of placenta accreta in subsequent pregnancies (a leading cause of maternal mortality), and a higher likelihood of repeat cesareans and future abdominal surgeries. But these complications unfold months or years later, creating no immediate accountability for the surgeon. All of this is to say, we do not want to regard the high rate of C-sections lightly, as it carries real risks.

By contrast, the obstetrician delivering a baby vaginally is devoting more time to that birth (often in the middle of the night) and ends up holding the bag for malpractice issues like stillbirth, shoulder dystocia (where the baby's shoulder becomes stuck during delivery, sometimes causing nerve damage to the arm), and meconium aspiration (where a newborn inhales its first stool during birth, which can cause breathing problems and lung complications). So obstetricians have several incentives to push a birth toward C-section, even if it sets the baby up for chronic illness down the road. Now, if we were presented with the choice, some of us might choose a higher risk of chronic health issues like eczema and autoimmune disorders in the long term over the low risk of an acute health issue like meconium aspiration at birth. But what we're lacking most of all is true informed consent in these cost-benefit decisions. While rates of catastrophic issues around birth are low (largely thanks to our obstetric heroics like C-sections), we are living in an epidemic of asthma, eczema, and autoimmune disease.

I don't envy obstetricians and their impossible position. These are tirelessly caring, hardworking professionals operating within a system that incentivizes intervention over patience. We're asking exhausted physicians—who work nights, weekends, and holidays—to repeatedly choose the slower, legally riskier path when their own human needs for rest and predictability pull in the opposite direction. In a culture with zero tolerance for bad outcomes, the defensive practice of medicine becomes almost inevitable. An obstetrician who allows a prolonged labor risks a heartbreaking outcome and a lawsuit if something goes wrong, while the long-term health consequences of unnecessary C-sections remain invisible and legally nearly consequence free. Not to mention that obstetricians have seen it all. Having witnessed how quickly births can turn perilous, I completely understand their bias toward caution.

Perhaps the solution isn't to expect superhuman resilience from individual doctors but to overhaul the incentive structure entirely. Countries like the UK and the Netherlands have created systems where low-risk pregnancies are managed by midwives as the primary care providers—whether in hospitals, birth centers, or at home—reserving obstetric intervention for truly high-risk situations. This approach honors the expertise of obstetricians (and midwives) and creates space for physiological birth to unfold naturally when appropriate.

Women's traditional birthing wisdom has often outperformed medical intervention, yet it remains systematically marginalized. When Hungarian physician Dr. Ignaz Semmelweis investigated maternal mortality in the 1840s, he discovered that women attended by midwives had significantly lower death rates than those delivered by physicians. The reason turned out to be that, at the time, physicians moved between autopsy rooms and delivery wards without washing their hands, spreading deadly infections, while midwives—who didn't perform autopsies—had cleaner practices and better outcomes. Today, this pattern of better outcomes persists. Even accounting for selection bias (with higher-risk pregnancies typically routed to obstetricians), research involving nearly 1.4 million women shows that midwife-led care consistently results in fewer unplanned C-sections and interventions, like instrumental deliveries and labor augmentation, while maintaining excellent safety outcomes. Yet despite this evidence, midwives struggle to practice freely in many states, facing barriers to hospital credentials, insurance reimbursement, and professional legitimacy. The marginalization of midwifery exemplifies our culture's pattern: institutional authority is privileged over women's wisdom, even when that wisdom gets better results.

Looking back at Helen's labor, I'm haunted by one thing: her belief that her body posed a threat to her baby. Treating birth as a medical emergency sends an insidious message to birthing women: you can't trust your body. As in Helen's experience, the modern obstetric narrative suggests: if you had been birthing on the proverbial savannah without modern medical intervention, you and your baby may have died.

When Helen told me that her doctor saved her baby's life, my initial thought was: maybe. It's true that modern obstetrics has made incredible strides toward reducing stillbirth and bad outcomes. It's true that infant and maternal mortality rates throughout human evolution used to be what we would consider untenable today. But also, we are not comparing apples to apples. When Helen's birth failed to progress, this was not an indication of what would have happened had she been birthing on all fours in the woods. This is what happened in the context of birthing on her back, immobilized by a fetal heart monitor and numbed legs, surrounded by strangers, in a foreign and alarming environment, with the chemical soup of Pitocin and an epidural. She felt that her body had failed her baby, but I'm not so sure.

Never mind that we are each the product of over ten thousand generations of successful human reproduction. Do we really believe that the buck stopped with Helen? Our modern births are not necessarily "failing to progress" because something is wrong with us, but because something is not quite right with modern medicine. This matters because birth is a critical lesson in either trusting or doubting our bodily wisdom. While we must remain grateful for lifesaving medical interventions and realistic about birth's genuine risks, we also shouldn't automatically assume our bodies are inadequate. Birth could be—should be—one of the most empowering experiences of a woman's life, an initiation into our own maternal strength. Instead, for many women like Helen, it becomes a lesson in fallibility and self-doubt.

12:50 A.M.

My own initiation into motherhood was also rocky, yet one of my most potent tastes of magic.

Despite my mom's quiet reservations, I'd planned for a home birth. I've always found it easier to make rebellious life choices if there are voices of reason around me who will let me know when I've gone too far. Although my mom's preference was for a hospital birth, she gave my home-birth plan her blessing. Then, after her death, my doubts crept in. My cabinet of trusted naysayers was missing a critical member. But given my years of disenchantment with conventional medicine, the pull toward a home birth remained.

In that vortex of acute grief in July 2015, exactly two weeks after my mom's sudden passing, my dad's sister also passed away. Here we were, a family shattered with grief, putting on the same suits and black dresses to attend another funeral. At my aunt's burial, the tombstone beside her grave bore a single, stark word: the unusual last name of my home birth midwife. The universe had carved its message in stone. The message wasn't lost on me, but I wasn't yet ready to listen. The plan was still a home birth. A few weeks later, we inflated a giant birth tub in our living room in preparation.

Then at 42 weeks' gestation, I still had not gone into labor. So my midwife made the choice for me: she discharged us from her practice for being two weeks past the due date.

My father happens to be a meticulous archivist. One evening, in those mournful early days after my mom's death, my husband emailed my dad: "Out of curiosity, do you have records of Ellen's conception and birth?" Did he ever. With that data, we calculated. I was born exactly 42½ weeks after conception. My mom went into labor around 1 P.M., and I was placed on her chest at 12:50 A.M. So if there's any genetic basis for these things, my daughter's gestation wasn't so off course.

Discharged from my midwife's practice, two weeks overdue, and suddenly without medical support, we were still attached to having a home birth. Our scramble for another midwife revealed an almost cosmic conspiracy: the regional home-birth conference was happening that exact weekend. Every midwife for hundreds of miles was unreachable. Even our backup was home sick with the flu. Door after door slammed shut until surrender was the only option left. We reluctantly checked in to a hospital for induction.

In the hospital, as the doctor prepared Pitocin, words tumbled out that I hadn't planned: "Do you think psychospiritual factors ever play a role in why someone doesn't go into labor?"

This stranger I'd met earlier that day, who was about to deliver my baby, paused, studying my face. With kind eyes, she responded, "Well, I don't know your *story*."

And with that word, something unlocked. I understood that my body had been holding on. It had all been too much to accept at once—loss compounded by more loss, a spiritual crisis, the complete upending of our carefully laid plans. Tears flooded my face, and in the same moment, before any Pitocin flowed through the IV tubing, my water broke. I went into labor. It was 1 P.M.

From that point on, I was on a different plane. Labor can be like that—a psychedelic ceremony, where time doesn't belong to clocks. In the ensuing swirl of sweat and moans and contractions, parts of me died and were reborn. I found myself pleading for an epidural after years of being the doctor who perhaps too readily dismissed my patients' requests for pharmaceutical relief. The epidural muted my contractions, forcing me to listen to my body in new ways—pushing during subtle rumblings I had to strain my senses to feel. I emerged from that in-between world some twelve hours later, when my daughter finally arrived.

She was placed on my chest. We'd made it. And I glanced at the clock. The red, illuminated digits felt like my mother's signature across time: 12:50 A.M., exactly 42½ weeks' gestation—the precise timing of my own birth decades earlier, as archived in my father's meticulous records. Coincidence? Senseless chaos? It certainly didn't feel that way. I perceived my mom's hand in this timing—it felt like divine storytelling and a hello from the beyond.

THE FOURTH TRIMESTER

In that first moment of my daughter looking up at me with her still-liminal gray eyes, I felt it—that primal surge of protectiveness that would forever change me. The postpartum period is one of our most profound gateways into witchy wisdom—if we reject the cultural mandate to "bounce back" and instead honor the transition. During pregnancy and birth, we've touched the veil between worlds, literally serving as the threshold between spirit and matter. In the weeks that follow, as we rock our babies in the moonlit hours, that veil remains particularly thin. Our heightened sensitivity and emotional attunement can be a powerful opening to deeper intuitive gifts. This is the true magic of motherhood—both the transcendence of this love, and how it initiates us into our own power.

Yet this is also a time of intense physical vulnerability. Our bodies have completed the monumental task of growing and birthing a baby. We might be healing from wounds or surgery, possibly feeding a baby with our bodies—all while operating on minimal and frequently interrupted sleep. This creates a perfect storm of nutritional and physical depletion that often manifests as anxiety and depression. When we frame these struggles purely as mental health issues, we pathologize a brain that's working exactly as it should—sending urgent signals about what the body needs. Our tendency is to once again put a sticker over the check-engine light instead of addressing why the light came on. And when we ignore these early warning signs, the consequences can cascade—setting women up for challenges like mastitis, autoimmune conditions, or chronic health issues that might take years to manifest. While supporting postpartum mental health is critical, we need to recognize that what presents as postpartum anxiety or depression is often our body crying out for replenishment and rest.

Cultures throughout history have recognized the postpartum period as a time requiring special protection and support, but modern American culture fails to understand this. Instead of being provided with what new mothers desperately need—a village of support, lactation guidance, pelvic floor physical therapy, state-sponsored childcare, parental leave for partners, warm, nourishing broths—women face isolation and pressure to return to "normal" while the clock ticks on their job security. Our tears, exhaustion, and raw sensitivity in this period are messages from a body seeking the deep nourishment and care it deserves. I don't mean to suggest that women experiencing postpartum depression or anxiety shouldn't seek treatment; rather, our society systematically fails to address the root causes. As the bearers of our species' future, postpartum women deserve comprehensive support that goes beyond symptom management.

HOW TO SUPPORT THE SACRED FOURTH TRIMESTER

The guiding principle is simple: everything should be in service of Mom, so Mom can be in service of baby without getting depleted.

Rest . . . Through Strategic Outsourcing

- "Sleep when the baby sleeps" sounds lovely in theory, but in practice, those precious nap minutes are consumed by dishes, emails, eating a snack, and finally getting to use the restroom alone. The real unlock for rest is outsourcing—whether that's accepting help from family, organizing meal trains with friends, or temporarily reallocating your budget to pay for support.

- While this may feel like privilege, remember: this expense is temporary, but strategic spending on help during these early weeks can transform your mental health and parenting trajectory. When Mom is depleted and exhausted, she's more vulnerable to mastitis, postpartum depression, and delayed recovery. Those conditions come with their own financial, time, and psychological costs. Sometimes we can't afford *not* to outsource.

Nourishment . . . Without the Work

- The postpartum period is a perfect storm of nutritional depletion. These deficiencies—particularly the loss of critical nutrients your brain needs to function—directly contribute to postpartum depression and anxiety.
- Focus on nutrient-dense foods: broths, egg yolks, red meat, chicken liver, starchy tubers, healthy fats, fruits, and vegetables. The crucial caveat: *someone else* needs to be preparing these foods so you can rest. Partners stepping up, mothers-in-law pitching in, and friends organizing meal trains are investments in your physical and mental health.

Drop the Obligations

- Matrescence means stepping into a new relationship with obligation. Thank-you cards can wait (forever?). Hosting duties are suspended. Many cultures encourage no visitors for the first forty days—from Chinese *zuoyuezi* (sitting the month) to Latin American *cuarentena* (the quarantine) to Korean *sanhujori* (recovery period). Even if you do things differently, consider the wisdom in that sacred boundary.

- When visitors do come, they should pass the full-body "yes" test and arrive ready to serve: taking out trash, bringing food, walking the dog. The priority isn't that they get to hold the baby while you make them a drink—it's that they support your recovery.

Embrace the Magic

- The fourth trimester is peak witch—a liminal space where the veil between physical and spiritual realms is gossamer-thin. In those hushed 3 A.M. moments rocking your baby in the darkness, you're developing an almost preternatural ability to sense their needs and read their cues. It is a magical capacity, amplified by necessity and love.
- To fully harness this heightened sensitivity, resist the urge to fill every quiet moment with Netflix or scrolling. Instead, sink into the silence. Let yourself feel the profound communion happening between you and your baby. Notice how your body responds to their rhythms, how you begin to anticipate their needs. This deep listening—to your baby, to your body, to the subtle energies moving through your home—is witchcraft in its purest form.

Chapter 13

THE GENERATIVE YEARS: WHERE IS OUR VILLAGE?

Generativity is primarily the interest in establishing and guiding the next generation.

—ERIK ERIKSON, *Identity and the Life Cycle*

There's a particular quality to our midlife years—a concentrated intensity that can feel supercharged and at times impossible. Psychologist and developmental theorist Erik Erikson identified this as the stage of "generativity versus stagnation," the phase of life when we're building, creating, nurturing, and making a contribution. These are the years when we're meant to channel our energy outward—raising children, mentoring protégés, making art, building things that outlast us.

Erikson defines this stage as spanning from our forties through our early sixties, but his framework—like most psychological theories of his era—was developed primarily by studying men. For women, this timeline doesn't map cleanly onto our experience. Our generative years often begin earlier as we're establishing careers and sometimes starting families, and they intensify through our forties. Then, just as we're hitting our stride, perimenopause arrives as an entirely different initiation, pulling us into the yin of the menopausal transition. As Miranda July's novel *All Fours* illuminates so well, women's hormonal trajectory across these decades doesn't follow the same arc as men's.

Up until this point, I've been making the case for embracing the yin—for protecting rest and resisting the cultural pressure to constantly produce. And I stand by that. But these generative years are inherently more yang. Relative to pregnancy, postpartum, and menopause—those yin initiations where the assignment is to slow down and turn inward—these middle years ask something different of us. They ask us to show up.

This is the time when you might be raising young children while simultaneously supporting aging parents. It's what we call the sandwich generation—fielding tech support calls from your seventy-something mother while packing school lunches, juggling work deadlines and school closures, coordinating a parent's medical appointments while remembering to schedule dentist appointments for several members of your family. All before breakfast. You're carrying a mile-long to-do list, pushing through exhaustion, managing the mental load of multiple dependent humans, and overstimulated to the point of a migraine.

And just when you think you've finally figured out your body—your cycles, your exercise and nutritional needs—perimenopause arrives to make everything unpredictable again. Your luteal phase brings increasing insomnia. Your energy levels become erratic. Your irritability verges on homicidal. There is simply no chill to a woman's life.

JUST GO AWAY FOR THE WEEKEND

Jamie, mother of three, sits on my office couch, dark circles under her eyes. She checks her phone anytime it vibrates, apologizing to me but adding that it might be the school nurse (there's a lice outbreak going on). Jamie is forty-three, works in operations at an airline company, and has a nine-year-old daughter, Mia, and six-year-old twins, Ben and Ellie. Her husband, Aaron, travels frequently for work. They moved closer to her parents specifically so they could help out, but even with that support, the logistics feel impossible.

"This week alone," she says, pulling up her color-coded calendar, "Mia has soccer practice Monday and Wednesday and the orthodontist on Thursday, Ellie has gymnastics, and Ben has OT and a speech appointment on Tuesday, and there's no school on Friday for staff development, so I need to figure out childcare."

Though the plan had been two kids, her second pregnancy was unexpectedly twins. And although the plan had been public school, they decided to pull Ben out and send him to a private school to support his special needs. "Which we can barely afford, by the way. But he's thriving there."

She's running a complex operation: coordinating three schedules that never align, making summer plans months in advance because the good camps fill up fast. Her work occasionally demands late nights with no warning. Her husband is good-natured and intends to be helpful (at least, when he's not traveling), but she's learned it's often easier to do things herself than to explain to him what needs doing. "When I do hand things off to Aaron, he forgets the permission slip or packs the wrong snack or doesn't notice Ben's meltdown brewing. So I end up cleaning up the mess. I resent doing damage control even more than just doing everything myself in the first place.

"I was telling a friend how tired I am, and she suggested a weekend wellness retreat," Jamie says with a bitter laugh. "Like a weekend would even touch this. I'm not 'I need a massage' tired. I'm so tired I would need to sleep for a year to feel human again."

She pauses, then admits something quietly: "Sometimes I have this shameful fantasy that I'll get really sick. Like, sick enough that I'd have to stay in bed all day, and everyone would have to . . . figure it out without me." She looks down, sheepish. "I know that's terrible. I know I should be grateful for my health. But I don't see any other way I'll ever get permission to rest."

Birthing three children drained something from Jamie that still hasn't been replenished. Even now, six years postpartum, she feels the cumulative depletion in her bones. Her body sends clear signals: slow down, rest. But there's always someone sick, someone up in the middle of the night with a bad dream or growing pains, someone calling out, "Mom . . . MOM!"

Jamie overrides her body's needs because she sees no alternative. It feels like, if she rested, everything around her would fall apart.

GENERATIVITY VERSUS STAGNATION

Erikson's psychosocial theory describes eight stages of human development, each defined by a core conflict that shapes personality, from trust versus mistrust at the beginning of life, all the way to integrity versus despair during the twilight years. The midlife stage is what he framed as generativity versus stagnation. The core question of this stage is whether we will contribute meaningfully to the next generation or retreat into stagnation and self-absorption.

Generativity can be thought of as channeling energy into nurturing and creating. It's energy flowing outward in service of something larger than ourselves. Stagnation is what happens when that energy has no outlet—when we're drifting through midlife without purpose. It's energy looping inward with nowhere to go.

Most of us automatically find ourselves in a state of generating during these years. We're building, teaching, and solving problems. Even if we're not consciously thinking, *I'm in my generativity phase*, our energy is flowing outward.

But what Erikson's framework doesn't fully capture is how brutally hard these years can be for modern women specifically. How structures that once supported women in these generative years are missing when we need them most.

WHERE IS OUR VILLAGE?

"It takes a village" is the oft-repeated refrain when we discuss how hard it is to raise a child. From anthropological research, and as something we know in our bones, we have an intuitive sense that we did not evolve to do this alone. And yet a day in the life of modern parents is a story of isolation and overwhelm. This season of a woman's life should be a time of deepening into our power and shaping the world. Instead, it can often feel like a crucible of defeat.

Community is in short supply in modern life. Our country is set up for life in cars—residential subdivisions (often without sidewalks) separated by great distances from the strip malls where commerce happens. The development of good public transportation in many parts of our country has been stymied by motor industry lobbyists wanting to ensure that commuters still rely on their cars rather than trains, even at the cost of traffic jams and long commutes. We are lacking "third spaces" like the European plaza where humans can gather in a venue that's not the workplace or the home (not that Americans would find the time to chill, even if we had the space).

Many households have two working parents and still barely make ends meet. Our days are spent rushing between work and the childcare arrangements that seem to drain much of the paychecks they enable. Sick days and school breaks are forever a pain point.

The village that once supported families has been dismantled. While grandparents used to figure into this equation, multigenerational living is fading out. We're having children later, when grandparents are often too frail to chase after rambunctious toddlers. The intimate work of caretaking—once woven through extended family networks—has been commodified. Villages have been replaced by daycare centers and after-school programs, while elders are parked in facilities rather than integrated into daily life. As Trevor Noah, former host of *The Daily Show*, puts it: "As a country becomes more and more 'developed,' the major thing that gets eroded is community. The village disappears . . . and you have to buy back the village."

Yes, these years are a time to lean into generativity. But generativity doesn't mean grinding yourself into dust. It means channeling your energy in ways that feel alive, that contribute to something beyond yourself, while maintaining the boundaries that keep you whole. Further, when we're overwhelmed, our inner guidance is muffled by the demands of survival mode. But when we have genuine support and our bodies feel safe, we create space to tune in to our intuitive wisdom. If we are to claim this most potent initiation into our witchiness, we need to start by intentionally rebuilding our villages.

MY MODERN COMMUNE

I can't say that my solution is applicable to all, but for what it's worth, I will share how I have done my best to solve this problem in my own life—how I've built back the village in order to protect pockets of yin in these yang years. I've attempted to re-create village life through what I call a modern commune—sharing daily life, meals, and childcare with another family. We're old friends who discovered over time that our families are uniquely compatible—similar parenting philosophies, shared values around food, daughters close in age, and we genuinely enjoy one another's company.

We moved close to each other. We do school drop-offs and pickups together, share cooking duties, and eat together. This setup alleviates the unpredictable challenges that come up: when a parent is sick or traveling, or a kid needs to be picked up from school early but parents are in meetings, the rest of us can pick up the slack. The commune improves mealtimes dramatically. Many of us have the best of intentions to serve home-cooked food to our families, but the mental and physical labor involved is monumental. In our commune, we share in this duty—meal planning (in particular, thinking through meal ideas that will satisfy all kids' preferences and dietary restrictions), grocery shopping, meal prep, cooking, and cleaning. Then we all sit down to a (mostly) phone-free family dinner every night at 6 P.M. It's a nonnegotiable.

Most importantly, our commune provides something that's devastatingly absent in modern American culture: authentic community. We share in the trials, tribulations, and joys of parenting. We bear witness to one another's journeys. And our children get the benefit of this community as well—not only do they have pseudosiblings but they also form a close bond with other trusted adults. I look forward to the biggest ROI from this in the teenage years, when my daughter will have questions that she does *not* want to come to me about, but she will need sage counsel from a trusted adult.

This arrangement has its own complexities and isn't feasible for every family, but I believe that it's an unsung strategy for improving modern life. Community is the salve to the impossible demands of these yang years. I leave this here not as a one-size-fits-all prescription but as a rough example of what becomes possible when we think creatively about how to rebuild the village.

WHEN GENERATIVITY FEELS OUT OF REACH

I want to name another land mine of this life phase: not everyone feels generative during these years. Maybe you don't have people depending on you—by choice or by circumstance. Maybe you wanted kids but couldn't have them. Maybe you haven't found a partner. Maybe your career feels stagnant or nonexistent. Maybe you look around at your life and think: *What am I building?*

Stagnation during these years is not the same as rest. It doesn't necessarily feel restorative or good.

At times what might look from the outside like stagnation is actually an undercover form of generativity—adopting rescue animals, working a twelve-step program, breaking a cycle, intergenerational healing, the quiet internal effort to build a foundation for future healthy relationships. That's real, even if it doesn't necessarily register as generativity to those around you.

But sometimes—and I say this gently—pseudogenerativity can exist in the form of endless cycles of self-improvement, wellness retreats, and healing modalities that never quite get us all the way to *healed*. It's the certifications piled on top of workshops, and the constant promise of a new modality that will finally fix us. It becomes a circuit of energy looping inward that masquerades as growth. And I believe the fuel for it comes from an unrealized yearning for generativity.

If you find yourself here, the question is not "What else do I need to do to heal?" A more useful thread to pull might be "How can I serve the collective?" Generativity doesn't require having children or a traditional career. But it does mean finding a way to contribute—teaching, mentoring, creating, building, and showing up for others. Satisfaction during these years of life lies on the other side of letting your energy flow outward instead of endlessly circling inward.

Whether we birth children, books, ideas, sobriety, or revolutions, these generative years call us into our power in new ways. This is when we most need our circles—not just for practical support, though that matters enormously, but to bear witness to this poignant phase of life. We need people around us who understand the impossible juggle, who can catch what's falling through the cracks, and who remind us that our exhaustion is a systemic bind that we're all in together. We need creative and often counter-mainstream solutions. Building back our villages in this fragmented modern landscape requires the same rebellious spirit that defines our witchiness.

Chapter 14

SEASON OF THE CRONE: WISDOM AND LIBERATION

> Though fairy tales end after ten pages, our lives do not. We are multi-volume sets.
>
> —CLARISSA PINKOLA ESTÉS, *Women Who Run with the Wolves*

When Nicole first came to see me, she was barely holding it together. At fifty-two, she hadn't slept through the night in what felt like years—she was waking regularly to use the bathroom or because searing hot flashes left her sheets drenched. Her teenage daughter was withdrawing from the family, losing weight, and glued to her phone day and night. Her son was recently off to college, her father's Parkinson's was rapidly progressing, and each of these developments came with its own kind of grief. Meanwhile, Nicole was finally up for an important promotion—a position she'd been working toward for years—but she could barely focus during important meetings, often excusing herself to splash cold water on her face in the bathroom.

"I feel like I'm disappearing," she told me in session, her voice catching. "The other day, presenting to the board, I had major brain fog. I started stumbling over my words, and I saw them exchange looks—these men who've known me for a decade. Suddenly I was reduced to this stereotype of the menopausal woman who can't keep it together."

What Nicole didn't realize was that she was standing at the threshold of a powerful era. Over the next several months we worked in collaboration with her functional medicine doctor to address her symptoms with a combination of hormone therapy and lifestyle adjustments. This took a few iterations and some troubleshooting, but eventually her discomfort eased, and something else emerged: a fierce clarity about who she was and what was important to her. She began speaking up in meetings without worrying about being "nice." She started a support group for other women in her firm navigating similar issues.

A year later, Nicole sat in my office with a different energy entirely. Yes, she still had mild symptoms, but they no longer defined her days. "You know what's strange?" she mused. "For the first time in my life, I don't care what anyone thinks of me. It's like all those hormones that kept me people-pleasing for decades have finally loosened their grip." She sat up a bit straighter on the couch. "I've earned every gray hair and wrinkle, and I'm done being invisible. I'm just getting started."

Nicole's evolution illustrates what I witness among many of my peri- and postmenopausal patients: that this physical metamorphosis can catalyze a spiritual awakening. If the luteal phase is the yin of our monthly cycle, the postmenopausal years represent the yin of our life cycle. The winding down of fertility opens up the witchiest time in our lives—a time when we become both more invisible to the outer world and more attuned to the invisible realm. Menopause is often framed as a loss—of fertility, vitality, desirability. But this transition is actually an opening. It's no wonder our image of a witch is a crone.

In fact, in our fertile years, our biological drives can block our magic. Hormones push us to maintain social harmony at the cost of our truth. Childbearing requires us to direct our vitality toward others' well-being, even at the expense of our own needs. But menopause brings liberation from this hormonal imperative to put others first. The ancient Sumerians understood this intuitively: they saw menstrual blood as life force—first, for making babies during our fertile years, then retained in the body to imbue a woman with wisdom during her menopausal years.

A DIFFERENT POSTPARTUM

During our reproductive years, hormones like estrogen and progesterone drive us to make nice and play well in the sandbox. As we've discussed, primate research shows that female likability directly correlates with reproductive fitness—we're hardwired to suppress our own needs in service of group harmony because, evolutionarily, belonging to the tribe meant desirability and survival.

But menopause poses an interesting plot twist. As estrogen levels wane, though we may experience physical challenges like hot flashes and insomnia, we're finally freed from the biological drive to prioritize others' needs. For once we can direct our nurturing energy toward *ourselves.*

This liberation is, surprisingly, a quirk of evolution. Most of our biological processes have been carefully refined over millennia through natural selection—that is, traits that help us reproduce successfully get selected for and passed down. But menopause exists outside this paradigm. Since it occurs after reproduction ends, evolution has no way to select for improvements. Over the course of human evolution, when a menopausal woman developed a beneficial trait—say, fewer hot flashes—that adaptation usually died with her, because it couldn't influence reproductive success. In other words, because menopause is *by definition* post-reproductive, it flies under the radar of evolution, and it's harder for any adaptations to get built into the genome. Sure, we can make a case for the grandmother effect (that is, a postmenopausal woman can be a source of wisdom and support, helping the survival of her kin), but this effect only accounts for her survival, not for her adaptation to the hormonal changes of menopause.

Because we haven't adapted to menopause, one theory is that our bodies respond to menopause using their existing "software" for hormone changes—specifically, the postpartum period. The precedent for a precipitous estrogen drop is the one that happens after giving birth. So, when menopause hits, the body falls back on that familiar programming. Our bodies mobilize calcium (great for making breast milk, problematic for bone density), we generate heat (perfect for warming babies, less ideal when it has us running out of a meeting in a sweaty panic), and we have interrupted sleep (essential for infant care, miserable in middle age).

This parallel between menopause and postpartum is biological but also deeply symbolic. Just as the postpartum period marks the birth of a child, menopause marks the birth of a new version of ourselves. In both transitions we experience physical changes, emotional upheaval, and a shift in identity. The night sweats, the mood swings, and feeling simultaneously powerful and invisible—these are the labor pains of our rebirth.

Freed from the hormonal imperative to subjugate our needs and "make nice," we can finally mother ourselves. This doesn't mean we become selfish or disconnected from others' well-being. Instead, we evolve into a more authentic form of service: doing what's right *because* it is right, not because it will make others like us. The menopausal transition gifts us with a deeper connection to our magic precisely because we're no longer bound by the need for approval.

While patriarchal culture taught us to fear and revile the warty old crones of our Halloween images, we're creating a new narrative. For the first time, perimenopausal and postmenopausal women are platformed and resourced. We're speaking openly about the nitty-gritty aspects of menopause, and we're recognizing that we deserve to feel better.

This shift matters more than we might realize. As Beth Berry, author of *Motherwhelmed*, writes, "Mature, embodied, well-resourced, and sisterhood-rooted women who know their worth are one of the biggest threats to patriarchy, capitalism, and white supremacy on the planet." And it comes not a moment too soon. If our hyperpolarized, extractive, oppressive, and endlessly warring world has any hope of righting itself before we fully capsize, it will be because the crones step forward, unleashing our magic, speaking our truth, and sharing what we know.

In the ancient Sumerian sense, we now retain our nurturing essence not for others' survival but for our own becoming. We are giving birth to our wild and mature selves. Our witch selves. Our wisest and most powerful incarnation. And this, in turn, births a new vision for the world.

FINDING RELIEF: A FRESH LOOK AT HORMONE THERAPY

While this transformation is profound and potentially revolutionary, the day-to-day experience can be incredibly challenging. As a practitioner who generally advocates for natural approaches to health, I've had to reckon with my own beliefs about medical intervention during menopause. Here's what I've come to understand: unlike other health conditions where symptoms indicate an imbalance needing correction (think anxiety signaling blood-sugar instability, brain fog signaling leaky gut), menopausal symptoms are different. There are limitations to addressing the symptoms of menopause at the root, because for the most part, they are not an indication that we've let our health slip—they're unavoidable consequences of outliving our reproductive capacity.

The list of symptoms reads like a witch's curse: insomnia, hot flashes, brain fog, and mood changes. Then there's the joint pain, frozen shoulder, and a range of urogenital issues (urinary tract infections, urinary urgency and frequency, incontinence, vaginal dryness and irritation, vaginal atrophy, decreased libido, and painful intercourse). There can also be serious medical issues like osteopenia and osteoporosis, and the postmenopausal years bring increased risks of dementia, broken bones, and cardiovascular disease.

One thing that makes this transition particularly harrowing is its timing. Modern women face these symptoms precisely when life demands the most from us. We may be raising children while caring for aging parents, all while hitting our career stride. Our professional success depends on being focused and effective, yet hormonal changes prevent us from thinking clearly or getting a full night's sleep. Add to this the role transition away from what society prizes as desirable. Many of us are also parenting tweens and teens who are experiencing their own hormonal changes just as we navigate this reverse puberty. It's a perfect storm: teenagers surging into their hormonal peak while we're on our hormonal decline, all under one roof.

The medical community's approach to hormone replacement therapy (HRT) has undergone a dramatic shift that's worth understanding.

It centers on the Women's Health Initiative (WHI), one of the largest U.S. health studies ever conducted. When results were published in 2002, they sent shock waves through the medical field: while HRT reduced menopausal symptoms, researchers claimed it increased risks of breast cancer, heart disease, blood clots, and stroke. Overnight, doctors pulled countless women off hormones.

Two decades—and immeasurable suffering—later, scientists revisited the data and found a more nuanced story. The key factor was timing. In some studies where healthy women began hormone therapy near the onset of menopause, HRT was associated with a *lower* risk of heart disease compared with women who never used hormones or who began treatment many years later. While the increased breast cancer risk with long-term combined HRT remains a consideration, short-term use for managing symptoms is now considered safe for many women. And emerging brain-imaging research led by Dr. Lisa Mosconi, director of the Weill Cornell Women's Brain Initiative as well as their Alzheimer's Prevention Clinic, and program director at the medical nonprofit Wellcome Leap, suggests that the menopause transition itself is an inflection point for brain aging in some women—a vulnerability thought to be influenced in part by declining estrogen levels. While it's too early to conclude that hormone therapy mitigates dementia risk, this line of research raises important questions about when, and for whom, estrogen therapy could protect the aging brain.

Think of hormone therapy as one of many tools in your witch's arsenal—alongside herbs like chasteberry, exercise, and dietary supports—for managing menopausal symptoms. Just as our ancestors used whatever plants and practices were available to them to navigate this transition, we can draw on both ancient wisdom and modern medicine. But bear in mind: you might find your first doctor isn't up to speed on this evolving understanding of HRT. If you hit a wall (when *haven't* we, as women in the medical system?), persist in searching for a practitioner who understands the current data and will work with your specific situation to find relief.

While I generally believe in addressing health issues at their root—and we should absolutely support our menopausal journey with nourishing food, lifestyle changes, and psychospiritual practices—menopause is a medical anomaly. Don't hesitate to seek individualized treatment for relief from symptoms that can significantly impact your quality of life, especially during years when you're juggling multiple demands and undergoing your most potent initiation into witchcraft.

A WITCH'S APPROACH TO MENOPAUSE

Symptom relief matters, but have we swung too far toward medicalizing this transition? Practitioners like Kimberly Ann Johnson (somatic experiencing practitioner and author of *Call of the Wild*) and Dr. Aviva Romm (midwife, herbalist, family physician specializing in OB/GYN, and author of *Hormone Intelligence*) are offering a different approach—one that makes space for the changes rather than reflexively medicating them away.

As Dr. Romm explains, "Menopause isn't a medical problem to be managed. Instead we should recognize it as a profound biological and spiritual turning point. Of course we deserve care—real care—for symptoms—but when we reduce menopause to hormone deficiency, something to fear, or something to 'fix,' we miss its deeper invitation. This is not an ending nor a failure of your body. It's a reorientation of power, perception, and purpose, of connection to self—another turn in the spiral of a woman's life."

Drawing from both practitioners' wisdom, here's how to approach this transition as the rite of passage it truly is:

- **Reframe the narrative.** Menopause marks the transition when women step into their greatest power as healers, leaders, and keepers of wisdom.
- **Honor the transformation.** Johnson describes menopause as "an underworld journey." Rather than "scrambling to stay" how you were, embrace the change. Let it be a "rewilding" process where you shed societal conditioning and return to your authentic self as you care less about pleasing others.

- **Rearrange**. As Johnson notes, "We are more rearrangable" during this hormonal upheaval, making menopause an "opportunity for healing." Use this time to shake things up and establish new patterns.
- **Support your nervous system**. Use breath work, somatic practices, and nervous system regulation techniques (e.g., yoga, biofeedback, Primal Trust, the Safe and Sound Protocol). Your body is recalibrating, and it may need extra support.
- **Nourish**. Following Romm's guidance, focus on hormone-supporting foods: healthy fats, phytoestrogen-rich plants, and nutrient-dense whole foods. When indicated, consider adaptogenic herbs like ashwagandha and holy basil.
- **Move with love, not rules**. Rather than following exercise "shoulds," Johnson learned to ask, "What is genuinely nourishing to me?" For her, that meant "dance and walking on the beach" rather than forcing herself into regimens that didn't feel right for her changing body.
- **Practice discernment**. Johnson emphasizes: "We have to get very clear about our energy and where we want to put it. There's nothing to waste. We don't have a margin of error anymore." Use this transition to eliminate what no longer serves and focus your precious energy intentionally.
- **Reclaim your sexuality**. Explore what pleasure means in this new phase. Johnson notes that "the physiological changes require that we get more specific, more creative, and more expansive with our definition of our sexuality."

COMING FULL CIRCLE

The Cycles card that once felt like a dud has revealed itself to be a map—a guide to navigating the phases of life. Each cycle, from the first blood of menarche to the liberation of the menopausal transition, offers a unique initiation into our witchcraft.

Circling back to Nicole: a year after she started gathering with other women in her company, she discovered exactly this kind of transformation. She had not only been promoted but had initiated a company-wide policy overhaul around women's health. She mused, "It's like the hot flashes were burning away everything that wasn't truly me."

Like the moon waxing and waning, like the seasons turning, we are always in motion, always becoming. We're ascending to our role as keepers of ancient knowing. The crone phase is the culmination of everything we've learned and experienced, distilled into wisdom that the world desperately needs.

Our culture is imbalanced toward yang, but a witch values the yin so that she can live in sync with nature, stay in balance, and move through the phases of the female life cycle with ease.

FOURTH PRACTICE: OPENING TO MYSTERY

Our Culture Prioritizes the Material. A Witch Is Open to Mystery.

For centuries, the Western world has built its understanding of reality on a simple premise: what can be measured is real. This materialist worldview, born from the Enlightenment's worthy pursuit of testing our hypotheses, has given us extraordinary advances in medicine, technology, and our understanding of the natural world. Yet, in our zeal to separate fact from fiction, we may have thrown the baby out with the bathwater.

Even when we witness the inexplicable firsthand, we rush to explain it away rather than letting ourselves be awed by what we don't understand—like when I first witnessed my patients benefiting from acupuncture and thought, *Show me the peer-reviewed study.* We have been conditioned to demand proof even of our own profound experiences. Today, we find ourselves spiritually starved in a culture that recognizes only what fits under a microscope or separates from placebo in an eight-week trial. We've been taught to deny our mystical experiences and any connection to the unseen currents of existence.

But what if our most advanced science is pointing us back toward mystery? What if the same rigorous inquiry that once seemed to disprove the magical is now revealing a universe far stranger and more interconnected than we can even imagine?

Chapter 15

LEAVING SPACE FOR MYSTERY

> The first gulp from the glass of natural sciences will turn you into an atheist, but at the bottom of the glass, God is waiting for you.
>
> —Attributed to WERNER HEISENBERG

As therapist and author Dené Logan writes in *Sovereign Love*, "The more I believe in wonder, possibility, divine timing, and a natural order and rhythm to the unfolding of life, the more life demonstrates to me the extent to which that is the precise nature of reality."

In the face of devastating grief, I came to understand that the psychospiritual questions of life are no place for the objective. It wasn't the time to apply my expertise with facts and data, searching for evidence like I was reading peer-reviewed papers in a journal. This was completely new terrain, and it required a different kind of discernment—one that could tolerate mystery rather than demanding proof. But that tolerance for mystery was hard won, given how deeply conditioned I'd been—not only by our culture but also by my medical training—to trust only what could be proven.

WAYS OF KNOWING

In Hinduism, there's a basic tenet: truth is one, paths are many.

Indeed, there are multiple ways to understand our world. There's the empirical way—the realm of measurement and microscopes, of repeatable experiments and falsifiable hypotheses. This is what is known as materialism—the philosophy that physical matter is the fundamental substance of reality, and that everything, including consciousness and thought, can ultimately be explained through material processes. From this perspective, the universe operates like an intricate machine: atoms colliding, neurons firing, chemical reactions cascading. There's no room for phenomena that can't be mapped.

Then there's what we might call a spiritual way of knowing—the insights that arise during mystical experiences, the resonance we feel with art or natural beauty, the truth we sense in our bodies. These too are *ways of knowing*. In fact, subjective, anecdotal reports are a form of evidence. While randomized controlled trials are the gold standard, sitting at the top of the evidence pyramid, anecdotes form its foundation—they're where inquiry begins.

As I write this, I'm well aware that the case I'm making in favor of believing in magic would be better received if I could back it up with science. Data-supported anecdotes have become de rigueur for serious nonfiction. *But isn't this exactly our problem?* It is our hyperrational world that has us beholden to objective explanations for our inherently valid subjective experiences. Truth is not the same as fact.

Our cultural predicament is this: when faced with mystery, we reflexively reach for rational explanations. Consider when you start noticing a meaningful number everywhere—on clocks, receipts, license plates. We are trained to call this frequency illusion: a combination of selective attention (our brains notice information we deem relevant) and confirmation bias (we prioritize things that confirm our beliefs). This scientific explanation has merit—our brains do notice patterns we're primed to see. But does that automatically negate other possibilities? This is exactly the either/or thinking that has us trapped.

Empirical and spiritual ways of knowing are not competing frameworks so much as complementary lenses through which to view reality. Like the right and left hemispheres, or yin and yang, they work best in partnership. Yet our culture has spent centuries elevating one while diminishing the other. The scientific way of knowing is still taken by most people as a *truer* understanding of the nature of reality than the knowing that comes from within.

Intrinsic to the scientific method is a spirit of openness. If we genuinely want the truth, this requires a willingness to be surprised by unexpected findings—that perhaps the world is not as we assume it is. When we shifted to the scientific method and first started testing our hypotheses, it rescued us from argument by assertion and untested medical treatments.

But, as astrophysicist Neil deGrasse Tyson points out, "scientists are human." He continues, "We have our blind spots and prejudices. Science is a mechanism designed to ferret them out. The problem is, we aren't always faithful to the core values of science." Indeed, our confirmation biases and human tendency to defend existing beliefs often override science's original purpose of uncovering truth.

These days, we've lost the spirit of the scientific method. Studies are tightly engineered to gain FDA approval for on-patent medications. We cherry-pick evidence to support whatever case we're making, whether or not it reflects the overall weight of the evidence. And while the peer review process is meant to function as quality control and a safeguard against bias, in practice it can reward conformity. If a study reveals a finding that runs counter to scientific consensus, the orthodoxy is more likely to get stuck in cognitive dissonance than adjust its worldview. When findings challenge the prevailing worldview, we dismiss them, shutting down the possibility of mystery in the name of logic and science. Academics are afraid to study mystical topics because they know they'd be laughed out of academia. Science itself has become like a religion.

In fact, our obsession with "the science" may be a product of our cultural pendulum swinging away from spirituality. We have so few frameworks for grappling with the mysteries of the universe that we try desperately to prove that our world makes concrete sense. As David Hawkins puts it: "The current elevation of science to the status of infallible oracle is an expression of our insecure compulsion to feel that there is some kind of a measurable, universally predictable, objective world 'out there' upon which we can truly rely."

To be sure, there is value in evidence. Evidence gives us antibiotics, GPS satellites, and bridges that don't collapse—reproducible knowledge that works regardless of our beliefs.

But not everything that exists lends itself to our current tools of measurement. In ignoring less falsifiable ways of knowing, what might we be overlooking? Do we really think we can perceive all that exists in our vast and mysterious universe with our current instruments? It would be hubris to assume we have developed all the tools of perception that can be developed, and we should not assume that what our six senses perceive is the full range of existence. For example, along the spectrum from radio waves to gamma rays, visible light (what we can see with the human eye) accounts for about 3×10^{-12} percent of electromagnetic radiation. Sharks and some species of birds can detect the earth's magnetic field. What other energies might be moving through space that we don't have a sense organ for and have yet to build an instrument to detect? As writer and mythologist Erick Godsey reminds us: "Humility is admitting anything is possible that doesn't violate the laws of physics." Wisdom, on the other hand, is the reckoning with the fact that "we don't know the limits of physics."

In an irreverent bit, comedian Pete Holmes exposes the false binary between theism and atheism. As he puts it, some people think God created the universe, others think "nothing" created it—but "if one of the things your 'nothing' does is spontaneously erupt into everything, that's a pretty magical nothing." He extends this logic to death itself: when atheists say, "You go into nothing," Holmes responds, "You mean . . . you merge back with your creator?" Whether we call it God, consciousness, the quantum field, or "nothing," we're invoking something mysterious and unprovable as the source of everything. Holmes reminds us that our choice isn't between the magical and the rational—it's between different names for the same unfathomable mystery.

The deepest truths of existence resist translation into words. When we attempt to capture the full, instantaneous reality of any given moment—what we might call right-hemisphere knowing—we encounter something like a fundamental law of consciousness: we can experience reality directly, or we can describe it, but we cannot do both well at the same time. There's a tension, like a delicate seesaw—we can either *inhabit* a moment or *analyze* it, but doing one inevitably dilutes the other.

I've learned this most vividly in psychedelic ceremonies, where my initial impulse is to bring along what I jokingly call my personal stenographer, frantically recording insights so I can bring back stories from the astral plane. I want to "eff" the ineffable—to take what's indescribable and somehow manage to describe it. But invariably, the medicine teaches me that if I want to go truly deep—if I want to soar—I must abandon this compulsion to translate and simply surrender to direct experience. The spirit of the medicine seems to say, "If you want me to show you the true nature of reality, you have to leave your personal stenographer behind." I comply, and then I fly—but I can only remember glimpses of it later.

We humans are storytellers by nature. The way we make sense of reality is by narrating it, encapsulating the infinite complexity of each moment in the dense container of words. In regular life, the left hemisphere serves an essential purpose in this dance between experience and expression. With its gift for language and analysis, it slows down the torrent of direct experience so we can define the events and the feelings—so consciousness can actually experience itself. But something is always lost in translation. When we transform the instantaneous all-at-onceness of our lived experience into cogent narrative, we lose so much of the texture of what actually occurred.

Perhaps our culture's obsession with analysis—this "left-hemisphere articulation or it didn't happen" mentality—has taken us out of the present moment. Perhaps it has stymied our ability to hold the ineffable aspects of the human experience without squirming away for proof. What if we could value the ineffable as much as the easily expressible? What if we could be fully present to the happening without always needing to preserve our capacity to describe it later, recognizing that this very preservation often pulls us out of the immediacy of direct experience? What if we could be comfortable with not knowing?

This creates a fascinating paradox: some of the people most committed to articulating reality are having experiences that resist articulation entirely.

THE FLIP

"If you build a prison out of rationality, all the exits look like going crazy," observes Malcolm Ocean, a systems thinker and behavior design expert. This captures the predicament facing some scientists and medical professionals—trained in the rigorous methods of measurement and verification—who are having experiences that shake their materialist foundations to the core.

Author, professor, and historian of religions Jeffrey J. Kripal uses the term "the flip" to describe the moment a convinced materialist or someone with a purely scientific worldview has a profound mystical, spiritual, or, in his words, "super natural" experience and suddenly realizes their worldview was never an absolute truth, but merely one interpretation among many.

Kripal documents numerous cases of this phenomenon—committed atheist Barbara Ehrenreich, the acclaimed journalist and social critic, who suppressed a powerful mystical experience for decades because it didn't fit her materialist worldview; neurosurgeon Eben Alexander whose near-death experience during a coma challenged everything he believed about brain-based consciousness; and Kripal himself, whose Kundalini-type experience during research in India forced him to rethink his entire scholarly framework. Each of these thinkers was forced to reconcile their training with experiences that don't fit the materialist model.

"We're not taught that there's a philosophy of science, but of course there is," explains Dr. Dean Radin, chief scientist at the Institute of Noetic Sciences, and a leading researcher in parapsychology and consciousness studies. "We assume that the world is made out of matter and energy, and that's the end of the story," he observes, adding, "It may be more than that."

At the heart of the tension between materialism and mysticism is how we understand consciousness—specifically, what philosophers call "the hard problem": how our inner experience of being aware, of feeling and perceiving, arises from physical brain matter. Following philosophers like William James and Aldous Huxley, Kripal offers one of the competing theories: consciousness isn't merely the brain's output, but reality's fundamental substance. "Mind is not what the brain does," he reflects. "Rather, the brain is what the mind looks like on its local journey through space-time."

Dr. Radin elaborates on this inverted model: "One way of thinking about the scientific model of reality is in the form of a pyramid. . . .

Most scientists would say that the bottom of the pyramid, the thing on which everything rests, is physics, and the next level up is chemistry, and the next thing up from that is biology, and then maybe psychology, and somewhere near the tippy top of this pyramid is awareness." But what if we've been looking at this pyramid upside down? In this revolutionary perspective, consciousness isn't the result of material building blocks—it's the *foundation* upon which everything else rests.

When confronted with phenomena that defy measurement—precognition, synchronicity, telepathy, near-death experiences—science often retreats to a familiar refrain: if it can't be measured, it isn't real. But this thinking has a logical flaw: while skepticism about unverifiable phenomena is healthy, dismissing them entirely is unwarranted. Kripal calls out the irony of this reflexive skepticism: "We live in a culture that prides itself on its skepticism, but that skepticism is often a kind of faith itself—a faith in the impossibility of the impossible."

The scientific method remains one of humanity's greatest achievements, but it was never meant to be the only path to truth. By acknowledging its limitations, we don't diminish science; we open ourselves to a more complete picture of reality. As Radin emphasizes, "Materialism . . . as a way of thinking about reality is not wrong. . . . We're not going to throw away the textbooks, but because it doesn't account very well for experience, we need something that's a little bit broader."

Yet this broader understanding bumps up against the same rationality-over-irrationality bias we've been exploring, where institutions systematically dismiss anything that challenges orthodox thinking. Biologist Rupert Sheldrake, formerly of Cambridge University, who has experienced significant pushback for his research on telepathy, observes that defenders of strict materialism "have an undue influence through universities and through the media, and their main influence is through trying to make people who disagree with them look stupid. They try and discredit their opponents. They don't look at the evidence, they just discredit them by saying they're pseudoscientists or charlatans or frauds." He articulates a crucial distinction: "There's a conflict in the heart of science between science as a method of inquiry . . . and science as a belief system or a worldview. And unfortunately, the worldview . . . has come to inhibit and constrict the free inquiry, which is the very lifeblood of the scientific endeavor."

SCIENCE'S OWN FLIP

These personal "flips" in worldview that scientists and scholars describe mirror what's happening at the frontiers of science itself.

For centuries, we used "God of the gaps" thinking—attributing to divine intervention whatever we couldn't yet explain through science. Then, as we developed a scientific understanding, there was less and less room for the supernatural. Mental illness was no longer demon possession but brain chemistry; epidemics became matters of germ theory rather than evidence of divine punishment; natural disasters reflected plate tectonics, not angry gods. For centuries, scientific progress meant increasing clarity—each discovery filled another gap in our understanding, each advance brought more precision and predictability. More knowledge meant less God.

But with the quantum revolution—the early-twentieth-century realization that matter and energy behave very differently at the atomic scale—this pattern has reversed. Today, the closer we look and the better our instruments, the *blurrier* things become. Light behaves as both a particle and a wave—not sometimes one and sometimes the other, but somehow both simultaneously. Atomic particles exist in what's called superposition—existing in multiple states or locations simultaneously until the moment we observe them, at which point they collapse into a single state. In other words, electrons don't decide where they are until we look. The act of observation itself shapes reality. Most bizarrely, we've demonstrated quantum entanglement—where two particles, once connected, remain instantaneously correlated across any distance, in ways that seem to violate our understanding of space and time—alongside other counterintuitive phenomena like quantum tunneling and quantum teleportation, which further challenge our everyday assumptions. We see that reality, at its most fundamental level, doesn't behave like solid ground. It's slippery, constantly in flux, and it even shapeshifts depending on how we look at it—as if the universe is playing an elaborate game of hide-and-seek.

Rather than eliminating the need for mystery, our most advanced science is revealing layers of reality that seem to *require* it. The more we know, the more we must admit that something incomprehensible undergirds our existence.

These discoveries suggest that reality, at its core, is not something to be conquered by logic alone. Though we're never going to put down our microscopes (nor should we), perhaps the wisest course is to stay open to uncertainty and something beyond the calculable. As science itself reveals a universe less amenable to the left-hemisphere, yang qualities of measurement and mastery, we're being invited to reincorporate the right hemisphere, the yin, and the magic: to embrace the wisdom of not knowing alongside rigorous inquiry.

If even our most rational disciplines are pointing toward mystery at the heart of existence, perhaps it's time to trust our own capacity to navigate that mystery directly.

BEYOND SECONDHAND SPIRITUALITY

For generations, many forms of organized religion have claimed exclusive access to the divine, with authority figures (usually male) dictating the supposedly right way to connect with spirit. While organized religion has provided access to guidance, community, and genuine transcendence for countless people, this model of religiosity has not been a safe spiritual home for all. And for many, it has interfered with direct spiritual experience.

What if we don't need intermediaries to interpret the divine? We are witches. We can do this work for ourselves. What if each of us can develop our own relationship with the unknown?

This requires trust—the kind my friend, the naturopathic doctor Erica Matluck, discovered one morning. She told me about a time when her son was very young and crying in protest at being strapped into his car seat. As she sat with his distress, she realized how often she herself had kicked and screamed against life's circumstances, and how the divine had held steady beside her—not out of cruelty, but because it could see the larger picture. When we resist our current circumstances, we're often like that protesting child, unable to see how our difficulty might serve our ultimate growth or protection.

If, like me, you grew up with skepticism presented as the only intelligent choice, or if you've been wounded by a religious institution that shamed or diminished you, consider reopening this case. We can write our own rules for connecting with spirit, reclaiming concepts that institutions have monopolized or that skeptics have dismissed. "Supernatural" simply refers to forces beyond current scientific understanding. But how much of nature's laws do we truly comprehend—if they are, in fact, laws at all?

A spiritual longing appears to be a birthright of conscious beings. As renowned essayist and travel writer Pico Iyer observes, there is "some religious intonation that many of us have, that there's something beyond the world that we see. And yet, what humans have done with that is cut it up into a thousand divisions and turned it into us-versus-them. When the whole basis of that intonation is something that connects us and that unites us." If you have been turned off by the way belief fuels conflict yet still feel a persistent spiritual longing, there may be a middle path.

THE ERASURE OF SACRED FEMININE LEADERSHIP

The systematic suppression of women's spiritual authority predates witch hunts—it reaches back to the very foundations of Western religious tradition. Consider Mary Magdalene, whose story illustrates how feminine spiritual power has been deliberately rewritten.

For centuries now, Mary Magdalene has been portrayed as a repentant prostitute, which diminishes her actual role as one of Jesus's most devoted disciples and, according to some early Christian texts, his closest confidant. Her characterization as a prostitute wasn't based on biblical evidence—nowhere in the canonical gospels is she described that way. Instead, Pope Gregory I created this identity in 591 C.E. by conflating her with other biblical figures, transforming a spiritual leader into a symbol of female sexual shame.

The Gnostic gospels, which reflect early Christian traditions outside the canonized Bible, tell a different story. In the Gospel of Mary, Mary Magdalene receives special teachings from Jesus and serves as a spiritual teacher to the other disciples. These texts portray her not as a fallen woman seeking redemption but as a religious teacher in her own right.

This pattern extends beyond Mary Magdalene. Early Christianity included numerous women in leadership roles—Phoebe was called a deacon, Junia an apostle, Priscilla a teacher of theology. But as Christianity became institutionalized and aligned with Roman power structures, women's authority was insidiously removed from the canon.

As usual, this erasure doesn't seem accidental. A spirituality that honored feminine wisdom would have threatened the emerging patriarchal church structure. Women who claimed direct spiritual revelation posed the same threat as the witches who would follow: they suggested that spiritual authority could exist outside institutional control.

Understanding this history helps explain why so many women feel spiritually homeless. This is why feminine ways of knowing the sacred—through embodied wisdom, connection to nature, and direct mystical experience—continue to be marginalized as "alternative" or "new age" when they are, in fact, among humanity's oldest spiritual traditions.

All I offer here is permission. Consider this your encouragement to start exploring, to find your own way of seeing across the bridge to other worlds, of staying connected with those who have crossed ahead of us. There's no how-to, but instead, a report back from someone who reopened the case. Through loss, I've gained so much from finding my way to this connection on my own terms.

But how do we move from permission to practice?

TRANSCENDENCE

Viktor Frankl quotes Friedrich Nietzsche in his book *Man's Search for Meaning*: "He who has a *why* to live can bear almost any *how*." This human condition is sure to bring us all to our breaking points one way or the other. But transcendence can make it more bearable. Transcendence—glimpsing beyond the veil of ordinary life, pointing toward something larger than ourselves—is the essential "why." When we have brushes with the rapture of this magical world, it fills our gas tank with the promise that something meaningful is occurring here, something not entirely accidental. It can help us trust in divine timing, even when we're inclined to be in resistance to our circumstances. May it also serve as a reminder not to be fair-weather friends of spirituality—to trust in greater forces not only when things feel charmed but also when we feel like we're being strapped into our car seats. Moments of transcendence feel like a wink from the universe saying, "What you're experiencing right now is not the whole story."

Even if we choose not to ascribe agency to the universe, transcendent experiences can infuse ordinary life with richness.

With life being as challenging as it is, when we have so many "hows" to endure, it helps to have a lot of "why." Transcendence is my "why," and it's there for the taking much more often than we realize. But it requires a certain priming. Admittedly, to touch transcendence, it helps to be at least open to its existence. As author Diane Duane writes in *So You Want to Be a Wizard*, "Magic does not live in the unwilling heart."

Transcendence and its first cousin, awe, humble us, instantly reminding us that we exist against a backdrop of vastness. When we recognize the implausible web of interconnections in our lives, we see the fingerprint of the divine. In words often attributed to philosopher Alan Watts: "Through our eyes, the universe is perceiving itself. Through our ears, the universe is listening to its harmonies. We are the witnesses through which the universe becomes conscious of its glory, of its magnificence." We can't help but bow. When we see ourselves in the fabric of a miraculous continuum, it at once lifts us into brushes with the divine and genuflects us into a posture of humility.

The paths to transcendence are as varied as we are, requiring only a genuine willingness to receive what wants to be revealed.

HOW CAN WE FIND MOMENTS OF TRANSCENDENCE?

What leaves you in awe? What art form feels sublime? The key is prioritizing opportunities for transcendence in your daily life. Here are reliable pathways:

- **Nature:** Seek the perspective that comes from hiking to a mountaintop or contemplate the steadiness of a tree. Even a sunset walk in your neighborhood can offer moments of awe at the natural world.
- **Music:** Rather than background noise, move music to the foreground. Do mindful listening with your favorite songs—they're favorites for a reason. Sing in the shower, join a choir, or gather friends for a casual sing-along. Create ritual around music: dedicated listening nights where you share songs that move you.
- **Art:** Whether it's painting, poetry, theater, or dance, identify which art forms take your breath away and seek them out intentionally.
- **Science:** Some touch transcendence through the deepest reaches of science: the uncanny interlocking of numbers in the geometry of a circle, the mind-boggling vastness of the galaxy. At its most developed, physics, the scientific explanation of the known universe, becomes practically spiritual.
- **Meditation:** When practiced with discipline, meditation reliably opens pathways to awe. Whether through mindfulness that cultivates loving awareness, metta meditation that extends compassion to all beings, or nondual practices that dissolve the illusion of separation and reveal awareness as the fundamental ground of being, meditation is a time-tested pathway to the transcendent nature of reality.
- **Creative Expression:** Writing, painting, cooking, crocheting, gardening, or any form of *making* connects us to the genera-

tive forces running through us. Notice how time disappears when you're fully absorbed in creating something. This flow state is a doorway to transcendence. You don't need to be "good" at it—the magic lies in the process of bringing something new into existence.

- **Acts of Service:** When we move beyond self-concern and genuinely serve others, we tap into something larger than ourselves. This might be volunteering at a shelter, caring for an elderly neighbor, or simply showing up for a friend in pain. Service dissolves the ego's boundaries and makes us aware of our fundamental interconnectedness. The transcendent moment often comes not in the grand gesture but in the quiet recognition that giving and receiving are a single movement.
- **Love:** Love is the ultimate superhighway to transcendence. Love for a child, partner, family member, friend, or pet activates the biochemical experience of the divine. Don't miss these moments by being distracted by grudges, busyness, scrolling, or numbing substances.

Materialism has served its purpose, carrying us through centuries of discovery and progress. But we've reached its limits. If our most rational disciplines can embrace the unknown, surely we can too. Rainer Maria Rilke captured this openness in his *Letters to a Young Poet:*

> Be patient toward all that is unsolved in your heart and try to love the questions themselves, like locked rooms and like books that are written in a very foreign tongue. Do not now seek the answers, which cannot be given you because you would not be able to live them. And the point is, to live everything. Live the questions now. Perhaps you will then gradually, without noticing it, live along some distant day into the answer.

This is the invitation of mystery itself—not to rush toward premature certainty, but to develop a tolerance for the unknown that allows us to *live everything* without ruling anything out. When I learned to *live the questions* with my mom, I found myself able to be receptive to whatever was unfolding. The mystery held space for hope, doubt, and spiritual surrender. In loving the questions themselves, we create room for experiences that definitive answers would foreclose.

Choosing to leave space for mystery requires courage—the willingness to release our death grip on certainty and step into a more spacious relationship with the unknown. It asks us to embrace a both/and perspective rather than an either/or mindset: one that allows for rigorous thinking *and* mystical experience, scientific inquiry *and* spiritual openness. But it's worth it. Opening to something vastly beyond our comprehension can enrich our lives. This willingness to be surprised by reality becomes the fertile ground from which authentic magic can grow. As the English writer Eden Phillpotts wrote, "The universe is full of magical things, patiently waiting for our wits to grow sharper."

Chapter 16

DON'T IGNORE THE VOICE

I'm sorry.

Please forgive me.

Thank you.

I love you.

—Ho'oponopono,
traditional Hawaiian
practice of reconciliation
and forgiveness

My dad and I were sitting at the back of the Public Theater in downtown Manhattan when he told me he had finally lost the fifteen pounds he'd been meaning to lose.

"But the funny thing is," he added, "I lost it over the course of two weeks. Without even trying."

Continuing with an inappropriately lighthearted tone, he added that he had suddenly started having abdominal pain so severe it would wake him from sleep. The moment he finished speaking this sentence, the curtain went up and the play began. I have zero memory of the play we saw that night, but I do remember spending the entire two hours in a full-body state of dread and certainty that my dad had cancer.

Two weeks later he was diagnosed, and shortly thereafter we were checking him in to Memorial Sloan Kettering for surgery.

It had been seven years since my mom died, which had left me, my dad, and my sister bereft. It was as though the fire had gone out in the hearth of our nuclear family. When she passed, my sister and I were in our thirties, at the beginning of our careers, with small babies and overflowing lives. We were heartbroken, drowning in the grief of motherless mothering. Yet, in our respective apartments, our lives marched forward at a breathless pace. For my dad, who had spent the past forty-one years in utter devotion to my mom, life had lost its sweetness. On a physical and emotional level, he was mightily resilient. But he lived alone in my childhood home, my mom's books stacked on her bedside table all these years. Even the most resilient among us can meet their match.

Now, seven years later, sitting in the hospital waiting room while my dad was in surgery, I kept hearing a single refrain in my mind: "Enough already." It was as though my mom was speaking to me, repeating it again and again, with a sigh of loving resignation. I understood it to be my mom essentially saying, "Your poor dad, he's not going to move on, he will continue to go through the motions as long as we let him, but at a certain point, enough already." I began to doubt myself, deciding that this was not my mom's voice but instead some projection of my own mind. Perhaps it was a hastily constructed coping mechanism that my brain had drummed up to be able to handle what would surely be a devastating path ahead.

The surgery went as expected—his primary tumor was removed to slow the cancer's progression and ease his pain, but we all knew this was about buying time, not curing anything. While he recovered from surgery, my dad stayed with us in our New York City apartment. I would attempt to work, my dad would watch Lifetime movies and attempt to stay ahead of the pain, and my husband would attempt to please multiple picky eaters at each mealtime.

Given that my husband, Vimal, is Indian (and I'm generally compulsive), we are one of those households where we take our shoes off at the front door. In those post-op recovery days, my dad and I took gentle walks around my neighborhood. In slippers, with a coat thrown over his pajamas, he would walk gingerly—hunched over, his body contracted by the November chill and the scaffolding of new scar tissue. When we'd return from our walks to my warm apartment, I'd watch my dad shuffle to the easy chair in his street slippers and collapse in exhaustion.

I'm not proud to admit that, trapped by my rigid need for order and control, I would insist that my dad change from outside slippers to inside slippers. But every single time I nudged him to do this, I would hear my mom's voice: "Your poor dad, give him a break." It was not like a voice in the room, but something almost clearer and more undeniable. It was like an instant noetic download of information, in her parlance, from her to me.

Though I could not deny it, I certainly did defy it. I don't know how many times I made my dad change his stupid slippers. And there are tears dripping onto my keyboard now as I reflect on it.

In the months that followed, my sister and I got into a rhythm of taking turns accompanying our dad to his chemo infusions every two weeks. He had a good response to chemo, and after a few very grim months, he was doing relatively well—better energy, feeling more like himself. "A new lease on life," we called it.

One Friday in June, I sat across from him in a chemo suite in White Plains, New York. He was in his blue padded chair, chemotherapy dripping into him through a jumble of IV tubing. I sat there feeling a combination of squeamishness, dehydration, overwhelm, and boredom. Was I cherishing this time with my dad? To be honest, I was not. There's nothing like the sting of losing your mom too young to make you not appreciate how good it is to still have your dad.

At one point I reflexively opened my phone and noticed several unread texts, emails, Instagram comments, and DMs. The brutal and shameful truth is that I paused the conversation with my dad, saying I had to attend to some work on my phone. He sat there, three feet from me, nothing to do, while I responded to Instagram comments from strangers with prayer-hand emojis.

That voice returned. This time it was the clearest message I'd received from my mom yet. She said, "You know, Ellen, one day your father isn't going to be here anymore, and you're going to regret being on your phone instead of connecting with him." At this point, I knew to trust this voice. I acknowledged it. I said to her in my mind, "Yes, I know. You're absolutely right. As the end of his life draws near, I'll be sure to put my phone down and be completely present." With that, I resumed scanning through my emails.

And that June afternoon was my last day with my dad.

I was learning to trust my mom's guidance, but always one crucial moment too late.

Let's pause. Some of you may be thinking you'd like to ease my guilt. It's a natural impulse, wanting to smooth away discomfort. And I thank you for the kind sentiment. But it makes me think of a moment in the Greek myth of Circe, as retold by Madeline Miller. Circe—incidentally, a witch—says to her visitor, "Do not try to take my regret from me."

My regret about those slippers, about scrolling during chemo and rushing home after appointments—I don't want to be absolved of it. It is etched into me. It keeps me alert to what matters. Regret, held rightly, is a teacher.

Though I ignored the voice when my mom urged me to stop with the goddamn slippers and to put down my phone, there was one moment—one pivotal moment—when I did manage to heed the call of spirit.

Shortly after that final chemo appointment, before I knew my dad would soon pass, I had a night of terrible insomnia. In the morning, I mumbled something about bad sleep as my daughter stirred my husband and me awake. Vimal quietly shepherded our daughter out of our bedroom and handled breakfast, leaving me to rest.

What followed wasn't mere sleep but a descent into the depths. I found myself caught in an uneasy dreamscape—fragmented scenes of my father's illness, of emergencies and catastrophes. While the specific images have faded, the feeling remains indelible in my memory: a persistent, gnawing urgency.

An hour or so later, as consciousness began to reassert itself through my half-opened eyes, something extraordinary happened. My mother's presence materialized, pulling me back into that liminal space between sleep and wakefulness. Her message came through like a primal knowing, transmitted directly from her spirit to my understanding: "If you take nothing else away from this dream, take this." Then, with crystal clarity, as tangible as if she stood in the room:

"Call your father."

I rose from bed with unusual purpose, dressed quickly, and discovered Vimal had taken our daughter out for breakfast. Untangling my headphones, I set out on a walk to catch up with them, my fingers already dialing my father's number. The details of our conversation have blurred with time—some catching up, some shared excitement about our upcoming family gathering—but its significance remains sharp and clear. It was the last time we spoke.

Some might call this a coincidence, a random impulse that happened to carry weight in retrospect. But I know differently. This physical plane we inhabit is indeed fraught—full of suffering and rife with loss. Yet I don't believe we're navigating this terrain alone. We have source, we have ancestors, and we have our lost loved ones to guide us. That dream, my mother's presence, her urgent message to call my dad, stand as testimony to the hidden currents flowing beneath the surface of our world.

Though that was my final conversation with my dad in this life, I believe my parents' spirits live on. This belief has transformed me. It's softened my heart's defensive walls; it's allowed me to loosen my grip and stop needing to control things quite so much. When fear arises, this belief offers an alternative view: If they live on, what is there, really, to fear? My tendency toward hypervigilance has gradually given way to a sense of ultimate safety.

THE VOICE

What I experienced with my mother's voice has a name: clairaudience, from the French, meaning "clear hearing"—the intuitive ability to receive auditory information from a source that isn't physically present. While mainstream medicine doesn't have a framework for this phenomenon, research into grief and consciousness suggests there's more happening than we can currently explain. Dr. Penny Sartori, a former intensive-care nurse who spent more than two decades studying near-death experiences, notes that many bereaved individuals report ongoing communication with deceased loved ones, often through distinct auditory messages that arrive with startling clarity.

In my moments of doubt, I try to convince myself that the voice I heard was my own internal dialogue, or my imagination gone wild. But what I feel in my bones is that this voice did not come from within me. It had a particular quality: it sounded like my mom (not just in tone but in diction and cadence), and it seemed to have prescience and access to information that I did not possess. Psychiatrist Elisabeth Kübler-Ross, who spent decades working with dying patients, wrote extensively about what she called "spiritual experiences" that grieving families reported—including clear messages from their deceased loved ones that provided comfort or crucial guidance. In fact, grief-related auditory experiences are well documented in mainstream psychology, with studies showing that about half of bereaved individuals report sensing the presence of their deceased loved one, including hearing their voice. These experiences often share common characteristics: they arrive unbidden, feel distinctly different from our own thoughts, and frequently contain information or perspectives we wouldn't have considered on our own. While science can't yet explain the mechanism, the consistency of these reports across cultures and throughout history suggests these experiences deserve serious consideration rather than reflexive dismissal. While traditional psychology frames these as "grief hallucinations," we can decide for ourselves if we believe they are coping mechanisms or something more.

THE CONVERSATION CONTINUES

The voices are a gift. In my view, they come from a place of wisdom well beyond the confines of our limited minds. I've come to cherish these voices—I only wish I had learned to trust them sooner.

We live on the fulcrum between fear and love. Our physical bodies, with their constant needs, and Earth's seemingly scarce resources, pull us toward fear. Will we have enough? Will we be okay? But our higher selves know a different truth: we are held, we are intrinsically resourced, the end is not absolute, and love is the fundamental force that connects us all. That foundational love is not bound by material constraints—it transcends life and death.

Awakening to magic allows us to shed fear and make space for love. We find the ability to trust and surrender, knowing that, even in pain and uncertainty, we are okay. While magic doesn't explain why terrible things happen, when we resolve conflict within ourselves by trusting, surrendering—moving out of our heads and into our hearts—we can play a role in creating less conflict in the external world.

When doubt overtakes me, I return to these moments—my mother's voice cutting through time and space with impossible prescience. It revives my trust in the magic and the mystery of it all.

And remember, this holy communication works in both directions. As I've learned to trust the voices I *hear*, I have also learned to speak directly to those I've lost, trusting they can hear *me* across whatever divide separates us. So I will say now: Dad, I am so sorry. I am so sorry about the slippers, about rushing home after every chemo appointment, about not being present when I was there, and for not cherishing you more. We all missed Mommy. But in being so focused on that, I missed that I had *you*. I miss you. I see you and everything that makes you unique and amazing. Grandma Gertrude, I see how hard you fought to keep your child healthy and well. He lived a full life, yet it still feels like it ended before its time. Dad, I appreciate absolutely everything. I'm sorry, please forgive me, thank you, I love you.

Chapter 17

WANTING THE REAL THING: STAYING CONNECTED TO THOSE WE'VE LOST

There are things you can't reach. But you can reach out to them, and all day long. The wind, the bird flying away. The idea of God. And it can keep you as busy as anything else, and happier.

—MARY OLIVER, "Yes! No!" in *House of Light*

My dad was a tax lawyer, and he was meticulous. In fact, he saved every single receipt ever. I mean ever. Over the course of a year, I would collect my receipts in a gallon ziplock bag, and then, come Christmastime, I would wrap it and place it under the tree for my dad.

"Receipts, oh goody!" he would say playfully.

This was not sarcasm—he was genuinely delighted to scurry away to his office on Christmas morning with this bag of receipts and reconcile them with my credit card statements.

As of this writing, it's been almost a year and a half since he passed away. I can't bring myself to stop collecting receipts in a ziplock bag. But who to bring them to? It turns out, these are not anybody else's idea of a good Christmas present.

Just this morning I went to put a receipt into the bag and noticed that it was bulging at the seams. I thought to myself, *That bag of receipts is getting pretty damn full*, and it dropped me to my knees with a sudden tidal wave of sadness. Glennon Doyle once wrote, "Grief is the receipt we wave in the air to remind everyone of the love we had." I looked down at this bulging ziplock bag and thought, *What a metaphor for grief: receipts that I have loved—with nowhere to go.*

TIME TO START WRITING

As my sister and I work through the arduous and impossibly nostalgic task of clearing out our parents' house, we've been uncovering pieces of their inner lives that we never knew existed. Tucked away on my mom's desk, beneath dusty hardcovers and personalized stationery, my sister discovered something utterly unexpected: the first half of an unfinished novel.

My mom—a librarian, a constant reader, a woman who had raised me to believe in the unmatched importance of books—had been secretly working on her own contribution to the canon. We had no idea.

The discovery sent me reeling back to that afternoon with Momoko, to my mom's message channeled through the acupuncturist: "It's time to stop reading books and start writing books." What I had interpreted as guidance meant uniquely for me suddenly revealed itself as something far more layered. My mom may have been speaking to herself as much as to me. She might have been relaying something she had said to herself many times. She might have hoped to live out her unfulfilled dream through me, or perhaps she understood something about the maternal line that I'm only now grasping—that we are all one continuous stream of dreams, some realized, some passed down like heirlooms.

And now, in this strange circularity of life, I write. In many ways, I write *because* of my parents' deaths. My first book, dedicated to my mom, was published seven years after her death. How I had ached at the time for her to be there to witness it. When milestone emails arrived from my literary agent or publisher, I found myself forwarding them to my mom's defunct email address. I couldn't let them pass without feeling I was sharing the news with her. Perhaps I needed her to see me step into the very dream she'd quietly harbored.

Writing, it seems, became our family's way of processing loss. My dad, who had never cooked a meal in forty-one years of marriage, suddenly found himself, at sixty-nine years old, learning to boil water for pasta. While grieving, he taught himself to cook—and then, wanting to help others in similar straits, he wrote *The Widower's Cookbook*. He self-published it, selling spiral-bound copies from the trunk of his car for twenty dollars each, Venmo accepted. Now my sister—an amazing cook—is considering refining and properly publishing his work.

Three grief-inspired writers. Are my mom's unrealized dreams finding their way into actualization through us all?

This is the alchemy of grief: what often seems like an ending later reveals itself as a continuation. Our dreams don't die with us—they flow forward through the people who love us, taking new forms, finding new vessels. My mom's unfinished novel was a seed planted in the mystery, and now something new is growing toward the sun.

A COVER IN A MINOR KEY

As we've discussed, I was pregnant when my mom passed away. At the time, my grief moved through my body like primal waves of energy. As a psychiatrist, I couldn't help but be aware of the disconcerting research about grief in pregnancy: the stress can have negative effects on the baby's long-term mental health. I felt as though the molecular signature of grief was coursing through my bloodstream, and I couldn't ignore the unsettling thought that I was incubating my baby in this stormy milieu.

It was my sister who came through with the sage advice. She told me that the placenta filters the grief. All that reaches the baby is love. This imagery eased my worries.

Over the last decade, my sister's words have shaped my understanding of grief even when there's no placenta involved. When we have experienced loss, we do indeed have a brew of chemical grief coursing through our veins. But, in our bodies, the neurochemical correlate of grief is love. In a sense, if love is a song, grief is a cover of that song in a minor key. The lyrics are still the same. Grief is just another way of singing about love.

To be sure, not all grief distills down to love. Nor is grief always about the death of a loved one. Grief can arise with divorce, with career changes, with kids moving out of the house, with pregnancy loss, even with birth. There are forms of grief, especially when we are grieving some violation of our dignity or personhood, that distill down to divine rage. Rather than restraining our emotions, we instead need to get in the habit of granting more permission and carving out more space for the genuine mourning process that comes with all these transitions.

This is where our culture fails us. We avoid the topic of death at all costs, and we lack sufficient grief rituals. This has left us blocked and brittle. When we have so much love and no place to put it—when our ziplock bag of receipts is bursting at the seams—we need rituals. We need ways of singing out the song of love in a minor key.

Many of us are understandably hesitant to dive headfirst into grief, because we fear the bottomless pit of sadness. And we're not wrong. Grief rituals can indeed bring on strong feelings. We may want professional support—such as working with a grief counselor or going on a grief retreat. Handing ourselves over to grief can feel like being knocked over unexpectedly by a tsunami of emotion. It can feel like a descent into the underworld. But in my experience, that descent is exactly the point. The pain of losing someone we love cracks open a portal to the spirit realm. Our loss necessitates that we confront certain questions: How did we show up in this relationship? How did the other person shape us? Where do we need to forgive others or ourselves? And, of course, the question that broke everything open for me: Does my person continue to exist in some form? Grief pushes us to contemplate: Is loss absolute, or is there something more occurring here than what we can explain with science? Grief can be an initiation into all that lies beyond. But for us to get there, we need to give ourselves over to grief fully.

Grief is love that is displaced, with no place to go. In the body, this translates to a well of energy that needs to move. When we don't release this energy, these uncried tears can make us irritable, likely to snap, and they may cut us off from the full range of our emotions. Our lack of ritual around grief and our cultural squeamishness about crying are stymieing our grieving processes and, I believe, causing a deterioration of our mental well-being. Attempting to hold back a tsunami turns out to be harder than swimming through it.

We can let grief harden us, or we can let it lead us on a quest into an underwater realm. Oftentimes, the witchiest ritual we can do is let tears pour down our faces, remaining open to what taps us from beyond.

WE WANT THE REAL THING

"But I don't want a vision, I want the real thing," Mahnaz laments.

Mahnaz, a thirty-eight-year-old mother of two, opens our session today by telling me about a vision she had while driving past the hospital where she'd given birth to her two sons. She saw her father—her humorous, bighearted, playful father with that enchanting sparkle in his eye—sitting in the waiting room with her mother and brother during her first son's birth. Yet, this was an impossible scene, as her beloved father had passed away two months before that day.

"I don't feel comforted by this, because . . . what's a vision going to do for me? I need the real him. I need a parent. I want the real thing."

While I share Mahnaz's yearning to have her parent here in the flesh—our shared yearning for the "real thing"—I've come to see it differently. Ever since I decided to believe that my mom continues to exist in spirit form, the way I experience it is that she is, in fact, right here. Though our earthly bodies fail, I have come to believe that consciousness persists. While of course I ache to have my parents physically present—to hug them, ask them questions, and watch them interact with my daughter—I've learned to decouple their physical form from "the real thing." The *real* thing is eternal, and it's right here. All the time.

During that day's session, I had Mahnaz do an exercise where she connected to her father in spirit form. I led us into a meditation, and then I gave her free range to dialogue with him in whatever way felt natural. Sitting there, deep in meditation, Mahnaz told her father the things she wished she could have said to him before he passed. She went on to tell him all about his two grandsons, who he never got to meet, and she asked him the questions she had been wanting to ask him. Incredibly, she "heard" answers. Naturally, she began to second-guess this, but I encouraged her to lean toward that initial sense of knowing. She wanted to know if he was suffering. She heard him respond, "I'm good." She felt as though he was trying to say more. We sat there, our eyes closed, and I encouraged Mahnaz to stay with this, to keep listening.

"It's almost like . . . what he's trying to tell me is that *he's* not the one we should be worrying about. It's like he's saying *I'm* the one we should be worrying about, because this physical life is hard, but on the other side, it's *good*."

When we've lost someone we love, we feel their absence acutely. But in my experience, it is possible to have a new kind of relationship with them—one that is ever present. It's important to accept that the new relationship will be different; it's a relationship with our loved ones in their spirit form, not in physical form. But when we cling too tightly, focusing on their physical absence and yearning only for what *was*, we risk missing out on this new kind of closeness.

Moving forward, Manhaz started to communicate with the spirit of her father on a regular basis. She stayed connected in a different but profoundly meaningful way.

PRACTICES FOR LIVING WITH GRIEF

Grief expert Claire Bidwell Smith, author of *The Rules of Inheritance* and *Anxiety: The Missing Stage of Grief*, reminds us that grief isn't something to "get over"—it's something to carry forward with intention. These practices help us process loss while staying connected to those we've lost.

Processing Grief

- **Allow the tears.** Cry. A lot. Whenever the urge arises. Tears are grief's natural expression and shouldn't be suppressed or scheduled.
- **Honor significant dates.** Create rituals for birthdays, death anniversaries, and holidays. Light candles, play their favorite music, or gather with others who loved them.

- **Seek grief-focused therapy**. Work with a grief counselor or consider grief retreats for dedicated processing time and connecting with a community of others who "get it."

Maintaining Connection

- **Write and talk to your deceased loved one**. Speak to them in whatever format feels comfortable—journaling, praying, or simply talking out loud. Share life updates and ask for guidance. Express gratitude, forgiveness, or unspoken feelings you wish you could have shared when they were alive.
- **Ask them to visit you in dreams**. I find that when I ask my parents to visit my dreams, I'm more likely to see them in my dreams—or at least to remember those dreams. When I encounter my parents, I don't feel like I'm dreaming *about* them—I feel like they're actually *there,* visiting me. Perhaps the liminality of sleep allows us to connect with spirit more readily than during waking life.
- **Stay open to their communication**. Their responses may come through signs: songs on the radio, words on a passing truck, tingling sensations. Laura Lynne Jackson's book *Signs* can be referred to for guidance on recognizing these communications.
- **Ask for help**. Want your loved one to help with something in your life? Make it explicit. As my friend and spiritual teacher Roya Darling has explained to me, we have free will, so spirit doesn't intervene unless we ask. My takeaway: it doesn't hurt to ask out loud.
- **Trust the sensations**. If you feel your loved one's presence, don't doubt it. Consider yourself lucky. Is it real? Nobody really knows. But if it brings comfort without harming anyone, receive the gift. Don't miss the magic.

Creating Meaning

- **Create an altar for remembrance.** Set up photos, place flowers. Sit in meditation and let yourself feel the presence of your loved one.
- **Cook their recipes.** Prepare their favorite meal or dishes that remind you of them.
- **Live their values.** Volunteer for causes they cared about or engage in activities that reflect what mattered most to them.
- **Visit sacred spaces.** Return to their favorite places or anywhere you feel their presence most strongly.

Remember: there's no timeline for grief and no "right" way to grieve.

BEYOND THE FAILING BRAIN

Although Mahnaz had a very positive relationship with her father, I've had many patients lose loved ones where the relationship was difficult, even abusive or traumatic. In my observation, when it comes to these strained relationships, the new relationship that we establish with our loved ones in spirit form is often liberated from whatever dynamics were challenging in the living years. It's as though our loved ones shed their wounds and baggage as they pass over, and they are communicating with us in a more fully actualized form.

The situation with Mahnaz's mom is more complicated. She is alive, but with severe dementia, and she gets particularly symptomatic every evening—a common symptom of dementia called sundowning. She will often get agitated and sad, insisting to her caregiver Lala that Mahnaz has an ear infection and needs help. She tells Lala, "I can hear Mahnaz crying." And she is known to shout at Lala, "Do something!"

Mahnaz did indeed have recurrent ear infections growing up. But that was some thirty-five years ago.

While Mahnaz can sit in meditation and dialogue with the spirit of her dad, the way to connect with her mom is more ambiguous. Mahnaz facetimes her mother every day, but that is often unsettling for both of them. I suggested that she connect with her mom on a different dimension, the way she does with her dad.

Dementia presents a unique challenge—which plane offers the clearest connection when the physical mind is compromised? Perhaps consciousness is an eternal energy, but the brain is simply the transmitter—the way we translate the signal of consciousness onto earth. Since Mahnaz's mom's brain no longer functions properly, I wondered if the best way for Mahnaz to connect with her consciousness was in another realm.

One night, Mahnaz did a little ritual where she lit a candle and then asked to connect to her mom's consciousness. In that dialogue, Mahnaz asked her mom why she thought she had an ear infection—why she cried for Mahnaz. After some moments of doubting the process, Mahnaz heard her mom answer: "I'm worried about you."

Mahnaz responded, "But I've told you, *I'm fine.* I have a good job, my husband is a wonderful man, I'm safe."

The spirit of her mom spoke back to her. "You tell me you're okay, but I don't think you're being truthful with me."

At this, Mahnaz broke down in tears. She admitted to her mom that she was carrying so much, that the world was heavy, and that there was a lot that felt hard right now. She began to vent to her mom, "Ramin [her husband] is worried about getting laid off, Reza [her younger son] is struggling in school. And for me, ever since my boss left, I no longer feel supported at my job. The political situation feels hopeless, and all of this triggers me, because I fled this kind of regime for a better life here, and now this country is turning into what we lived through back home."

Mahnaz wept. Incredibly, she felt as though her mom was listening—was holding her—if not physically, then in some other sense.

"And," Mahnaz added, "I'm going through all of it without a parent. And I just really wish I had a parent right now." With this, a subtle but unmistakable tingling pressure enveloped her body, starting at her shoulders and spreading down her back, as though she was being held. She stayed perfectly still, tears flowing freely, allowing this ethereal embrace to cradle her until her breath finally steadied and deepened.

And here's what defies logic. After this dialogue, Mahnaz got a report from her mom's caretaker. Her mom had stopped saying that Mahnaz had an ear infection, or that she could hear her crying. Apparently, they both received exactly the message they needed from each other that night.

THE CIRCLE GAME

Even though I'm writing a book about trusting the magic, of course I also have my own moments of missing the "real thing." But I'm learning to ride the uncertain terrain of this new relationship with my parents.

One Mother's Day, eight years after my mom's passing, I took my daughter to Jane's Carousel at the foot of the Brooklyn Bridge. Jane was my mom's name, and it has become its own kind of calling card. Whenever I encounter "Jane," I feel her presence, a gentle "Hi, I love you" from beyond.

As my daughter and I rode the painted ponies, going up and down, round and round, I found myself teaching my daughter the words to Joni Mitchell's "The Circle Game." I kept getting stuck in the refrain. Unable to recall Mitchell's lyrics, I couldn't bring the song to resolution. The irony wasn't lost on me. Afterward, walking through Brooklyn Heights, my daughter and I holding hands and singing our imperfect version, I felt tears of a particular quality streaming down my face. They were the same tears I'd cried while dancing with my mom on that precious last day with her, my daughter still in my belly—tears with the salty taste of God in them.

Circling around the refrain of "The Circle Game" on my mom's namesake carousel, three generations brought together on Mother's Day—I was starting to find my footing in this art of staying connected. The universe seems to delight in offering these connections, whether through songs, signs, or the sacred geometry of generations turning through time. And I took comfort in it.

But then, seven weeks after that carousel ride, I lost my father. It was July 2023—eight years and two days from my mom's sudden passing.

Here we were, sitting shiva in my childhood home once again. The suburban house that had once been my true north now felt strange—buzzing with relatives and friends, but suddenly ownerless. Who was hosting? Did anyone know how to work the AC? I found myself retreating to my childhood bedroom, pulling close friends with me to cocoon in familiar comfort. I cherished being held this way, though now I regret not spending more time with beloved relatives who'd flown in or driven ten hours from rural Pennsylvania. I thought I had time. We always think we have more time. But shiva, like life itself, develops a concluding momentum and ends without warning.

My sister and I did our best to hold court: bereft, with our own families to care for, embodying this vortex of grief. As the long day wound down and our children grew restless, the relentless question arose: What's for dinner?

It felt right to return to our dad's favorite restaurant, which was situated next to a pond we called "the dragonfly pond," where, decades ago, my sister and I attended day camp. The food there was unremarkable, but the staff knew our dad, made him feel seen. To be known, we realized, nourishes something deeper than fancy food ever could.

As kids we'd sit on the grassy slope next to the restaurant eating ice cream sandwiches, scratching mosquito bites. The counselors taught us to sing "The Circle Game." In those 1980s summers, without a care in the world, I would sing along, "Caught a dragonfly inside a jar," while learning to braid hair. Given the abundance of dragonflies around this pond (and the fact that it would be more than a decade before I even knew who Joni Mitchell was), I assumed this lovely little song was something the counselors had made up about that tiny, algae-covered pond.

As dinner was winding down, our husbands wrangled our exhausted children while my sister and I got wrapped up in a conversation with the restaurant staff, who were sharing their condolences and memories of our dad. When we emerged from the restaurant, the July sun had set, and we found the kids running through the same meadow where we had spent countless summer days as children, catching fireflies just as we once had. The circle game was playing out before our eyes, past and present merging in a dance of magic, light, and memory.

A month after my dad's shiva, Vimal, my daughter, and I were celebrating a special occasion with a day at Coney Island and a fancy dinner in Brooklyn. In those days of new, fresh grief, we tried to find joy in this finale to summer. As we worked through the tasting menu, Vimal got that look he gets when he senses something from the beyond.

"Wait," he said, studying the dishes before us. "Crab fried rice, s'mores . . . these were your dad's favorite foods." Then, with absolute certainty: "Your dad is here."

I felt goose bumps rise, followed immediately by my habitual skepticism trying to deflate the magic. But then Vimal pointed out that these weren't just my dad's favorite foods—they were, through a strange series of coincidences, what he happened to have eaten during his last two days of life. The providence of it all—the timing, the specific connection to his final meals—felt potent. I thought about what would be the ultimate sign of my mom's presence from the early days of that loss. With my willing heart, I said a prayer: *Okay, Mom and Dad, if you're really here, if you still exist and you're watching over us, please play "Spirit in the Sky."*

We took a few more bites of our s'mores and then, moments later, the familiar guitar riff began playing over the restaurant speakers. My whole body tingled with chills as Vimal and I exchanged looks of amazement. In that moment, I felt cradled—held in the certainty that my parents were still bearing witness to our lives.

As the German-Swiss writer and poet Hermann Hesse writes in *Siddhartha*, "The river is everywhere at once, at the source and at the mouth, at the waterfall, at the ferry, at the rapids, in the ocean, and in the mountains, everywhere, and . . . there is only the present time for it, not the shadow of the past, not the shadow of the future." These themes—of songs and signs, of dragonflies and s'mores—are the ways our loved ones wink to us from their perch in the Fibonacci sequence of existence. It's as though they're looking down from a higher spot on a spiral staircase, seeing us and sending love. Like Siddhartha's river that exists everywhere at once, perhaps this story has no true beginning or end—perhaps all moments exist simultaneously, and what we perceive as linear time is merely our limited way of experiencing an infinite whole. Our loved ones, no longer bound by time's illusion, can be everywhere at once: at the source and at the mouth, in memory and in the present, in loss and in reunion. A spirit simultaneously in the sky and playing over restaurant speakers.

When we can trust this, what is there to fear?

And so we keep moving through this spiral existence: round and round, in the circle game.

Our culture prioritizes the material, but a witch is open to mystery so that her life can be enriched with meaning and she can stay connected to those she has lost.

FIFTH PRACTICE: SERVING THE COLLECTIVE

Our Culture Is Hyperindividualistic. A Witch Serves the Collective.

The fifth and final cultural bias that severs us from our magic is our obsession with individual achievement at the expense of collective well-being. We've been trained to see ourselves as isolated units competing for scarce resources rather than interconnected beings whose well-being is inextricably tied up in the liberation of all. This hyperindividualism shows up in our tireless self-optimization, our tendency to hoard rather than share, and our belief that we must figure everything out alone. As psychotherapist and author Esther Perel has observed, "The language speaks for itself: it puts 'self' in front of everything"—self-care, self-love, self-reliance, self-actualization, and endless variations that quietly train us to turn toward our own navels. A witch remembers that she is part of an unbroken chain of ancestors whose wisdom flows through her, that she is embedded in a community, and that her greatest power comes from aligning her gifts with service to the larger whole.

Chapter 18

FROM ANCESTORS TO SERVICE: MOVING BEYOND THE SELF

> I slept and dreamt that life was joy. I awoke and saw that life was service. I acted and behold, service was joy.
>
> —Attributed to RABINDRANATH TAGORE

Many years since Momoko channeled my mother and Daniela told me I was a witch, I'm now the practitioner working over the acupuncture table, and my patient, Janice, is lying in a supine position. I've placed needles, and now I'm standing by her side doing a bit of energy work. I notice something I identify as tension in the energetic field over her left hip, and I pause there, hands hovering over the slope of her hip. It feels as though energy pours out of her body, into my hands. The energy then courses through my body, and down through my feet into the ground. I "listen" from my right hemisphere, opening up the channel of diffuse awareness. I remain there for several minutes, until it feels like the movement of energy has dissipated and I sense that the process is complete.

In an email the next day, Janice shares that her hip and lower back pain are much better. She adds that she had a dreamlike experience during the treatment where she saw a slideshow of images, many of them centered on her stepmom. She felt like she was metabolizing some of the resentment she had carried toward her since childhood—and for the first time, she could extend compassion to this woman. "I realize now, she has not had an easy life herself, and she was just doing her best." Janice felt that her burden was lightened, and that she walked out of that session physically and emotionally transformed.

Sometimes, when you deal in the unmeasurable and unseen, it can seem as though miraculous things happen. As we all develop our witchcraft, it can be tempting to go to an egoic place in response—thinking we're personally responsible for the healing, that our individual gifts created the transformation. But remember, the work we do here on earth is not done alone. Whether you're a health practitioner treating mental or physical ailments, or you're an artist creating original work for others' elevation, or even if your work feels more mundane, none of this is done alone. We are all channels bringing visions and ideas into the material world. And all work is a collaboration with source. To do it well, we must practice getting out of the way. Developing our craft means cultivating our ability to be a portal for powerful energies to work through us.

Over the years, I've learned to rightsize my role in this work. Like many practitioners, I began with imposter syndrome: Who was I to do this healing work? As I honed my craft and felt more potent in my abilities, ego crept in. But eventually, I came to understand that any transformative work I facilitate happens because I've managed to step aside and allow greater forces to work through me. This book is no exception.

This realization is both humbling and disorienting. If larger forces are doing the work, what role do I actually serve? This question reveals how thoroughly we've been conditioned to see ourselves as isolated actors. In time, the deeper truth emerges: we have an essential role as the ones who translate spirit into material form.

YOU HAVE HANDS

Back in 2015, a few weeks after my mom's passing and my treatment with Momoko, I saw another practitioner named Swaranpal. After doing some beautiful Kundalini energy work—a hands-on practice working with spiritual energy—she told me a story about her late sister, who came to her in a dream, asking Swaranpal to do energy work on her daughter (Swaranpal's niece). Not from a place of resistance, but out of genuine curiosity, Swaranpal asked the spirit of her sister: "If you can come to me in a dream, why don't you do the energy work on your daughter yourself?" Her sister's response: "Because I don't have hands."

Those of us in human form do not necessarily have the omniscient wisdom to always know what needs to be done. But we do have hands. When you are doing your work, making your art, interfacing with patients, students, clients, or an audience, I recommend pausing for a moment before you begin. Ask spirit/source/ancestors/guides to work through you. Let them know that your intention is to be in service of everyone's highest good, and that your aim is to be a channel for them to work through you on earth. That willingness allows for a magical collaboration between *their* wisdom and *your* hands.

After that session with Swaranpal, six months pregnant and in the altered state that follows deep energy work, I wandered down the block in a daze. Something pulled me toward Golden Bridge Yoga, a Kundalini yoga center with a small gift shop at the entrance. Bronze Buddha statues and the scent of essential oils were comforting, softening my transition between the sacred space I'd left and the jarring sounds and smells of the Lower East Side of Manhattan.

A woman approached me—someone I didn't know personally, but I recognized. Gurmukh Kaur Khalsa, a legendary Kundalini teacher and the center's founder. Seeing my pregnant belly, she placed her hand directly on it, a gesture our culture has trained us to avoid but one I've always appreciated—that moment of tactile connection celebrating the spirit growing just beneath the surface. "Jai guru!" (Hail to the teacher!) she proclaimed. Then her eyes traveled up from my belly, met my eyes, and seemed to stare into my soul. "Girl or boy?" she asked.

"Girl," I replied.

Her response was a sentence that has stayed with me: "Aah. A girl. It's a harder path, but it's a higher calling."

Those words hit me with a gale force of recognition. They validated something I'd felt my entire life—that being a woman is hard. It doesn't feel fair. This acknowledgment from a wise elder at once vindicated and released a lifetime of grievances I carried about the challenges of womanhood—while simultaneously reframing that difficulty as purpose. Gurmukh opened my eyes to the gift hidden within the struggle: we carry a high calling. In that moment, I could finally fully embrace being a woman.

Being a witch is the harder path—you'll face skepticism, dismissal, the constant pressure to prove what can't be proven. Some will feel threatened by your rebelliousness and power. Others will patronize and judge. But it's also a high calling. It means having the courage to trust your intuition when the world demands data; to remain present, soft, and embodied, honoring the wisdom of your body; to value mystery when everyone around you worships evidence; to serve forces greater than yourself when the culture lauds individual achievement.

Now I see the invisible web of guidance that led to that moment. Spirit moved through Swaranpal to tell me her sister's story about having hands. That story left me in exactly the receptive state necessary for me to wander into Golden Bridge, where spirit could work through Gurmukh to deliver the message I needed to hear. Each interaction prepared me for the next, all leading to this book, where I can pass the message forward: Embrace your witchiness. It may be a harder path, but it's a higher calling. And you have hands—use them in service of what wants to be born through you.

CONNECT TO ANCESTORS

There's a Chinese proverb that tells us, "To forget one's ancestors is to be a brook without a source, a tree without a root." The historic National Black Theatre (NBT) stands as a testament to this ancient wisdom. Occupying an entire city block in Harlem, it serves as what its CEO and director Sade Lythcott calls "a temple of liberation to both the past and the Afro future." But the brook of ancestral waters has taken a winding path to this ambitious vision.

Sade and I met at a women's retreat, where we connected over our shared identity as motherless mothers. Through a sprawling late-night conversation, we discovered we both find comfort in our ongoing connection with our mothers' spirits. For Sade, this connection would prove transformative not just personally but for an entire community.

Sade's mother, Dr. Barbara Ann Teer, a champion of the Black Arts Movement, founded NBT in 1968 to help course-correct pervasive, inaccurate, and incomplete narratives about Black life. After her passing in 2008, Sade stepped up to continue her mother's legacy and the work of NBT—assuming a mantle of responsibility that carried both grief and the charge of carrying forward her mother's vision.

Like her mother, Sade is a force of nature. For more than a decade, she guided the theater with sensitivity and purpose. But even the strongest leaders face moments of doubt. Sade's breaking point came in her eleventh year of running the theater, as the COVID-19 pandemic unraveled almost every industry, with few hit harder than theater—an impossible medium to maintain through the constraints of social distancing. Stakeholders and board members battled over imperfect solutions. Actors, directors, and crew grappled with existential fears about their livelihood. And Sade stood at the front lines of it all, questioning whether she could truly honor her mother's legacy. The responsibility had grown to include not just her mother's memory but a community of artists, colleagues, peers, and even neighbors who had come to rely on the artistic and liberatory programs of NBT, at a time when it all felt especially critical.

The question of legacy had been with Sade from the beginning. Dr. Maya Angelou, a dear friend of the family, had written a poem to be read at Dr. Teer's funeral. In Dr. Angelou's words, "There is not nor can there be another Barbara Ann Teer and no one can follow her or step in her footprints and fill them. The world is paled by her absence and the company of us who cared for her are weakened by her departure." Sitting at her mother's funeral, hearing these words, Sade was left to wonder: How was she going to not only survive the immediacy of this loss but simultaneously fill the impossibly gigantic footprints left behind?

In her moment of deepest despair, Sade had no choice but to drop to her knees and pray. She did what she had watched her mother—a spiritual, witchy woman—do her whole life: she created a simple altar, hoping it would "act as a tuning fork to those on the other side." On it she placed a picture of her mother, a candle, fresh flowers, a glass of water, and a small bell. She rang the bell and began to ask her mother for guidance.

In the silence, she felt her way to the answer. Her mother told her to revisit her auntie Maya's poem, adding that "on the other side of whatever scares you the most are the keys to your freedom." Sade returned to the poem, her eyes now gravitating to the ending: "We must be assured that she is surrounded by loving peers and that on this plane she will never be forgotten." Could this simple prompt be the blueprint for what came next? Could it be possible that Sade's job here on earth went beyond taking on the labor of NBT—that it was to ensure that her mother's work would never be forgotten?

Throughout her professional life, Dr. Teer had fought to maintain ownership of her visionary work—battling men who tried to take credit for her ideas or write her out of her own narrative. Suddenly, Sade saw her assignment clearly: she would write her mother back into the story.

As Sade sat with these words, the air in the room seemed to thicken with presence. What came through the stillness wasn't just her mother's spirit but her entire maternal line of ancestors. Sade sat motionless and in awe as this visitation unfolded. Her ancestors expressed their pride in her work and assured her that everything would be okay. But they didn't stop there—they addressed what she had been wondering in her quiet moments. Was the theater going to make it? Should she downsize in order to survive?

They told her that scaling back or contracting in the face of challenge would "rustle their spirit." Rather than downsizing the theater, they urged her to *expand*. She could hear seven generations back and seven generations forward singing her mother's wisdom, like a choir of guardian angels—repeating the words her mother often told her when she was facing monumental life moments: "Where there is love, there is no fear."

Her ancestors had the wisdom and vision, but they needed Sade's hands to build it into reality. This was the sacred collaboration—*their* guidance flowing through *her* physical action in the world.

Sade took this "divine listening" to heart. She launched a program called NBT Beyond Walls, which has brought the theater's transformative work everywhere from the Kennedy Center to the Royal Shakespeare Company, even taking two shows to Broadway and winning the company's first Tony Award. The theater made it through the pandemic, stronger than ever.

But there was one more frontier that gave Sade pause. It was what her mom had been wrestling with when she passed: the idea of demolishing the entire city block where the theater sat in order to rebuild it. Dr. Teer's vision, Sade told me, was an "ecosystem where artists can live, work, create, and serve." Or, in Sade's words, "a living land acknowledgment to all of our good angels and ancestors whose shoulders we proudly stand on and a testimony to the Black imagination." Sade was being called to build an altar in theater form. But it was an enormous undertaking.

These ancestral voices left Sade at a crossroads. Finding comfort in spiritual guidance during prayer and meditation is one thing—what harm can come from it? But to break ground on an ambitious construction project and put others' jobs on the line as a result of this counsel? That seemed like a bold change to make in response to what some might call an apparition. Yet as she reflected, she remembered her auntie Maya's words: "never be forgotten." By staging authentic Black stories—the traumas, the private struggles, the impossible power, resilience, and rejoicing—she was creating a container for healing future generations. This theater was, at its core, *for* and *from* and *about* her ancestors. So how could she go against their wishes?

ANCESTRAL ARCHITECTURE

Sade's experience reflects what many cultures have known for millennia, and what science is now beginning to confirm. Living with a moment-to-moment connection to our ancestors has measurable impact on our well-being. Research by clinical psychologist Simon Choi and colleagues revealed that what they call "self-transcendence"—a strong awareness of ancestors and forces greater than oneself—correlates with lower rates of depression and anxiety across cultures. This protective effect was particularly pronounced in India and China, where people report the strongest perceived relationships with ancestors. Yet in the West we've largely dismissed ongoing connection with ancestors as a primitive superstition. This dismissal reflects our culture's broader bias toward valuing only what can be seen and quantified, and the omnipotence we ascribe to the individual, without regard for the shoulders we stand on. Indeed, the United States showed the weakest ancestral connections. Choi's research suggests that our contemporary focus on individualism and self-reliance may come at a steeper psychological cost than we realize.

As Austrian spiritual teacher and author Thomas Hübl explains, "When a person feels especially disconnected from their family of ancestors, an essential energy resource gets cut, as if they are suddenly unplugged. . . . Frequently, the lack of ancestral resourcing results in a quality of rootlessness, disembodiment, and/or an unstable sense of personal, cultural, or social identity."

But our ancestors remain present, whether we acknowledge them or not. They live on in our bodies, our habits, our mannerisms. Our connection to ancestors is even written in our biology. Recall that the field of epigenetics makes a case for physiologic continuity between us and those who came before us. Each of us began as a follicle in our mother's ovaries while she was still a fetus in our grandmother's womb. We were, in a sense, *physically* present in our grandmother's womb. Whatever our grandmother was going through while pregnant impacts us *directly*. Through a process called methylation, our DNA expression was modified in response to our grandmother's experiences. We are impacted by her stressors, her traumas, and her triumphs. Our DNA—what makes us *us*—lived inside our grandmother and carries the imprint of her experiences. This is one of those instances where the boundary between science and spirit is blurred. Our very genetic makeup carries the echo of our ancestors' lives. We hold a dusting of their lived experience in each building block of our DNA.

Today, Sade's mother's theater fulfills her ancestors' vision. What was once a small building has transformed into a twenty-two-story structure spanning the full city block. It is a creative ecosystem with performance spaces, a tech storytelling lab, and artist housing. The expanded version serves as what Sade calls "a grand dedication" to those who came before, honoring their dreams, while training the next generation of theater professionals.

On a crisp March evening in 2025, Sade and I made a pilgrimage to the theater. As we rounded the corner of East 126th Street and Fifth Avenue, a sudden gust of wind swept across our faces and the clear sky darkened, releasing an unexpected downpour. We took cover under the marquee, and Sade nodded with quiet recognition. "One of my mother's nicknames was *kālāhonua*, from the Hawaiian word for 'one who brings water.'" The synchronicity hung between us, undeniable. Then she shared something even more profound: each brick forming this towering edifice had been cut from the clay of the river where her mother's ashes were scattered. The very molecules that once composed Dr. Barbara Ann Teer's physical form were now part of the structure of the theater itself, a literal embodiment of ancestral presence. As if through methylation, a dusting of her lived experience in each building block of the theater.

Sade maintains daily communication with her ancestral guides, finding direction and purpose in their counsel. "Now more than ever," she reflects, "we are charged to be vessels/portals/stewards of the divine, and support others through our wisdom—bestowed on us from all of the entities and spirit guides that continue to light our way." All Sade has to do—all any of us has to do—is ask . . . and then trust what comes through. Dr. Teer's spirit lives in every brick. But it was Sade's hands that brought them into form, one by one, as this monument to ancestral dreams made manifest.

BE OF SERVICE

But what if, unlike Sade, we feel as though we've lost touch with both our lineage and our calling? This is where many of us find ourselves—caught between the ego's demands for security and the soul's directive toward service.

My patient Charlotte was in her mid-thirties, living in San Francisco, and in the early days of a promising relationship. She'd grown up in the South, in the rural outskirts of an otherwise affluent school district. Her household struggled, and at school she was surrounded by families who always seemed to have it better. Charlotte had childhood memories of feeling excluded by the other girls who would come to school in trendy jeans, while Charlotte was stuck wearing hand-me-downs from her cousins. School supply lists and playdates at the movies or the mall meant household tension—knowing her parents would argue over how to come up with the money. In high school, when Charlotte would creep into the kitchen at 9 P.M. to get a snack, she would overhear her parents arguing about their financial stress while doing dishes. She was certain of one thing: when she grew up and had a family of her own, she didn't want money stress.

Now Charlotte worked for an animation studio. She spent long hours in her dimly lit workspace, her face illuminated by the glow of dual monitors, perfecting the subtle facial expressions and fluid movements that make animated characters feel real. Through some alchemy of skill and magic she transformed pixels and polygon meshes into characters capable of moving us to tears. Despite working in a notoriously competitive industry, Charlotte had carved out a solid career, with steady projects and respectable compensation. And yet, a comfortable life in the Bay Area does not come cheap. From dinner parties to group hikes in Marin County, Charlotte was constantly confronted with her peers' envy-inducing lives. They drove fancy SUVs, lived in homes with panoramic views, and drank third-wave cortados. Charlotte, financially secure by any measure, felt like the pauper of her friend group. Again.

Charlotte was checking in with me over Zoom because she was considering breaking up with her boyfriend and making drastic changes in her career. That was a lot for us to tackle in fifty minutes, but we gave it a try.

I'm always looking for my patients' microexpressions and the tenor of their mood when they describe their partners. Charlotte smiled broadly and her body relaxed when she discussed her boyfriend, Greg: "We're compatible, we have good chemistry, he's intellectually curious, he makes me laugh, and he's a really good guy." So why was she considering ending the relationship?

"Because he's a starving artist."

Greg was an experimental jazz composer whom critics adored but venues rarely booked. Charlotte was hell-bent on creating financial security for her future family, and Greg, a brilliant musician without any prospects for career stability, was not going to be her meal ticket.

"What happens when we have kids? What if I want to take some time off to be with them? I would be our sole breadwinner. This isn't going to work."

Charlotte had also been considering making sweeping changes to her job, because, though she felt creatively satisfied, again, there was no shot at a financial windfall. It paid the bills, but would she ever be able to buy a house?

Let's acknowledge that Charlotte came by her uncertainty honestly. Her parents' frequent fights over money had left her with a childhood wound around financial scarcity. Before she was old enough to know better, she equated her parents' stress over their finances with genuine survival fears. She was hypersensitive to money stress, and her idea of security was having financial abundance.

"I'm trying so hard to manifest the life I want. Is the universe even listening?" Charlotte wondered aloud.

Her question revealed the trap of hyperindividualism: how we focus on what we can get rather than what we can give. Charlotte added, her voice shaky, "I mean, ultimately, I just make *cartoons.* I'm not even sure my work matters."

Here's how I advised Charlotte. I think "the universe" couldn't care less about what we want. I imagine that when we tell the universe what we want for ourselves, it thinks to itself, *That's cute.* In my experience, the universe perks up its ears and listens to our prayers when we show up with the intention to be of service. That is, how can we use our gifts to make a contribution? How can we use our passions, creativity, privilege, power, or influence to be a force for good in this world? Or, as the quote popularly attributed to Martin Luther King Jr. goes, "Life's most persistent and urgent question is, 'What are you doing for others?' "

The soundtrack of the lower self is: I need more. Charlotte was understandably stuck in this valence. Meanwhile, the higher self wonders, How do I serve? Our gifts exist not for our own benefit but as offerings to the world. In my own experience, anytime I put this intention of service into my prayers, there's a fundamental shift—I become a co-conspirator with larger benevolent forces. The universe no longer responds with the dismissive "That's cute" but seems to say instead, "You have my attention, go on."

Charlotte had grown up praying before bed. After this conversation, she dusted off this old habit. In her prayers, she stopped focusing on what she *wanted*, and she instead started asking: What are my unique gifts? What is my contribution? Insights and downloads started popping into her awareness. She pulled out a notebook to capture everything that was coming through. Charlotte found that the pen was moving in a way that felt beyond voluntary control. What poured forth were her *intentions*. She wanted her movies to open people to the deeper questions about life. She wanted her work to inspire others to make art. She wanted her characters to make people *feel*. Most of all, she wanted her movies to do for others what great art did for her: it made her feel less alone.

Charlotte stayed with her boyfriend and began to shift her focus from what she lacked to what she could give. In full transparency, this shift was nonlinear and had its ups and downs. Some mornings, she would wake up in a panic about their financial future, scrolling through real estate listings she knew they couldn't afford. "This intention-setting practice feels like magical thinking," she confessed during one session. "Last night I found myself calculating how much we'd need for a down payment, and the number made me physically ill."

For weeks, she would alternate between moments of creative flow and paralyzing anxiety. She'd catch herself judging Greg when he turned down a wedding gig to focus on his original music, then feel ashamed of her resentment. "I believe in his talent," she said. "I really do. But then I look at my bank account and I'm stressed." Even as she continued her daily prayers about service, part of her clung desperately to the old belief that wealth was all that could provide true safety.

It was only after receiving recognition for a new animation technique she'd developed—along with a modest promotion—that she began to see the first hints that her new approach might be bearing fruit. "Maybe there's something to this intention setting after all," she admitted cautiously.

Instead of asking, "Who am I to make art?" she began to ask herself, "Who am I to block the creative energy that wants to flow through me?" She realized that her imposter syndrome was lying to her. True humility isn't about making ourselves small—it's about being willing to be a channel for something greater than ourselves. The real audacity isn't in creating; it's in refusing to create when we're called to do so.

During one session, Charlotte reflected on how her artistic process was beginning to feel different. She shared a quote from the pioneering abstract artist Hilma af Klint: "The pictures were painted directly through me, without preliminary drawings and with great power. I had no idea what the pictures would depict and still I worked quickly and surely without changing a single brush-stroke." Charlotte hesitated, then admitted that something similar was happening to her at the computer. There were moments when she entered a flow state, and it felt as though unseen forces were guiding her fingers across the trackpad. She laughed self-consciously as she said this, quickly adding, "I realize this sounds ridiculous." But the experience was undeniable.

With Greg, we took the approach of the "next right step." Was it time to break up, or was this relationship still compelling? The next right step always seemed to be to stay together, and this feeling went on for months and then years. Though Greg never made a lot of money, a short time after Charlotte started her intention-setting practice, she was involved in a movie that won accolades and awards. In time, her income became enough to support them both. This wasn't without complexity in terms of their dynamic, but ultimately, they ended up moving outside of the city to experience a lower cost of living and better proximity to nature. Charlotte never fully outgrew her habit of worrying about their finances, but she was able to continuously remind herself that they had enough. She would see her movies in theaters alongside other moviegoers, and she witnessed how her work moved people, how it mattered.

Charlotte came to understand that she was a vessel for something greater. The magic wasn't coming from her ego's striving or grasping but from her willingness to be a clear channel, to let the universe work through her hands. This was how she served.

Years after that initial conversation about service, Charlotte opened a session by telling me a story from the day before. "I was seeing my movie in the theater. Sitting next to me was a mom and her grown daughter." Charlotte explained that during a particularly poignant scene, one which she had a direct hand in, the mother was sobbing. "Like, ugly crying." Charlotte continued, "While the credits were rolling, the mother and daughter hugged and held that embrace for maybe . . . a solid minute. I have no idea what that scene meant to them, but clearly it struck a chord." Charlotte knew she was on her path, living out her intention, serving others with her art. Spirit provided the guidance, and Charlotte offered what only she could—her hands moving across the trackpad, translating inspiration into animated life.

When we offer our gifts, the world has a way of taking care of us in return. This is the paradox our individualistic culture overlooks: real security flows not from self-focused striving but from the web of relationships, mutual aid, and collective care we're all held within.

GOING BEYOND THE SELF

When it comes to connecting to forces beyond ourselves, there are no rules—you should simply do what feels right to you. Here are some strategies that have worked for me and my patients:

- **Connect to ancestors**. Create a small altar with photos, flowers, or objects that connect you to your lineage. This does not have to be limited to blood relatives; it can include spiritual teachers, mentors, and anyone beloved.
- **Set an intention to be of service**. Before starting your day's work, pause and ask, "How can I be of service through what I do?"

- **Notice when you're operating from scarcity** (trying to control outcomes) **versus trust** (allowing outcomes to unfold). Have a lot of patience with yourself with this one; it's a practice.
- **Notice when you're operating from insecurity**. Do you overhear yourself thinking, *I'm an imposter; What if I fail?;* or *Who am I to do this?* When these arise, reframe: *Who am I to block the creative force that wants to be birthed through me?* If you're aligned with your intention to be of service, you cannot go wrong (and the critics can't get under your skin quite so easily).

These small practices of connection, intention, and surrender help us release our grip on controlling the outcome and instead focus on being of service. This is the doorway through which we move beyond the self and into our larger purpose.

Whether we're doing energy work, building theaters, or creating art that moves audiences to tears, we are all translating spirit into form, one careful gesture at a time. The task at hand is to get out of our own way and trust what wants to come through. Ancestral connection reminds us that we are part of an unbroken chain. Service transforms our gifts into offerings for the collective good.

We are never working alone. We are held by an invisible web of wisdom and support, available to us whenever we pause to ask for guidance. There are forces that want to birth art, healing, and transformation through us—but they need our participation. They need our willingness to show up, to trust, to act. Never underestimate the role we have in this. In the words of Swaranpal's late sister, you have hands. Use them to craft something that ripples out well beyond the self.

Chapter 19

THE LESSONS OF GRIEF

If we're not supposed to dance,
Why all this music?

—GREGORY ORR, *Concerning the Book That Is the Body of the Beloved*

*O*m—that ancient, resonant sound that ripples through Hindu temples, Buddhist monasteries, Jain sanctuaries, and yoga classes—is said to be the primordial vibration of the universe itself. It feels like no accident that this sacred syllable echoes through some of our most primal words: "home" and "mom" and "womb" in English, the word for mother in multiple languages ("amma" and "ima"), perhaps even "amen." Each one carries that same vibrational medicine, striking at the heart of belonging.

I felt this connection viscerally last night, cradling my daughter as she cried. We had been reading together before bed when a simple line about parents leaving for work tripped a wire in her. I paused to reassure her. "Even though I go to work, you are my number one priority." Her response knocked the wind out of me—she said she didn't always feel that was true.

Then her body shuddered with the full force of held-back tears, and between gasping sobs she said something that caught me completely off guard: "I want to go home."

The words hung in the air, strange and powerful. Here she was, in her own bed, in the only home she'd ever known. "You *are* home," I wanted to say. But I sensed that she was reaching for something deeper. She wasn't yearning for these four walls, but for "home" in its most primal sense—the safety of Mom, the completeness of the womb, the unity of *om*. She longed for that earlier time when my arms were her whole world, before school and schedules and all the necessary separations of growing up began to dissolve our merged existence.

My daughter's plea to "go home" was really a yearning to return to source—to Mom, to womb, to *om*. This is territory I know well. After my mom passed, my tears took on a particular quality. Each time I cried, I felt myself regressing to infancy, becoming again that small creature whose very survival depended on a mother's response.

In those raw days of early grief—bent over my pregnant belly in the shower, hands on knees, heaving guttural pleas—my tears would echo back to me in the cold bathroom. I wanted to go home—to a time, a place, a wholeness that no longer existed. And that singular question would surface: Was she truly gone?

As I've awakened to the magic in my life, I see that bathroom scene differently now. My mom was there, reassuring me through the silence: You *are* home. And I was experiencing my own version of my daughter's plea—yearning for home from my own bed. Yearning for my mom when she was, in fact, right there.

Individual grief and universal longing aren't so different after all. Perhaps this universal yearning reveals a clue about existence: we enter this life through the portal of our mother's *womb* and find our way to source—*om*—at its end.

In a modern parable often attributed to Henri Nouwen, twins converse in the womb. One asks, "Do you believe in life after delivery?" The other dismisses this as nonsense. "No one has ever returned after delivery. Delivery is the end of life." But the first twin wonders about Mother:

"I think we will meet Mother and she will take care of us."

"Mother? You believe in a mother? Where is she now?"

"She is all around us. We are of her. It is in her that we live."

"I don't see her, so she doesn't exist."

"Sometimes, when we're silent, I can feel her presence."

Our longing for our mothers echoes our most primal yearning—to merge again with the oceanic mother of creation. Yet there's wisdom in the universe's design: before we can return to that perfect unity, before we can be "delivered," we must complete our journey through what the mystics call earth school—this long gestation, where we experience ourselves as heartbreakingly separate. Where we've forgotten who we are. And where we feel, in the background of our hearts, an aching awareness that "there's no place like home."

My daughter's yearning to go home that night embodied the same ancient pull my father would follow just months later—the soul's inevitable wish to journey back to source.

RAPTURE

My dad's last day of life was the Fourth of July. There's that time of year again—that sacred fulcrum in my life, with my husband's birthday, my first psilocybin ceremony, the Cycles card, my mother's passing, and now this. My sister and I held our dad's hands and our husbands gathered around as we held our breath in the moments before the flat line appeared on the monitor. There was a point when we collectively exhaled. The room came to stillness. Moments after my father's heart stopped having any electrical signals, a blue glare moved across my glasses, and I felt what I can only describe as an invisible shift.

A distant boom drew my eyes toward the window. The sun had set, and on the horizon the Fourth of July fireworks had just begun—at what seemed to be the very moment my dad's soul left his body. My dad was transported to whatever lies beyond. And in that instant, after so sorely missing my mom for so long, he was reunited with his one true love. Like a first kiss, it was fireworks.

Death may represent something far beyond our mortal comprehension. Though we naturally grieve, our heaviness may simply reflect our own earthbound perspective. While we remain here, processing our loss, our loved one might be crossing a threshold into realms of rapture and light. When I've been proximal to it, death has carried this quality—as if the soul crossing over is witnessing the edge of something vast, luminous, and holy.

SIGNS

As with my daughter's birth time at 12:50 A.M., I felt my mom's hand in the timing of my dad's death—eight years and two days from her own. Close enough to be unmistakably connected, but a couple days off to avoid napalming my husband's birthday. And because it was that pivotal weekend in July, the time of year that my family gathers to be together for the anniversary of my mom's passing, my dad was not alone. Yet even these reassurances don't inoculate me against doubt. And each loss seems to teach me different lessons. My mother's death broke open my spiritual worldview. My father's death tested me in entirely new ways.

When my mom died, it brought my sister and me closer. Nobody can understand what you're going through during the loss of a parent the way a sibling can. I was comforted by the ways my sister looked and sounded like my mom. Her laugh and her sneeze had the timbre of maternal source, familiar since the womb. I cherished the ways my sister was the keeper of family knowledge, recipes, references, memories. My sister was the new matriarch, the new hearth, and I gathered around her to keep warm in that devastation.

But the death of our father introduced an unexpected source of tension. With my mom's death, my dad was the grown-up in the room. He was the point person for the funeral home and the hospital. He made decisions about autopsies and coffins. He did the heavy-duty adulting. My sister and I were shielded in that way that one often is—invisibly—when they still have an involved parent. But with our dad's death, there was no grown-up in the room. My sister and I, geriatric orphans that we were, busy raising our families and building our careers, were left to divvy up the adulting between the two of us. There were life insurance companies to call, electricity bills to pay. An attic to clear, a house to sell. Logistics and practicalities took up most of our time together, eclipsing our role as each other's emotional sanctuary. This loss introduced more distance than closeness.

A few months after my dad's passing, I was introduced to a woman named Mara at a dinner party. She was in her mid-thirties, and she radiated a polished composure, from her fitted navy cardigan and cloth headband to her expressive green eyes that held both warmth and keen intelligence. We made unremarkable small talk until dessert was winding down, when we stumbled upon our commonality: we had both lost parents too early.

Mara recommended the book *Signs* by Laura Lynne Jackson. I had heard of it before, but this was the first time someone recommended it to me directly. I downloaded the audiobook on my walk home. Following its guidance, I decided to ask my parents to send me a sign—a specific symbol or occurrence that would let me know they were still present in my life. The freshness of the "Spirit in the Sky" moment in that Brooklyn restaurant (crab fried rice, s'mores, the song coming on the restaurant speakers) was fading, and my doubts were resurfacing. Jackson suggests setting aside quiet time to make this request, ideally before sleep when the mind is most receptive. She advises choosing "something specific and unusual enough"—an object or creature so distinct that when you encounter it, you'll have no doubt it's a message from your loved one. That evening, as I lay in bed with my eyes closed, trying to open myself to whatever image might arise, repeating to myself that it needed to be unusual and specific, what popped into my mind was . . . an armadillo. Unusual indeed. I decided to go with it.

"Okay, Mom and Dad," I said out loud. "Could you please send me three armadillos as a sign?"

This was met by the cosmic shrug and radio silence you might expect. But then, sure enough, the signs started coming. First it was an armadillo logo on a delivery truck that flashed past me on my way to drop my daughter at school. Then, while I was in Florida visiting my in-laws, I went out for a walk and spotted what looked like armadillo roadkill. I walked home questioning it, wishing I had documented it somehow. Do armadillos even live in the Tampa area? Had I seen my second sign? Maybe? Maybe not.

Many weeks of scanning the horizon ensued, without an armadillo in sight. It started to feel like the exercise was a bust. In moments of hope I thought, *They must have a reason for making me wait.* But most of the time, doubt took over. *That roadkill could not have been an armadillo,* I thought, *and there's no way I'm ever going to get my third sign. Armadillo was a stupid thing to pick.* But self-blame was only a tranquilizer from the more painful thought going through my mind: *I was foolish to be hopeful.*

Theologian and philosopher Paul Tillich, known for bridging traditional faith with modern existential questions, tells us, "Doubt is not the opposite of faith; it is one element of faith." Perhaps my doubts were a vital part of my relationship with hope. When we're clouded in uncertainty, we might desperately want proof that magic exists—but perhaps that assurance only arrives when we're truly ready to receive it.

In a moment of self-reflection, I pondered if perhaps my parents were making me wait for the last sign for a reason. Was there an action I needed to take? Was there a lesson I hadn't yet learned? One image that came through repeatedly in my meditations was a scene of my dad sitting by a lake back in 2015, one month after my mom's death. We had made a pilgrimage to our favorite campground in Vermont—the site of many childhood family vacations. My dad had reserved the campsite months earlier. (The original intent was a vacation for him and my mom.) But everything had changed, and now we were in Vermont together to spread my mom's ashes instead. My dad and I sat together on the beach of the small lake, watching my niece splashing at the water's edge. Around us were families with young kids—the parents applying sunblock, blowing up floaties, managing meltdowns. My dad turned to me and shared a single sentiment: "Those were the golden years."

My throat caught. I felt his wrenching nostalgia for a time, a hearth, a goldenness that was now forever out of reach. And I shared it. I looked back at my childhood, feeling how irretrievably lost that time was.

Seven months pregnant but not yet a mother, I didn't realize that I was embarking upon my own version of the golden years. Even further out of my awareness at the time, I certainly never thought to recognize *this* moment—pregnant, grieving, sitting next to my dad, my niece still a toddler—as its own kind of golden years.

Coming back to 2023 and my daily search for missing armadillos, I sat with doubt. Slowly, an insight began to come through: if we learn nothing else from losing the people we love too soon, it's to at least appreciate the people we still have. When my dad was alive, I was so fixated on my mom's absence that I missed out on fully relishing that I had him. I had a parent—an anchor to my childhood memories, a keeper of family stories and traditions, a human being who I loved. But I was looking past it, focused on what was missing. In my meditations, I would ask, *But what do I do with this lesson? It's too late to go back and appreciate my dad.* I would sit there dumbly, drawing a blank. Time passed. I waited for clarity. And waited for more armadillos.

The leaves changed from green to yellow to papery brown crunching underfoot, and winter break arrived. It was time for us to pack up and train down to D.C. to spend the Christmas holiday with my sister and her family. This was our first Christmas without our dad. Sadness, stress, and ongoing death-related logistics were at an all-time peak.

When my sister came to the front door, we met each other's gaze, tearful. We took an afternoon walk together, stepping gingerly, the sidewalk brittle and slippery from a recent freeze. We weaved our way through the chilled D.C. streets, shaking our heads at how surreal it all felt, holding steady through long stretches of silence, both wordlessly weeping.

On that first night together, we took the kids to ZooLights at the National Zoo—an LED winter wonderland against the solstice darkness. We wandered through the maze of glowing paths—kids manic from sugar and late bedtimes, tongues prickly from burning hot chocolate—until the evening culminated with a carousel ride. When I noticed that the carousel was not horses but an assortment of zoo animals, my mind went immediately to thoughts of my incomplete request for armadillos. Maybe, just maybe, there would be an armadillo on this carousel. I trained my eyes on the carousel as it went round: a zebra, a lion, a giraffe, a panda, a gazelle . . . I realized an armadillo was not on brand for this carousel. It was, once again, far too random. Why had I asked for such an implausible sign?

And then I spotted it. Amid the tigers and elephants, utterly out of place, was a squat little armadillo. Waiting in line for the carousel, surrounded by our buzzing children, I told my sister the whole story of the *Signs* book and the armadillos. When we got to the front of the line, I walked straight to the armadillo and took a seat. It finally happened: my third armadillo. (Or was it my second, because the roadkill was suspect? But it turns out, armadillos *can* be found in the Tampa area. Who knew?)

I was already satisfied. But as we walked toward the parking lot, in an embarrassment of riches, there was a whole exhibit about armadillos, with a neon family of exactly three armadillos as we exited the zoo. I so appreciated this final armadillo pile-on. As an overthinker, an utter lack of ambiguity is always helpful in assuaging my doubts. No matter how I measured it, this was the complete sign.

The timing felt purposeful. Of course my parents waited until this moment, when all remnants of our family were together. But there was more to it—to why my parents made me wait.

About to exit the zoo, I lingered for a moment in front of the neon armadillos. The rainbow lights refracted through my tears, scattering into a swirl of armadillo fractals. I thought of the cover of the Pink Floyd album *The Dark Side of the Moon.* White light enters a prism and emerges as a spectrum of color.

For so long, I thought of this world as two-dimensional white light—straightforward, measurable, linear. Losing my mom became my prism. The white light of my understanding entered the portal of grief and exploded into an array of multicolor light. The universe revealed itself as infinite and mysterious, more colorful and strange than I had previously believed. This is what happens when we reclaim our witchiness. To see the world through witches' eyes is to put white light through a prism. Reality was only ever appearing flat or mechanistic. The truth is an explosive array.

If parents in another realm can send armadillos at exactly the right moment, magic is undeniable. Their ongoing presence serves as a reminder: this human experience does not represent the totality of reality—it's one minor slice of our vast and eternal consciousness, a brief chapter in an endless story. But it's a chapter with purpose.

Earth is the prism for consciousness. It takes the primordial stew of source consciousness—unified white light—and refracts it into separate, individual experiences. In this realm, we are consciousness experiencing itself in all its multidimensional color. But this requires that we live under the illusion of separation. We forget that we are one and the same as each other, as source. We forget that we are divine. This forgetting is by design—it's a necessary precondition. Only when we're refracted into our individual components—the subjective experience of being a specific individual, with preferences and stories, memories and wounds—can we begin this work. Only when we know ourselves as one shade of indigo, rather than the whole rainbow, can we truly learn about love. Only then can we do the alchemy we came here to do.

What unfolds here isn't senseless chaos but curriculum. We study love in all its forms. Even when relationships challenge us; even when they fracture us open. Especially then. There are times in our relationships when love comes easily. In these moments, our assignment is not to learn to love but to stay awake to the present and ease our attachment. To hold love loosely. To let it breathe. To tolerate impermanence.

And then there are the challenging times. When things get hard, the path of least resistance is to diffuse away. But often, our relationships only trigger us because they hold up a mirror to something we haven't fully resolved within ourselves, to our densities and shadows that we still need to alchemize. These moments are actually what we came here for.

Our work is to shift fear and separation, against all odds, into love. Both within ourselves and in our relationships with those around us. For me, the aftermath of losing my parents has been my hardest lesson, but not just because of the sting of loss. I was yearning for my mom, and missing out on what I had with my dad. Now, mourning both of them, I'm doing it again—missing out on what I have with my sister. Missing the fact that we are not separate but one unified light. Missing that these, too, are golden years.

Perhaps the most profound gift of seeing magic is learning to apply that vision to our material lives—to the relationships we're still lucky enough to have. My parents waited until my sister and I were reconnecting, our distinct watercolor hues blending together through the medium of tears, before revealing the armadillos. Through signs and timing, my parents are right here, continuing to raise us.

There are moments when I revert to seeing only the flat white light and forget the fuller picture. That's the work of being here—to keep putting our experiences back through the prism of witchiness, to keep seeing the refraction. To know in our bones that we are not separate.

To remember that we are all part of the same unified white light, having a temporary refracted experience. I don't know why. I suspect it's not our job to know why. But I do know that every time we choose love over separation, we participate in something sacred.

When we open ourselves to the possibility of something beyond our understanding, we're not abandoning reason or pledging allegiance to any particular belief system. We're simply creating space for wonder and meaning. This openness enriches our lives in tangible ways. It helps us navigate loss and experience everyday moments with greater depth. It reminds us that even in our most alone moments, we're part of something vast and possibly benevolent—something that might be trying to send us an armadillo when we need it most.

I'm not sure how long I was standing there in front of those neon armadillos. My reverie broke when I heard my sister's voice in the distance.

"This way," she called out, worried that perhaps I had gotten lost among the winding paths of the zoo.

I wiped the tears from my eyes, and the fractals slowly resolved.

They're right here, I thought. *Don't miss the magic.*

But there was something about my parents' timing—the longest night of the year, my sister and I together. They weren't just saying: *we're right here.* They were also saying: *so is she. Don't miss that either.*

I took a final glance at the armadillos and walked through the solstice dark toward her voice.

☾ ☾ ☾

Our culture is hyperindividualistic, but a witch is connected to the collective so that she can live a life of service and love.

CONCLUSION

Season of the Witch

A year after my dad's passing, I was invited to a women's retreat in the tropics. It was a gathering of movers and shakers—the kind of women who close eight-figure deals and win Olympic gold medals, whose calendars are booked solid with board meetings and keynote speeches. We arrived with the standard armor of successful women: media training, jewel-toned suits, and Dyson Airwraps. We were ready to optimize our leadership potential and trade strategies for winning in a male-dominated world.

But the jungle had other plans. Within hours, we were frizzy and shvitzy. Any airs we'd maintained in our normal lives—the blowouts, the carefully crafted talking points, the unflappable composure—dissolved in the humidity.

For three days, we workshopped entrepreneurship tactics. We were women who had understood the assignment—rational, evidence-based, jumping through any hoop the world held up before us. But something else was happening beneath the surface of those workshops.

We started telling the truth. Our confessions and reflections were unrehearsed and unpublishable. Women who ordinarily go through their lives without a hair out of place were moving through messy emotions and uncertain territory. And the truth that kept surfacing was that we were done. Done performing and apologizing. Done compressing our full spectrum of light into something two-dimensional. Done shrinking ourselves to fit a world that was never designed for our wholeness.

On the final evening, we gathered for the closing ceremony. The workshop task: write a haiku summarizing our time together. As we went around the circle reading them aloud, a theme emerged. We were all talking about the same things. Intuition. Mystery. Magic.

A charismatic woman named Steph, ever the social arbiter, leaned forward with a knowing smile. "It's the Season of the Witch, y'all."

The room erupted in collective recognition. We didn't have to keep squeezing ourselves into a mold that never fit, that couldn't contain the full spectrum of our capacities.

This retreat was never really about learning to be better at performing the part of ourselves that the world wanted. We were there to remember our suppressed truth: that our real power doesn't come from analyzing the data or backing up our arguments with evidence. It comes from the golden compass of our intuition and embracing the parts of ourselves we'd been conditioned to dismiss.

In that candlelit circle, we expanded into our witchiness, and it felt like coming home. These were women who had mastered the game of succeeding in a man's world. And in that moment, we realized: we're done straining to fit into that world. It's time to build a witch's world instead.

Perhaps you can feel it too—that slight shift in the air, that opening to something more magical than what you were taught to believe. You've been conditioned to doubt yourself and dismiss your intuition. This is no accident. A woman who stands firmly in her witchy nature challenges the established order, because she carries within herself an impervious sense of wholeness.

This witchiness that we've been taught to disavow connects us to an ancient lineage of women who have carried these gifts through generations of persecution. It attunes us to the subtle currents of energy that can guide personal and collective healing. It shores up our pieces in a world designed to keep us fragmented.

A witchy woman doesn't require rational explanations for her knowing or constant productivity to feel worthy. Instead, she is emboldened by connection—to her ancestors, to source, to the sacred cycles that govern both our bodies and our natural world, to her internal compass that somehow knows the way through the dark. She recognizes that the "worst-case scenario" is an illusion. What we should fear most isn't some external outcome but the suffering created by our resistance to life's unfolding. She holds up a prism and sees that our material lives represent a sliver of our enduring consciousness.

My hope is that more of us can see this universe as fundamentally magical. We acknowledge that this is unprovable, but we feel it, and that's enough.

Our culture systematically devalues so much of what is natural to us—favoring analysis over intuition, dissociation over embodiment, distraction over presence, yang over yin, the individual over the collective, materialism over mystery. This is the invisible cage that taught us we were somehow inferior, that convinced us to stay quiet in self-doubt. The generation of women rising now refuses to hide half of who we are for acceptance in a system built to deny us.

When we reclaim our magic, we see reality in its full spectrum—not just the narrow band of what can be measured and proven but the dazzling, baffling richness that exists beyond the visible.

We thought this world was a stream of two-dimensional white light. Losing my mom was my prism. When grief forced me to expand beyond the narrow band of rational materialism, I discovered that I was guided and held. I was able to find meaning in the unfolding. And my hope is that this book can serve as a prism for you.

COMING OUT OF THE BROOM CLOSET

I didn't set out to become someone who believes in magic. As a psychiatrist, I was trained in evidence-based medicine and scientific skepticism. But when my parents died, that worldview couldn't hold the fullness of what I experienced. The choice became: ignore the voices, dismiss the impossible synchronicities, miss out on the sense of ongoing relationship, or expand my understanding of what's possible.

The writer Elizabeth Gilbert describes a similar crossroads in her memoir *All the Way to the River*, reflecting, "I believe there is a right and natural order of things—the Tao, the path, a way of living in easeful alignment with the drift and movement of the universe—and I was moving in exactly the opposite direction. If the universe can be said to want anything from us, I now believe, it is that we position ourselves to exist in harmony with reality—to sway in accordance with destiny, without excessive argument or struggle."

It may not be for us to understand why the current flows as it does, but what is certain is that it's easier to float downstream than to hold back a river. Opening to mystery has helped me find a way to "sway in accordance with destiny." That choice changed everything for me. And I want the same for you.

Don't miss the magic.

The magic has been there for you all along. Our culture has conditioned us to dismiss these experiences as wishful thinking or delusion. But the Season of the Witch is upon us. After centuries of persecution and silence, it is imperative that we now emerge from the shadows. Our world desperately needs people who can feel what's out of alignment, sense the guidance of spirit, and respond without regard for outdated social convention. You are, in fact, precisely what this moment in history requires—a woman who sees beyond the veil and who is brave enough to stand in her power without apology.

My hope for you is that you will stop feeling shame for believing in what cannot be proven. That you will clear your channels to better hear your intuition, and help other women rise into their power. That you will connect to your ancestors and find both guidance and humility in that connection, and feel the proximity of those you have lost.

If pure materialism is genuinely your truth, then honor that. But if you harbor a buried truth that includes magic—if you've been shaming yourself out of insights from your deeper knowing—then consider this your permission slip to reopen to it.

This is my answer to a call I received from spirit. It is my case for women to believe in magic—for our own wholeness and for the collective healing of our world. When we reclaim our witchiness, we remember that we are not separate from nature but are nature itself in human form; that we are not disconnected from source but are source refracted through a prism and expressing itself through us; that we are loved, and that we *are* love.

The time for hiding is over. The Season of the Witch is here.

ACKNOWLEDGMENTS

Vimal—My love, nothing is possible without you. Thank you for holding down our world and for the essential (and endless) help with the book. But most of all, thank you for going all the way to the river with me. You are my original magic, and I love you.

J—It is the joy of my life to know you and to learn from you. Thank you for being so patient while I worked on this book. It's a blessing to be your mom, and I love you infinitely.

Mom—I miss you. Thank you for every sign and instance of support. In the sky and over the speakers, you have taught me about the inexplicable nature of reality. See you later, I love you.

Dad—I miss you, and it feels like you should be here with us. Thank you for so much stability and support. I hope you are reconnected with Mommy and that it's fireworks. I'm sorry, please forgive me, thank you, I love you.

Anne—This book is a love letter to you and to all the lessons I learn through our soul contract. I love you.

Whit Frick—Thank you for your brilliance and the extraordinary care you brought to this book. You have a rare gift for helping authors translate lessons of the heart into words that can heal. Working with you has been a dream come true.

Sam Zukergood—Thank you for your careful eye and deep insights. It has been a delight to work with you, and I hope that this is the beginning of a much longer journey together.

Sarah Passick, Mia Vitale, and the whole team at PF&B—I have always felt so held by your immense expertise. Deep gratitude to you all.

Leila Tejani, Avideh Bashirrad, Rachel Parker, Christina Tatulli, Debbie Aroff, Michelle Jasmine, Luke Epplin, Leah Sims, Meghan O'Leary, Mimi Lipson, Jo Anne Metsch, and the entire team at Dial Press—I am so grateful to each and every one of you for your expertise and care with this book. You are truly the best in the biz.

To my patients—Thank you for entrusting me with your care and for being my forever teachers. It's an honor to be on this journey with each and every one of you.

Baba and Dada—Thank you for treating me as one of your own and for being a source of sweetness and love for J. I'm so grateful to you both.

Manish—Thanks for being a true brother. Your generosity and genius enrich all our lives. I hope you know how much we appreciate you.

Ankur, Nisha, and S—You bring the humor and the warmth. I love you all.

Decker—Welcome to the family. I look forward to so many adventures ahead.

Adam—Thank you for being an incredible brother-in-law, uncle, and grounding presence in our lives. Next time around, I'll send you a manuscript early so that I can get your superb editorial advice.

VMS crew—There is no better family on the planet. I am so lucky to have you all in my life.

Raina—Thank you for your critical insights and for taking the time in spite of your brutal hours. I can't wait to celebrate you very soon.

Sutcliffes—Thank you for your pure hearts and your central role in the magic of this wild life.

To my dear, soul-level friends—You teach me about love and everything that matters, and I'm so lucky to be on this ride alongside you.

Thank you Morquists, Mashins, Omri, Jeremy, Jenny, Elise, Jennifer & Rendy, Andrew & Roya, Paul & Erica, Liz & Zach, Kayvon &

Elena, Jay & Julia, Cat & Carl, Seanna & Brady, Tara & Jonathan, and the entire favorite child and 305 crews.

Amely and Marisa—To the original coven that got this project off the ground, thank you for tapping into your witchy knowing to point this book in the right direction.

Darshana Avila, Melissa Lowenstein, Sarah Messmore, and Janet Fowler—Thank you for sharing your indispensable expertise.

Daniela—Thank you for naming something in me that has shaped the trajectory of my life.

Momoko Uno, Swaranpal, and Katinka Locascio—Thank you for sharing your gifts for bridging the worlds.

Mark Ferlito—A healer in the truest sense of the word, thank you for seeing me and helping me on every level—mind, body, and soul.

Gwyneth—You're a visionary with a giant heart. Thank you for helping me spread my message and for always pushing the culture forward.

Expand—The coming together of so many magical people has shaped this book and my life. Thank you all for helping me expand. GP and Brit, I am forever grateful for the love you poured into this experience.

Sade Lythcott—Every word you speak is poetry. Thank you for sharing your story. I'm so grateful to call you a friend.

De'Ara Balenger—When we're together, the spirits surround us. I cherish your friendship.

Laura Lynne Jackson—The way you share your gift has changed countless lives. I appreciate your guidance and your friendship. You are a true force for the light.

Amy Griffin—Your generosity knows no bounds, and your truth-telling serves as a guiding light. The work you do is medicine.

Kate Bowler—You are brilliant and hilarious, and you're a national treasure (we claim you).

Sima Sistani—You're a generous friend and my exact brand of Beyoncé-loving witch.

Julia Hartz—You are a powerful witch, and I'm so grateful to you for taking the time to connect.

Ingrid Fetell Lee—You are gentle, powerful, and wise, and I am so lucky to count you as a true friend.

Steph Simon—Your ability to put your finger on the pulse of culture is virtuosic. It was one of these genius moments that provided the title for this book. I am forever in your debt.

Dr. Iain McGilchrist—Thank you for your scholarship and for taking the time to bring me up to speed on the current understanding of the science.

Hoda Kotb and the Joy 101 team—You're making an incredible contribution to the world, and I'm so honored to be a part of it.

Pilar Guzman—Thank you for your friendship and support. Here's to many more cappuccinos and cultural musings together.

Kimberly Ann Johnson—Your insights cut straight to the core of what holds our culture back. Thank you for all you do.

Aviva Romm—The OG, you have done so much for women's health. Thank you for taking the time to support this project. I cannot wait for your next book.

To all the guides at Alpha NYC, thank you for the most incredible year. I'm grateful for your hard work and deep attunement. Here's to building something beautiful together.

Gratitude for allowing me to showcase your work and for your insights on the text: Esther Perel, Jonathan Haidt, Alexa Arnold, Zach Rausch, Jean Twenge, Lisa Mosconi, Jeffrey Kripal, Julia Ross, Dean Radin, Vanessa Cornell, Mara Feil, Mory Fontanez, Stephanie Arnold, Dené Logan, Azra Bertrand, Claire Bidwell Smith.

To my readers, thank you for coming along this journey with me. I hope this book can be your prism.

NOTES

INTRODUCTION

xviii **book I'd been reading at the time:** Drew Ramsey and Jennifer Iserioh, *Fifty Shades of Kale: 50 Fresh and Satisfying Recipes That Are Bound to Please* (Harper Wave, 2013).

xxiii **"climbed to the top":** Joseph Campbell, *The Hero's Journey: Joseph Campbell on His Life and Work*, ed. Phil Cousineau (New World Library, 2003), 63.

CHAPTER 1

3 **relationship between spirituality and mental health:** Lisa Miller, *The Awakened Brain: The New Science of Spirituality and Our Quest for an Inspired Life* (Random House, 2021), doi:10.3390/geriatrics 3030035.

3 **lower rates of depression and suicide:** Arjan W. Braam and Harold G. Koenig, "Religion, Spirituality and Depression in Prospective Studies: A Systematic Review," *Journal of Affective Disorders* 257 (2019): 428–38, doi:10.1016/j.jad.2019.06.063; James B. Wade et al., "Associations Between Religiosity, Spirituality, and Happiness Among Adults Living with Neurological Illness," *Geriatrics* 3, no. 3 (2018): 35, doi:10.3390/geriatrics3030035.

4 **associated with emotional regulation and resilience:** Lisa Miller

et al., "Neuroanatomical Correlates of Religiosity and Spirituality: A Study in Adults at High and Low Familial Risk for Depression," *JAMA Psychiatry* 71, no. 2 (2014): 128–35, doi:10.1001/jama psychiatry.2013.3067.

4 **"Subtle is the Lord":** Abraham Pais, *Subtle Is the Lord: The Science and the Life of Albert Einstein* (Oxford University Press, 1982), vii.

5 **"strong back, soft front, wild heart":** Brené Brown, *Dare to Lead: Brave Work. Tough Conversations. Whole Hearts* (Random House, 2018), 90.

6 **characteristic of the left hemisphere of the brain:** Simon M. McCrea, "Intuition, Insight, and the Right Hemisphere: Emergence of Higher Sociocognitive Functions," *Psychology Research and Behavior Management* 3 (2010): 1–39, doi:10.2147/prbm.s7935.

6 **characteristic of the right hemisphere:** McCrea, "Intuition, Insight."

13 **"more here than I ever was before":** Andrea Gibson, "Love Letter from the Afterlife," *Things That Don't Suck* (Substack), December 21, 2023, https://andreagibson.substack.com/p/love-letter-from-the-afterlife.

CHAPTER 2

15 **"an archetype, a cluster of powerful images":** Margot Adler, *Drawing Down the Moon: Witches, Druids, Goddess-Worshippers, and Other Pagans in America* (Penguin, 2006), 60.

16 **"*witch* deriving from the word *wit*, meaning wise":** Clarissa Pinkola Estés, *Women Who Run with the Wolves* (Random House, 1995), 89.

16 **"heretic in league with the Devil":** Michael D. Bailey, ed., *The Cambridge History of Magic and Witchcraft in the West: From Antiquity to the Present* (Cambridge University Press, 2015), 373.

16 **"both artifacts are symbols of a housewife":** Elise Loehnen, *On Our Best Behavior: The Seven Deadly Sins and the Price Women Pay to Be Good* (Random House, 2023), 76.

17 **the need for scapegoats intensified:** Loehnen, *On Our Best Behavior*, 22.

17 **"were persecuted as witches":** Loehnen, *On Our Best Behavior*, 16.

17 **Dominican monk Heinrich Kramer:** Heinrich Kramer, *Malleus Maleficarum* [Hammer of Witches], trans. Montague Summers (London: John Rodker, 1928).

18 **an estimated forty to sixty thousand people:** "Estimates of Executions (Recorded and Estimated)," The Crossroads and the Summerlands, accessed August 21, 2025, Table of Executions section, Summerlands website, www.summerlands.com/crossroads/remembrance/current.htm#Table%20of%20Executions.

18 **predominantly women:** Robert A. Rapley, *A Case of Witchcraft: The Trial of Urbain Grandier* (McGill-Queen's University Press, 2001).

18 **"friends turned on friends, daughters their mothers":** Loehnen, *On Our Best Behavior*, 17.

18 **"willing to watch each other get cut down":** Loehnen, *On Our Best Behavior*, 17–18.

19 **well documented in animal studies:** Asli Aykac and Rasime Kalkan, "Epigenetic Approach to PTSD: In the Aspects of Rat Models," *Global Medical Genetics* 9, no. 1 (2022): 7–13; Stanley Krippner and Deirdre Barrett, "Transgenerational Trauma," *The Journal of Mind and Behavior* 40, no. 1 (2019): 53–62.

19 **stressors like famine:** Bastiaan Heijmans et al., "Persistent Epigenetic Differences Associated with Prenatal Exposure to Famine in Humans," *Proceedings of the National Academy of Sciences* 105, no. 44 (2008): 17046–49, doi:10.1073/pnas.0806560105.

19 **and war:** Zara Raza et al., "Exposure to War and Conflict: The Individual and Inherited Epigenetic Effects on Health, with a Focus on Post-Traumatic Stress Disorder," *Frontiers in Epidemiology* 3 (2023), doi:10.3389/fepid.2023.1066158.

22 **"self-abandon are a coincidence":** Dené Logan, *Sovereign Love: A Guide to Healing Relationships by Reclaiming the Masculine and Feminine Within* (St. Martin's Essentials / Sounds True, 2024), 34.

CHAPTER 3

26 **characteristic of the left hemisphere of the brain:** Simon M. McCrea, "Intuition, Insight, and the Right Hemisphere: Emergence of Higher Sociocognitive Functions," *Psychology Research and Behavior Management* (2010): 1–39, doi:10.2147/prbm.s7935.

26 **characteristic of the right hemisphere:** McCrea, "Intuition, Insight."

27 **right hemisphere of the brain:** McCrea, "Intuition, Insight."

31 **being a "father's daughter":** Maureen Murdock, *The Heroine's Journey: Woman's Quest for Wholeness* (Shambhala, 1990), 20.

32 **British psychiatrist and author of *The Master and His Emissary*:** Iain McGilchrist, *The Master and His Emissary: The Divided Brain and the Making of the Western World* (Yale University Press, 2019).

32 **explicit instruction and logical sequences:** Jean-François Démonet et al., "Renewal of the Neurophysiology of Language: Functional Neuroimaging," *Physiological Reviews* 85, no. 1 (2005): 49–95, https://doi.org/10.1152/physrev.00049.2003; Michael S. Gazzaniga et al., *Cognitive Neuroscience: The Biology of the Mind*, 4th ed. (W. W. Norton, 2013), 153.

33 **in contrast, sees the big picture:** Anastasia V. Flevaris and Lynn C. Robertson, "Spatial Frequency Selection and Integration of Global and Local Information in Visual Processing: A Selective Review and Tribute to Shlomo Bentin," *Neuropsychologia* 83 (2016): 192–200, https://doi.org/10.1016/j.neuropsychologia.2015.10.024.

33 **grasps the implicit:** Leonard F. Koziol, "The Novelty–Routinization Principle of Brain Organization," in *The Myth of Executive Functioning*, ed. Leonard F. Koziol and Deborah Ely Budding (Springer, 2014), 27–31, https://doi.org/10.1007/978-3-319-04477-4_8.

33 **excels at pattern recognition:** Geoffrey Wolford et al., "The Left Hemisphere's Role in Hypothesis Formation," *Proceedings of the National Academy of Sciences of the United States of America* 97, no. 4 (2000): 1933–37, https://doi.org/10.1073/pnas.97.4.1933.

33 **learns by experience:** Elkhonon Goldberg and Luciano D. Costa, "Hemispheric Differences in the Acquisition and Use of Descriptive Systems," *Brain and Language* 14, no. 1 (1981): 144–73, https://doi.org/10.1016/0093-934X(81)90014-9.

33 **a unified symphony:** Robert J. Zatorre, Virginia B. Penhune, and Peretz Isabelle, "Spectral and Temporal Processing in Human Auditory Cortex," *Trends in Neurosciences* 25, no. 5 (2002): 255–62, doi:10.1093/cercor/11.10.946.

33 **emotional intelligence:** Guido Gainotti, "The Role of the Right Hemisphere in Emotional and Behavioral Disorders," *Frontiers in Psychology* 10 (2019): 249, https://doi.org/10.3389/fnagi.2019.00055.

33 **connection, timelessness, and peace:** Jill Bolte Taylor, "My Stroke of Insight," TED, February 2008, www.ted.com/talks/jill_bolte_taylor_my_stroke_of_insight.

33 ***It believes it's right:*** V. S. Ramachandran, "Anosognosia in Parietal Lobe Lesions," *Consciousness and Cognition* 4, no. 1 (1995): 22–51,

https://doi.org/10.1006/ccog.1995.1002; McGilchrist, *The Master and His Emissary*, xxiii.

33 **comfortable with ambiguity:** Mark Jung Beeman, "Coarse Semantic Coding and Discourse Comprehension," in *Right Hemisphere Language Comprehension*, ed. Mark Jung Beeman and Christine Chiarello (Psychology Press, 1998), 255–84.

34 **"much more likely to be correct":** Iain McGilchrist, personal email communication with the author, January 9, 2026.

34 **"right hemisphere has literally no voice":** McGilchrist, *The Master and His Emissary*, xxiii.

34 **left and right hemispheres:** Madhura Ingalhalikar et al., "Sex Differences in the Structural Connectome of the Human Brain," *Proceedings of the National Academy of Sciences* 111, no. 2 (2014): 823–28, doi:10.1073/pnas.1316909110.

34 **different types of thinking:** Ingalhalikar et al., "Sex Differences."

34 **"coordinated action":** Ingalhalikar et al., "Sex Differences."

34 **"intuitive processing modes":** Ingalhalikar et al., "Sex Differences."

34 **"My personal definition":** Jensen Huang, episode of *A Bit Personal with Jodi Shelton*, podcast, accessed January 28, 2026; original release January 2026.

38 **terrible at once:** Kate Bowler, *Everything Happens for a Reason: And Other Lies I've Loved* (Random House, 2018).

39 **surgeon:** Education and Employers, "#RedrawTheBalance—Inspiring the Future," posted March 8, 2016, YouTube, www.youtube.com/watch?v=kJP1zPOfq_0.

39 **salaries decline in lockstep:** Researchers analyzed fifty years of U.S. census data and found that pay drops when professions move from predominantly male to predominantly female—in short, if women do a job, it's likely to be low-paid, for no other reason than that women's work is undervalued. Asaf Levanon et al., "Occupational Feminization and Pay: Assessing Causal Dynamics Using 1950–2000 U.S. Census Data," *Social Forces* 88, no. 2 (2009): 865–91, https://doi.org/10.1353/sof.0.0264.

FIRST PRACTICE

46 **more sensitive to environmental cues than men:** Donald McFadden, "Sex Differences in the Auditory System," *Developmental Neuropsychology* 14, nos. 2–3 (1998): 261–98, https://doi.org/10.1080

/87565649809540712; Moa Lillqvist et al., "Comparable Responses to a Wide Range of Olfactory Stimulation in Women and Men," *Scientific Reports* 13 (2023): 9059, https://doi.org/10.1038/s41598-023-35936-5; Sami Karjalainen, "Thermal Comfort and Gender: A Literature Review," *Indoor Air* 22, no. 2 (2012): 96–109, https://doi.org/10.1111/j.1600-0668.2011.00747.x.

46 **connectivity between hemispheres:** Madhura Ingalhalikar et al., "Sex Differences in the Structural Connectome of the Human Brain," *Proceedings of the National Academy of Sciences* 111, no. 2 (2014): 823–28, https://doi.org/10.1073/pnas.1316909110.

47 **thirty to forty trillion cells:** Yusuf Khan and Aisha Farhana, "Histology, Cell," in *StatPearls [Internet]* (StatPearls Publishing, 2025), available from www.ncbi.nlm.nih.gov/sites/books/NBK554382.

47 **one hundred thousand or more:** Jianying Yang and Michael Reth, "Receptor Dissociation and B-Cell Activation," *Current Topics in Microbiology and Immunology* 393 (2016): 27–43; Beth A. Schodin et al., "Correlation Between the Number of T Cell Receptors Required for T Cell Activation and TCR–Ligand Affinity," *Immunity* 5, no. 2 (1996): 137–46, https://doi.org/10.1016/S1074-7613(00)80490-2; Sudish C. Murthy et al., "Interleukin-3 Down-Regulates Its Own Receptor," *Blood* 73, no. 5 (1989): 1180–87, https://doi.org/10.1182/blood.V73.5.1180.1180.

47 **neurons:** Frederico A. C. Azevedo et al., "Equal Numbers of Neuronal and Nonneuronal Cells Make the Human Brain an Isometrically Scaled-Up Primate Brain," *Journal of Comparative Neurology* 513, no. 5 (2000): 532–41, doi.org/10.1002/cne.21974.

47 **we're drunk:** Jia Luo, "Effects of Ethanol on the Cerebellum: Advances and Prospects," *The Cerebellum* 14, no. 4 (2015): 383–85.

CHAPTER 4

50 **microbiome:** Hamad Khalili et al., "Oral Contraceptives, Reproductive Factors and Risk of Inflammatory Bowel Disease," *Gut* 62, no. 8 (2013): 1153–59, doi:10.1136/gutjnl-2012-302362; Hamad Khalili et al., "Hormone Therapy Increases Risk of Ulcerative Colitis but Not Crohn's Disease," *Gastroenterology* 143, no. 5 (2013): 1199–206, doi:10.1053/j.gastro.2012.07.096; William V. Williams, "Hormonal Contraception and the Development of Autoimmunity: A Review of the Literature," *Linacre Quarterly* 84, no. 3 (2017): 275–95, doi:10.1080

/00243639.2017.1360065; Tessa Flood et al., "The Effect of Sex, Menstrual Cycle Phase and Oral Contraceptive Use on Intestinal Permeability and Ex-Vivo Monocyte TNFα Release Following Treatment with Lipopolysaccharide and Hyperthermia," *Cytokine* 158 (2022): 155991, doi:10.1016/j.cyto.2022.155991.

50 **impacts mood:** Therese Johansson et al., "Population-Based Cohort Study of Oral Contraceptive Use and Risk of Depression," *Epidemiology and Psychiatry Sciences* 32 (2023): 39, doi:10.1017/S2045796023000525.

50 **libido:** Amanda Boozalis et al., "Sexual Desire and Hormonal Contraception," *Obstetrics and Gynecology* 127, no. 3 (2016): 563–72, doi:10.1097/AOG.0000000000001286.

50 **vaginal lubrication:** Ariel B. Handy et al., "Reduction in Genital Sexual Arousal Varies by Type of Oral Contraceptive Pill," *The Journal of Sexual Medicine* 20, no. 8 (2023): 1094–102, doi:10.1093/jsxmed/qdad072.

50 **gut health:** Jovana Mihajlovic et al., "Combined Hormonal Contraceptives Are Associated with Minor Changes in Composition and Diversity in Gut Microbiota of Healthy Women," *Environmental Microbiology* 23, no. 6 (2021): 3037–47, doi:10.1111/1462-2920.15517.

50 **potential adverse effects:** Mohammed Miqdad et al., "Isotretinoin-Induced Inflammatory Bowel Disease: Is There a Real Association?" *Cureus* 14, no. 10 (2022): e29825, doi:10.7759/cureus.29825; J. Douglas Bremner et al., "Retinoic Acid and Affective Disorders: The Evidence for an Association," *The Journal of Clinical Psychiatry* 73, no. 1 (2012): 37–50, doi:10.4088/JCP.10r05993; "Isotretinoin 20mg Capsules," Alliance Pharmaceuticals, Internet Archive's Wayback Machine, last modified July 25, 2017.

50 **gut flora:** Mi Young Yoon and Sang Sun Yoon, "Disruption of the Gut Ecosystem by Antibiotics," *Yonsei Medical Journal* 59, no. 1 (2018): 4–12, doi:10.3349/ymj.2018.59.1.4.

51 **spinal cord:** Meenakshi Rao and Michael D. Gershon, "The Bowel and Beyond: The Enteric Nervous System in Neurological Disorders," *Nature Reviews Gastroenterology and Hepatology* 13, no. 9 (2016): 517–28, doi:10.1038/nrgastro.2016.107.

51 **body's serotonin:** Jeremy Appleton, "The Gut-Brain Axis: Influence of Microbiota on Mood and Mental Health," *Integrative Medicine* 17, no. 4 (2018): 28–32.

51 **our mood:** Anna-Chiara Schaub et al., "Clinical, Gut Microbial and Neural Effects of a Probiotic Add-On Therapy in Depressed Patients: A Randomized Controlled Trial," *Translational Psychiatry* 12 (2022): 1–10, https://doi.org/10.1038/s41398-022-01977-z.

51 **cravings:** Solveiga Samulėnaitė et al., "Gut Microbiota Signatures of Vulnerability to Food Addiction in Mice and Humans," *Gut* 72, no. 12 (2023): 2381–95, doi:10.1136/gutjnl-2023-331445.

51 **metabolism:** Andrew M. Martin et al., "The Influence of the Gut Microbiome on Host Metabolism Through the Regulation of Gut Hormone Release," *Frontiers in Physiology* 10 (2019): 428, https://doi.org/10.3389/fphys.2019.00428.

51 **chronic bloating:** Aynur Unalp-Arida and Constance E. Ruhl, "The Burden of Digestive Diseases in the United States Population," medRxiv (2023), https://doi.org/10.1101/2023.08.16.23294166.

51 **more microbial than human:** "NIH Human Microbiome Project Defines Normal Bacterial Makeup of the Body," NIH News, National Human Genome Research Institute, last modified June 13, 2012, www.genome.gov/27549144/2012-release-nih-human-microbiome-project-defines-normal-bacterial-makeup-of-the-body.

51 **antibiotics:** Martin J. Blaser, "Antibiotic Use and Its Consequences for the Normal Microbiome," *Science* 352, no. 6285 (2016): 544–45, doi:10.1126/science.aad9358.

51 **chlorinated tap water:** Katherine E. Fish et al., "Uncharted Waters: The Unintended Impacts of Residual Chlorine on Water Quality and Biofilms," *npj Biofilms Microbiomes* 6, no. 34 (2020): https://doi.org/10.1038/s41522-020-00144-w.

51 **gut lining:** Pere Puigbò et al., "Does Glyphosate Affect the Human Microbiota?" *Life* 12, no. 5 (2022): 707, doi:10.3390/life12050707.

52 **natural environment:** Martin Blaser, *Missing Microbes: How the Overuse of Antibiotics Is Fueling Our Modern Plagues* (Henry Holt, 2014). Blaser explains that the widespread use of antibiotics, changes in diet, increased sanitation, and reduced contact with natural environments have all contributed to a decline in microbial diversity. This, in turn, has been linked to the rise of various chronic diseases and conditions, as our bodies are deprived of the beneficial microbes that play essential roles in maintaining health.

52 **deep within the body:** David A. Seminowicz et al., "Regional Gray Matter Density Changes in Brains of Patients with Irritable Bowel

Syndrome," *Gastroenterology* 139, no. 1 (2010): 48–57, doi:10.1053/j.gastro.2010.03.049; Mathieu Piché et al., "Thicker Posterior Insula Is Associated with Disease Duration in Women with Irritable Bowel Syndrome (IBS) Whereas Thicker Orbitofrontal Cortex Predicts Reduced Pain Inhibition in Both IBS Patients and Controls," *The Journal of Pain* 14, no. 10 (2013): 1217–26, https://doi.org/10.1016/j.jpain.2013.05.009; Susrutha Narayanan et al., "Sex- and Gender-Related Differences in Common Functional Gastroenterologic Disorders," *Mayo Clinic Proceedings* 96, no. 4 (2021): 1071–89.

55 **alcohol:** Christiane Bode and J. Christian Bode, "Effect of Alcohol Consumption on the Gut," *Alcohol Research and Health* 27, no. 2 (2003): 575–92, https://doi.org/10.1016/S1521-6918(03)00034-9.

55 **gluten:** Giacomo Caio et al., "Effect of Gluten-Free Diet on Gut Microbiota Composition in Patients with Celiac Disease and Non-Celiac Gluten/Wheat Sensitivity," *Nutrients* 12, no. 6 (June 18, 2020): 1832, https://doi.org/10.3390/nu12061832.

55 **seed oils:** Chris Kresser, "How Industrial Seed Oils Are Making Us Sick," *Chris Kresser* (blog), February 19, 2019, https://chriskresser.com/how-industrial-seed-oils-are-making-us-sick.

55 **dairy:** M. F. Brandao Gois et al., "Role of the Gut Microbiome in Mediating Lactose Intolerance Symptoms," *Gut* 71, no. 1 (2022): 215–17, doi:10.1136/gutjnl-2020-323911.

55 **eggs:** Michimasa Fujiwara et al., "New-Onset Egg Allergy in an Adult: A Case Report," *Frontiers in Allergy* 1, no. 5 (2024): 1395807, doi:10.3389/falgy.2024.1395807.

55 **corn:** Giacomo Pasini et al., "IgE-Mediated Allergy to Corn: A 50 kDa Protein, Belonging to the Reduced Soluble Proteins, Is a Major Allergen," *Allergy* 57, no. 2 (2002): 98–106, doi:10.1034/j.1398-9995.2002.1o3413.x.

55 **soy:** Lei Wang et al., "Soybean Glycinin and β-Coglycinin Damage the Intestinal Barrier by Triggering Oxidative Stress and Inflammatory Response in Weaned Piglets," *European Journal of Nutrition* 62, no. 7 (2023): 2841–54, https://doi.org/10.1007/s00394-023-03188-8.

55 **eggplants:** Rebecca Kuang et al., "Nightshade Vegetables: A Dietary Trigger for Worsening Inflammatory Bowel Disease and Irritable Bowel Syndrome?" *Digestive Diseases and Science* 62, no. 11 (2023): 5051–59, doi:10.1007/s10620-023-07955-9.

55 **increase permeability:** Damian Maseda and Emanuela Ricciotti,

"NSAID–Gut Microbiota Interactions," *Frontiers in Pharmacology* 11 (2020): 1153, https://doi.org/10.3389/fphar.2020.01153.

55 **beneficial microbiota:** Dhrati V. Patangia et al., "Impact of Antibiotics on the Human Microbiome and Consequences for Host Health," *MicrobiologyOpen* 11, no. 1 (2022): e1260, https://doi.org/10.1002/mbo3.1260.

55 **microbiota balance:** Osamu Dohi et al., "Alterations in Gut Microbiota and Stool Properties Following Treatment with Potassium-Competitive Acid Blocker and Proton Pump Inhibitor," *Digestive Diseases and Sciences* 70 (2025): 3705–15, https://doi.org/10.1007/s10620-025-09228-z.

55 **altered microbiota:** Julian Brito et al., "Hormonal Birth Control Is Associated with Altered Gut Microbiota β-Diversity in Physically Active Females Across the Menstrual Cycle: A Pilot Trial," *Journal of Applied Physiology* 138, no. 3 (2025): 739–45, https://doi.org/10.1152/japplphysiol.00008.2025.

55 **some studies:** Khalili et al., "Oral Contraceptives, Reproductive Factors and Risk of Inflammatory Bowel Disease."

55 **motility changes:** Yasmine Ait Chait et al., "Unravelling the Antimicrobial Action of Antidepressants on Gut Commensal Microbes," *Scientific Reports* 21, no. 10 (2020): 17878, doi:10.1038/s41598-020-74934-9.

56 **immune-gut interaction:** Gen Zheng et al., "Corticosterone Mediates Stress-Related Increased Intestinal Epithelial Permeability in Rats," *Scientific Reports* 3 (2013): 2430, https://doi.org/10.1111/nmo.12066.

56 **SIBO:** Chunchun Yang et al., "Small Intestinal Bacterial Overgrowth and Evaluation of Intestinal Barrier Function in Patients with Ulcerative Colitis," *American Journal of Translational Research* 13, no. 6 (2021): 6605–10.

56 **Parasites:** Ahsan Naveed and Sabahat Abdullah, "Impact of Parasitic Infection on Human Gut Ecology and Immune Regulations," *Translational Medicine Communications* 6, no. 1 (2021): 11, https://doi.org/10.1186/s41231-021-00091-4.

56 **Dysbiosis:** Uday Ghoshal and Ujjala Ghoshal, "Small Intestinal Bacterial Overgrowth and Other Intestinal Disorders," *Gastroenterology Clinic* 46, no. 1 (2017): 103–20, doi:10.1016/j.gtc.2016.09.008.

56 **Bone broth:** Ayah Matar et al., "Bone Broth Benefits: How Its Nutrients Fortify Gut Barrier in Health and Disease," *Digestive Diseases and Sciences* 70 (2025): 1951–61, https://doi.org/10.1007/s10620-025-08997-x.

56 **apple cider vinegar:** Natasha K. Leeuwendaal et al., "Fermented Foods, Health and the Gut Microbiome," *Nutrients* 14, no. 7 (2022): 1527, https://doi.org/10.3390/nu14071527.

56 **yucca:** Zhao Chen et al., "Resistant Starch and the Gut Microbiome: Exploring Beneficial Interactions and Dietary Impacts," *Food Chemistry: X* 21 (2024): 101118, https://doi.org/10.1016/j.fochx.2024.101118.

56 **clarified butter:** Deepshikha Kataria and Gurmeet Singh, "Health Benefits of Ghee: Review of Ayurveda and Modern Science Perspectives," *Journal of Ayurveda and Integrative Medicine* 15, no. 1 (2024): 100819, https://doi.org/10.1016/j.jaim.2023.100819.

56 **collagen:** Mariette Abrahams et al., "Effect of a Daily Collagen Peptide Supplement on Digestive Symptoms in Healthy Women: 2-Phase Mixed Methods Study," *JMIR Formative Research* 6, no. 5 (2022): e36339, https://doi.org/10.2196/36339.

56 **L-glutamine:** Brett J. Deters and Mir Saleem, "The Role of Glutamine in Supporting Gut Health and Neuropsychiatric Factors," *Food Science and Human Wellness* 10, no. 2 (2021): 149–54, https://doi.org/10.1016/j.fshw.2021.02.003.

56 **lactoferrin:** Weiru Yu et al., "Lactoferrin Promotes Intestinal Stem Cell–Mediated Recovery After Gut Injury in Mice and Organoids," *Food Frontiers* 5, no. 5 (2024): 2290–304, doi:10.1002/fft2.408.

56 **beta-glucan:** Ravendra Pal Singh et al., "β-Glucans: A Potential Source for Maintaining Gut Microbiota and Immune Homeostasis," *Frontiers in Nutrition* 10 (2023): 10198134.

56 **bovine colostrum:** Maciej Hałasa et al., "Oral Supplementation with Bovine Colostrum Decreases Intestinal Permeability in Subjects with Mild Gut Barrier Impairment," *Nutrients* 9, no. 4 (2017): 370.

56 **DGL (deglycyrrhizinated licorice):** Elham Zaeif Khorasani et al., "Efficacy of Glycyrrhiza glabra on Peptic Ulcer Disease: A Systematic Review and Meta-Analysis," *Advances in Integrative Medicine* 12, no. 4 (December 2025): 100485, https://doi.org/10.1016/j.aimed.2025.100485.

56 **prebiotics:** Paulina Markowiak and Katarzyna Śliżewska, "Effects of Probiotics, Prebiotics, and Synbiotics on Human Health," *Nutrients* 9, no. 9 (2017): 1021, https://doi.org/10.3390/nu9091021.

56 **magnesium glycinate or citrate:** Sepideh Mahboobi et al., "Effects of Probiotic and Magnesium Co-Supplementation on Mood, Cognition, Intestinal Barrier Function and Inflammation in Individuals with Obesity and Depressed Mood: A Randomized, Double-Blind Placebo-Controlled Clinical Trial," *Frontiers in Nutrition* 9 (2022): 1018357, https://doi.org/10.3389/fnut.2022.1018357.

56 **fiber:** Jiongxing Fu et al., "Dietary Fiber Intake and Gut Microbiota in Human Health," *Microorganisms* 10, no. 12 (2022): 2507, https://doi.org/10.3390/microorganisms10122507.

56 **kiwi:** Richard Gearry et al., "Consumption of Two Green Kiwifruits Daily Improves Constipation and Abdominal Comfort: Results of an International Multicenter Randomized Controlled Trial," *American Journal of Gastroenterology* 118, no. 6 (2023): 1058–68, https://doi.org/10.14309/ajg.0000000000002124.

56 **triphala:** Pulok K. Mukherjee et al., "Clinical Study of Triphala—a Well-Known Phytomedicine from India," *Indian Journal of Experimental Biology* 44, no. 5 (2006): 414–17.

56 **aloe:** Seung Wook Hong et al., "Aloe Vera Is Effective and Safe in Short-Term Treatment of Irritable Bowel Syndrome: A Systematic Review and Meta-Analysis," *Journal of Neurogastroenterology and Motility* 24, no. 4 (2018): 528–35, https://doi.org/10.5056/jnm18077.

56 **chanting:** Bangalore G. Kalyani et al., "Neurohemodynamic Correlates of 'OM' Chanting: A Pilot Functional Magnetic Resonance Imaging Study," *International Journal of Yoga* 4, no. 1 (2011): 3–6, https://doi.org/10.4103/0973-6131.78171.

56 **humming:** Henna Korkalainen, *The Use of Humming: A Narrative Literature Review on Nasal Humming in Stress and Anxiety Alleviation* (master's thesis, University of Jyväskylä, 2025), https://urn.fi/URN:NBN:fi:jyu-202506195539.

56 **gargling:** "What Is the Vagus Nerve?" Food for the Brain Foundation, https://foodforthebrain.org/supporting-vagus-nerve-function-is-this-the-missing-link-to-improving-mental-health.

56 **meditation:** Ying Sun et al., "Alteration of Faecal Microbiota Balance Related to Long-Term Deep Meditation," *General Psychiatry* (2023): e100893.

CHAPTER 5

61 **before the age of eighteen:** David Finkelhor et al., "The Lifetime Prevalence of Child Sexual Abuse and Sexual Assault Assessed in Late Adolescence," *Journal of Adolescent Health* 55 (2014): 329–33.

61 **at some point in their lives:** Kathleen C. Basile et al., "The National Intimate Partner and Sexual Violence Survey: 2016/2017 Report on Sexual Violence," Centers for Disease Control and Prevention, 2022, www.cdc.gov/nisvs/documentation/nisvsReportonSexualViolence.pdf.

63 **excluded women from clinical trials:** Henry A. Waxman et al., "Women's Health. FDA Needs to Ensure More Study of Gender Differences in Prescription Drug Testing," U.S. Government Accountability Office, 1992.

64 **heart attacks:** Kevin A. Bybee and Tracy L. Stevens, "Matters of the Heart: Cardiovascular Disease in U.S. Women," *Missouri Medicine* 110, no. 1 (2013): 65–70.

64 **fatal ones:** "Heart Disease Death Rate by Sex Chart, 2023," Kaiser Family Foundation website, accessed May 7, 2024, www.kff.org/other/state-indicator/heart-disease-death-rate-by-sex.

64 **non-Hispanic white women:** Donna L. Hoyert, "Health E-Stat: Maternal Mortality Rates in the United States, 2021," U.S. Centers for Disease Control and Prevention, 2023, accessed December 18, 2025, www.cdc.gov/nchs/data/hestat/maternal-mortality/2021/maternal-mortality-rates-2021.pdf.

65 **"keeping the score":** Bessel van der Kolk, *The Body Keeps the Score: Brain, Mind, and Body in the Healing of Trauma* (Penguin, 2015).

67 **7 percent of men:** Nathalie Conrad et al., "Incidence, Prevalence, and Co-Occurrence of Autoimmune Disorders over Time and by Age, Sex, and Socioeconomic Status: A Population-Based Cohort Study of 22 Million Individuals in the UK," *The Lancet* 401, no. 10391 (2023): 1878–90, doi:10.1016/S0140-6736(23)00457-9.

67 **epidemic of autoimmune disorders is multifactorial:** Huihui Xu et al., "The Dynamic Interplay Between the Gut Microbiota and Autoimmune Diseases," *Journal of Immunology Research* 2019, no. 1 (2019): 7546047, doi:10.1155/2019/7546047.

69 **higher ACE (adverse childhood experience) scores:** Shanta R. Dube et al., "Cumulative Childhood Stress and Autoimmune Diseases

in Adults," *Psychosomatic Medicine* 71, no. 2 (2009): 243–50, doi: 10.1097/PSY.0b013e3181907888.

69 **chronic stress:** Huan Song et al., "Association of Stress-Related Disorders with Subsequent Autoimmune Disease," *JAMA* 319, no. 23 (2018): 2388–2400, doi:10.1001/jama.2018.7028.

69 **genetics:** Adem Akçakaya, "Hashimoto's Thyroiditis from the General Surgeon's Perspective," *Bezmialem Science* 12, no. 1 (2024): 1–6, doi:10.14235/bas.galenos.2024.21704.

69 **inflammation:** Karolina Wrońska et al., "The Role of the Immune System in the Course of Hashimoto's Thyroiditis: The Current State of Knowledge," *International Journal of Molecular Sciences* 25, no. 13 (2024): 6883, doi:10.3390/ijms25136883.

69 **environmental triggers:** Wrońska et al., "The Role of the Immune System in the Course of Hashimoto's Thyroiditis."

69 **thyroid transglutaminase:** Gregory A. Brent, "Environmental Exposures and Autoimmune Thyroid Disease," *Thyroid* 20, no. 7 (2010): 755–61, doi:10.1089/thy.2010.1636.

69 **immune function:** Janice Kiecolt-Glaser et al., "Inflammation: Depression Fans the Flames and Feasts on the Heat," *American Journal of Psychiatry* 172, no. 11 (2015): 1075–91, https://doi.org/10.1176/appi.ajp.2015.15020152; Janice Kiecolt-Glaser et al., "Emotions, Morbidity, and Mortality: New Perspectives from Psychoneuroimmunology," *Annual Review of Psychology* 53 (2002): 83–107, doi:10.1146/annurev.psych.53.100901.135217.

72 **"puzzle to be solved":** Kate Bowler, *Everything Happens for a Reason: And Other Lies I've Loved* (Random House, 2018), 119.

72 **"the math doesn't math":** Kate Bowler, conversation with the author, May 22, 2024.

73 **little by little:** Madeline Miller, *Circe* (Little, Brown, 2018), 85.

CHAPTER 6

80 **your gut:** Michael D. Gershon and Jan Tack, "The Serotonin Signaling System: From Basic Understanding to Drug Development for Functional GI Disorders," *Gastroenterology* 132, no. 1 (2007): 397–414, doi:10.1053/j.gastro.2006.11.002.

80 **clotting:** Jessica A. Maclean and Simone M. Schoenwaelder, "Serotonin in Platelets," in *Serotonin: The Mediator That Spans Evolution,*

ed. Paul M. Pilowsky (Academic Press, 2019): 91–119, doi:10.1016/B978-0-12-800050-2.00005-X.

80 **serotonin levels and depression:** Joanna Moncrieff et al., "The Serotonin Theory of Depression: A Systematic Umbrella Review of the Evidence," *Molecular Psychiatry* 28 (2023): 3243–56, https://doi.org/10.1038/s41380-022-01661-0.

81 **our life circumstances:** Julia Ross, *The Mood Cure: The 4-Step Program to Take Charge of Your Emotions—Today* (Penguin, 2002).

86 **may not be his:** This quotation is widely attributed to Jiddu Krishnamurti, though the Krishnamurti Foundation notes it does not appear verbatim in his works. The closest source is *Commentaries on Living, Series III* (Harper & Brothers, 1960), where he wrote, "Why should the individual adjust himself to an unhealthy society? If he is healthy, he will not be a part of it." The phrase may have been popularized by Mark Vonnegut in *The Eden Express: A Memoir of Insanity* (Praeger, 1975).

88 **"sweat, tears, or the sea":** Isak Dinesen, *Seven Gothic Tales* (Knopf Doubleday, 1991), 39.

89 **leucine-enkephalin:** Hao Liang et al., "Non-Targeted Metabolomics Analysis Reveals Distinct Metabolic Profiles Between Positive and Negative Emotional Tears of Humans," *Cureus* 15, no. 8 (2023): e42985, doi 10.7759/cureus.42985.

89 **stress response:** Emily Nagoski and Amelia Nagoski, *Burnout: The Secret to Unlocking the Stress Cycle* (Ballantine Books, 2019).

95 **take antidepressants:** Tara A. LeGates et al., "Sex Differences in Antidepressant Efficacy," *Neuropsychopharmacology* 44, no. 1 (2019): 140–54, doi:10.1038/s41386-018-0156-z.

CHAPTER 7

98 **As Mory Fontanez, author of *Higher Self*:** Mory Fontanez, *Higher Self: Reclaiming the Power of Your Intuition* (Dey Street Books, 2025).

98 **"to happen to you":** Mory Fontanez, remarks during a women's retreat attended by the author, Ojai, California, October 2024.

99 **"difference":** Fatima Khadijah, Instagram post, August 26, 2025.

99 **"even exciting":** Mory Fontanez remarks during a women's retreat attended by the author, Ojai, California, October 2024.

100 **"so peaceful":** Ayesha Ophelia, Instagram post, November 10, 2025.

101 **love, joy, peace:** David R. Hawkins, *The Map of Consciousness Explained: A Proven Energy Scale to Actualize Your Ultimate Potential* (Hay House, 2020).

101 **brain's electrical activity:** HeartMath Institute, "Energetic Communication (Science of the Heart)," HeartMath Institute website, accessed August 26, 2025.

102 **"'for the highest good'":** Roya Darling, conversation with the author, November 30, 2025.

102 **"most powerful offering":** Roya Darling, Instagram post, September 23, 2025, www.instagram.com/p/DO6E4WCkYDM.

103 **vagus nerve:** Björn Vickhoff et al., "Music Structure Determines Heart Rate Variability of Singers," *Frontiers in Psychology* 4 (2013): 334, https://doi.org/10.3389/fpsyg.2013.00334. Singing produces slow, regular, and deep respiration, which in turn triggers respiratory sinus arrhythmia (RSA). This causes a pulsating vagal activity, which, together with sympathetic activity, is interpreted in the context of Porges's polyvagal theory of communication.

103 **stress a nervous system:** Uwe Geier, "Practical Investigation of the Impact of Classroom Lighting on Student Behaviour: A Comparison of LED and Incandescent Light," *ROSE: Research on Steiner Education* 9, no. 2 (2018): 73–83.

104 **"Anchor oneness within you":** Roya Darling, Instagram post, September 13, 2025.

105 **"affects the whole":** Roya Darling, conversation with the author, October 21, 2025.

106 **"heat death":** Gordon F. W. Drake, "Thermodynamics," Britannica, www.britannica.com/science/thermodynamics/Entropy-and-heat-death.

CHAPTER 8

113 **makes us feel sleepy:** Seithikurippu R. Pandi-Perumal et al., "Role of the Melatonin System in the Control of Sleep: Therapeutic Implications," *CNS Drugs* 21, no. 12 (2007): 995–1018, https://doi.org/10.2165/00023210-200721120-00004.

113 **suppresses melatonin release:** Christian Cajochen et al., "High Sensitivity of Human Melatonin, Alertness, Thermoregulation, and Heart Rate to Short-Wavelength Light," *Journal of Clinical Endocri-*

nology and Metabolism 90, no. 3 (2005): 1311–16, https://doi.org/10.1210/jc.2004-0957.

113 **keep us engaged:** Luke Munn, "Angry by Design: Toxic Communication and Technical Architectures," *Humanities and Social Sciences Communications* 7, no. 53 (2020): 1–11, https://doi.org/10.1057/s41599-020-00550-7.

114 **take a back seat:** Amy F. T. Arnsten, "Stress Signalling Pathways That Impair Prefrontal Cortex Structure and Function," *Nature Reviews Neuroscience* 10, no. 6 (2009): 410–22, https://doi.org/10.1038/nrn2648.

114 **survival-driven functions:** Kerry Ressler, "Amygdala Activity, Fear, and Anxiety: Modulation by Stress," *Biological Psychiatry* 67, no. 12 (2010): 1117–19, doi:10.1016/j.biopsych.2010.04.027.

114 **as well as empathy:** Matt T. Richins et al., "Incidental Fear Reduces Empathy for an Out-Group's Pain," *Emotion* 21, no. 3 (2021) 536–54, doi:10.1037/emo0000714.

114 **big-picture thinking:** Alexander J. Shackman et al., "Stress Potentiates Early and Attenuates Late Stages of Visual Processing," *Journal of Neuroscience* 31, no. 3 (2011): 1156–61, doi:10.1523/JNEUROSCI.3384-10.2011.

114 **"unhappiness has burned out":** Andrea Gibson, "Post-Election Letter to a Friend," *Things That Don't Suck* (Substack), November 14, 2024, https://andreagibson.substack.com/p/post-election-letter-to-a-friend.

115 **"show up to the world's pain":** Gibson, "Post-Election Letter to a Friend."

115 **"radical choice we can make":** Roya Darling, Instagram post, September 15, 2025, www.instagram.com/royadarlinghealing.

117 **second wind of energy:** Nora A. O'Byrne et al., "Sleep and Circadian Regulation of Cortisol: A Short Review," *Current Opinion in Endocrine and Metabolic Research* 18 (2022): 178–86, https://doi.org/10.1016/j.coemr.2021.03.011.

117 **better quality sleep:** Helen J. Burgess and Charmane I. Eastman, "Early Versus Late Bedtimes Phase Shift the Human Dim Light Melatonin Rhythm Despite a Fixed Morning Lights on Time," *American Journal of Physiology–Regulatory, Integrative and Comparative Physiology* 286, no. 5 (2004): 115–18, https://doi.org/10.1016/j.neulet.2003.11.032.

117 **helps with sleep:** Reza Abbasi et al., "The Effect of Magnesium Supplementation on Primary Insomnia in Elderly Patients: A Double-Blind Placebo-Controlled Clinical Trial," *Journal of Research in Medical Sciences: The Official Journal of Isfahan University of Medical Sciences* 17, no. 12 (2012): 1161–69.

117 **headaches:** Lisa A. Yablon and Alexander Mauskop, "Magnesium in Headache," in *Magnesium in the Central Nervous System*, ed. Robert Vink and Mihai Nechifor (University of Adelaide Press, 2011), 125–34, www.ncbi.nlm.nih.gov/books/NBK507271.

117 **menstrual cramps:** Fabio Parazzini et al., "Magnesium in the Gynecological Practice: A Literature Review," *Magnesium Research* 30, no. 1 (2017): 1–7.

117 **anxiety:** Susan Anderson and George Williams, "Does Magnesium Supplementation Decrease Anxiety in Adults?" *Evidence-Based Practice* 24, no. 2 (2021): 21–22.

117 **digestion:** Lili Zhang et al., "Association of Dietary Magnesium Intake with Chronic Constipation Among U.S. Adults: Evidence from the National Health and Nutrition Examination Survey," *Food Science and Nutrition* 9 (2021): 6634–41.

117 **deficient:** Jeroen H. F. de Baaij et al., "Magnesium in Man: Implications for Health and Disease," *Physiological Reviews* 95, no. 1 (2015): 1–46, https://doi.org/10.1152/physrev.00012.2014.

117 **progesterone levels:** Marek Milewicz et al., "Vitex Agnus Castus in the Treatment of Luteal Phase Defects Due to Latent Hyperprolactinemia," *Arzneimittel-Forschung* 43, no. 3 (1993): 752–56.

118 **"image of your mind":** Byron Katie, *Loving What Is: Four Questions That Can Change Your Life* (Three Rivers Press, 2002), 76.

119 **Be Still, and Know:** Psalm 46:10, *The Holy Bible* (King James Version).

121 **"sell nylons":** Alan Taylor, dir., *Mad Men*, Season 1, episode 1, "Smoke Gets in Your Eyes," AMC, July 19, 2007.

123 ***Quit Like a Woman:*** Holly Whitaker, *Quit Like a Woman: The Radical Choice to Not Drink in a Culture Obsessed with Alcohol* (Dial Press, 2019).

124 **coming back for more:** Anahad O'Connor, "Many of Today's Unhealthy Foods Were Brought to You by Big Tobacco," *The Washington Post*, September 19, 2023, www.washingtonpost.com/wellness/2023/09/19/addiction-foods-hyperpalatable-tobacco.

125 **antioxidants:** Monika Sztretye et al., "Astaxanthin: A Potential Mitochondrial-Targeted Antioxidant Treatment in Diseases and with Aging," *Oxidative Medicine and Cellular Longevity*, no. 1 (2019): 3849692, doi:10.1155/2019/3849692; Ezgi Dogan et al., "Relationship Between Color and Antioxidant Capacity of Fruits and Vegetables," *Current Research in Food Science* 2 (2019): 1–10, doi:10.1016/j.crfs.2019.11.001.

127 **"suffering in paradise":** Katie, *Loving What Is*, 76.

CHAPTER 9

131 **"It was a disguise":** Anaïs Nin, *The Diary of Anaïs Nin, 1944–1947*, vol. 4 (Harcourt Brace Jovanovich, 1971), 138.

134 **"lies we tell ourselves":** Geneen Roth, *Love Finally: Choosing Yourself in a World of Endless Options* (Dial Press, 2018), 138.

134 ***Choosing Wholeness over Goodness:*** Elise Loehnen and Courtney Smith, *Choosing Wholeness over Goodness: A Process for Reclaiming Your Full Self* (Dial Press, 2025).

139 **"learned how to please":** Glennon Doyle, *Untamed* (Dial Press, 2020).

140 **faced greater risks than men:** Tracy Vaillancourt et al., "Behavioral and Neural Responses to Social Exclusion in Women: The Role of Facial Attractiveness and Friendliness," *Scientific Reports* 14, no. 1 (2024): 15135, doi:10.1038/s41598-024-65833-4.

140 **physical pain:** Ethan Kross et al., "Social Rejection Shares Somatosensory Representations with Physical Pain," *Proceedings of the National Academy of Sciences* 108, no. 15 (March 28, 2011): 6270–75, https://doi.org/10.1073/pnas.1102693108.

140 **stronger in women:** Theodoris Giovazolias and Eirini Paschalidi, "The Effect of Rejection Sensitivity on Fear of Intimacy in Emerging Adulthood: A Moderated-Mediation Model," *European Journal of Psychology Open* 81, no. 1 (2022): 1–12, doi:10.1024/2673-8627/a000019.

140 **Among female primates:** Joan B. Silk, Susan C. Alberts, and Jeanne Altmann, "Social Bonds of Female Baboons Enhance Infant Survival," *Science* 302, no. 5648 (2003): 1231–1234. https://doi.org/10.1126/science.1088580. Research has shown that in some primate species, particularly those with complex social structures, such as certain species of monkeys and apes, female-female relationships and

social bonds can have an impact on reproductive success. Here are some key points from relevant research:

- Social bonds and cooperation: Female primates often form social bonds and alliances with other females within their group. These bonds can be important for various reasons, including protection against predators, access to resources, and support during conflicts.
- Access to mating opportunities: In some cases, having strong social bonds with other females can provide a female with access to mating opportunities. For example, dominant females in some primate groups may allow subordinate females to mate with high-ranking males.
- Infant care and assistance: Female primates may cooperate in the care of infants. Having a network of females who provide support and assistance with raising offspring can contribute to higher reproductive success.
- Social status and reproduction: Social status within a group can also play a role in reproductive success. High-ranking females may have better access to resources and may be more successful in raising offspring to maturity.

140 **dominance rank:** Joan B. Silk et al., "The Benefits of Social Capital: Close Social Bonds Among Female Baboons Enhance Offspring Survival," *Proceedings of the Royal Society B: Biological Sciences* 276, no. 1670 (2009): 3099–104, doi:10.1098/rspb.2009.0681.

141 ***The Anxious Generation:*** Jonathan Haidt, *The Anxious Generation: How the Great Rewiring of Childhood Is Causing an Epidemic of Mental Illness* (Penguin, 2024).

141 **52 percent increase:** Jean M. Twenge, "Increases in Depression, Self-Harm and Suicide Among U.S. Adolescents After 2012 and Links to Technology Use: Possible Mechanisms," *Psychiatric Research and Clinical Practice* 2, no. 1 (2020): 19–25, doi:10.1176/appi.prcp.20190015.

141 **36 percent for boys:** Jonaki Bose et al., "2015 National Survey on Drug Use and Health," Detailed Tables, Substance Abuse and Mental Health Services Administration, September 8, 2016, www.samhsa.gov/data/data-we-collect/nsduh-national-survey-drug-use-and-health/national-releases/2015#detailed-tables.

141 **from 2009 to 2015:** Melissa C. Mercado et al., "Trends in Emergency Department Visits for Nonfatal Self-Inflicted Injuries Among Youth Aged 10–24 Years in the United States, 2001–2015," *JAMA* 318, no. 19 (2017): 1931–33, doi:10.1001/jama.2017.13317.

142 **likability penalty:** Madeline E. Heilman and Tyler G. Okimoto, "Why Are Women Penalized for Success at Male Tasks?: The Implied Communality Deficit," *Journal of Applied Psychology* 92, no. 1 (2007): 81–92, https://doi.org/10.1037/0021-9010.92.1.81.

144 **social conditioning:** Abdul-Fattah Yafai et al., "Social Conformity and Autism Spectrum Disorder: A Child-Friendly Take on a Classic Study," *Autism* 18, no. 8 (2014): 1007–13, https://doi.org/10.1177/1362361313508023.

144 **synaptic pruning:** Guomei Tang et al., "Loss of mTOR-Dependent Macroautophagy Causes Autistic-Like Synaptic Pruning Deficits," *Neuron* 83, no. 5 (2014): 1131–43, https://doi.org/10.1016/j.neuron.2014.07.040.

144 **documented correlation:** Carolina Baeza-Velasco et al., "Autism in the Context of Joint Hypermobility, Hypermobility Spectrum Disorders, and Ehlers-Danlos Syndromes: A Systematic Review and Prevalence Meta-Analyses," *Autism* 29, no. 8 (2025): 1939–58.

144 **"neurotypical people filter out":** Laura Lynne Jackson, *Guided: The Secret Path to an Illuminated Life* (Dial Press, 2025), 92.

145 **"single linear channel":** Kristina Kyser, Instagram post, November 23, 2025, www.instagram.com/kristina.kyser.phd.

146 **"hunted and smeared":** Jameela Jamil, Instagram post, April 22, 2020, www.instagram.com/jameelajamil/p/B_SubIoDASW/?img_index=1.

147 **"trained for power":** Elise Loehnen, *On Our Best Behavior: The Seven Deadly Sins and the Price Women Pay to Be Good* (Random House, 2023), 11.

147 **"'I don't care'":** Elise Loehnen, conversation with the author, May 18, 2023.

148 **A fascinating metastudy:** Tania A. Reynolds et al., "Bless Her Heart: Gossip Phrased with Concern Provides Advantages in Female Intrasexual Competition," *Journal of Experimental Social Psychology* 116 (2025): 104670, https://doi.org/10.1016/j.jesp.2024.104670.

148 **spread information maliciously:** Reynolds et al., "Bless Her Heart."

CHAPTER 10

161 **"behind all life":** Mehul Kiritkumar Nayak, *The Divine Path to Motherhood: Seven Spiritual Laws for a Blissful Pregnancy* (OrangeBooks Publication, 2024), 31.

164 **declines throughout the day:** Michael J. Diver et al., "Diurnal Rhythms of Serum Total, Free and Bioavailable Testosterone and of SHBG in Middle-Aged Men Compared with Those in Young Men," *Clinical Endocrinology* 58, no. 6 (2003): 710–17, https://doi.org/10.1046/j.1365-2265.2003.01772.

165 **affect women differently:** Sushil Kumar and Gurcharan Kaur, "Intermittent Fasting Dietary Restriction Regimen Negatively Influences Reproduction in Young Rats: A Study of Hypothalamo-Hypophysial-Gonadal Axis," *PLOS One* 8, no. 1 (2013): e52416, https://doi.org/10.1371/journal.pone.0052416.

165 **hormonal cascades:** Chayarndorn Phumsatitpong et al., "Neuroendocrine Interactions of the Stress and Reproductive Axes," *Frontiers in Neuroendocrinology* 63 (2021): 100940, https://doi.org/10.1016/j.yfrne.2021.100928.

165 **seasonal cycles:** Azra Bertrand, conversation with the author, November 7, 2024.

165 **adopted in 1582:** Editors, "Gregorian Calendar," Britannica, www.britannica.com/science/Gregorian-calendar.

166 **lunar and menstrual cycles:** Dwayne Meisner, "The Evolution of the Roman Calendar," *Past Imperfect* 15 (2009): 290–309.

171 **nonverbal understanding:** Elseline Hoekzema et al., "Pregnancy Leads to Long-Lasting Changes in Human Brain Structure," *Nature Neuroscience* 20 (2017): 287–96, https://doi.org/10.1038/nn.4458.

CHAPTER 11

177 **impact mood:** Charlotte Wessel Skovlund et al., "Association of Hormonal Contraception with Depression," *JAMA Psychiatry* 73, no. 11 (2016): 1154–62, https://doi.org/10.1001/jamapsychiatry.2016.2387.

178 **antidepressant:** Skovlund et al., "Association of Hormonal Contraception with Depression."

178 **reduce vaginal lubrication:** Ariel B. Handy et al., "Reduction in Genital Sexual Arousal Varies by Type of Oral Contraceptive Pill,"

The Journal of Sexual Medicine 20, no. 8 (2023): 1094–102, https://doi.org/10.1093/jsxmed/qdad072.

178 **decrease libido for some:** Y. Zimmerman et al., "The Effect of Combined Oral Contraception on Testosterone Levels in Healthy Women: A Systematic Review and Meta-Analysis," *Database of Abstracts of Reviews of Effects (DARE): Quality-Assessed Reviews, Human Reproduction Update* 20, no. 1 (2014): 76–105, www.ncbi.nlm.nih.gov/books/NBK164632; Amanda Boozalis et al., "Sexual Desire and Hormonal Contraception," *Obstetrics and Gynecology* 127, no. 3 (2016): 563–72, doi:10.1097/AOG.0000000000001286.

178 **stopping the Pill:** Claudia Panzer et al., "Impact of Oral Contraceptives on Sex Hormone–Binding Globulin and Androgen Levels: A Retrospective Study in Women with Sexual Dysfunction," *The Journal of Sexual Medicine* 3, no. 1 (2006): 104–13, doi:10.1111/j.1743-6109.2005.00198.x. Long-term follow-up at six months and even at twelve months after cessation of the Pill showed sustained changes in circulating androgen levels, implying lowered libido long after oral contraceptive use. The science behind this is that exogenous hormones prompt the liver to secrete a substance called sex hormone–binding globulin (SHBG), which then binds the circulating androgen (the male sex hormone, more colloquially called testosterone), making it unavailable. Thus the Pill effectively reduces a woman's androgen, or male sex hormone, level. Since both male and female libido relies primarily on androgen levels, this effect of the Pill might give us clear skin, but it also reduces libido and vaginal lubrication. While there haven't been studies to examine whether SHBG remains elevated beyond a year after cessation of the Pill (which is itself disconcerting—why isn't it a priority to get this information?), it stands to reason that this impact on libido might be an enduring adverse side effect of the Pill.

178 **evade medical research:** Martha K. McClintock, "Menstrual Synchrony and Suppression," *Nature* 229, no. 5282 (1971): 244–45. https://doi.org/10.1038/229244a0. The original theory, proposed by Martha McClintock in 1971, suggested that pheromones could be responsible for synchronizing menstrual cycles. According to the theory, these chemical signals are subconsciously detected through smell and could influence the timing of menstrual cycles in close-living females. The mechanism has often been speculated to be evo-

lutionary, perhaps serving to facilitate communal childcare or mate selection in ancestral environments.

178 **connection:** Claus Wedekind et al., "MHC-Dependent Mate Preferences in Humans," *Proceedings of the Royal Society B: Biological Sciences* 260, no. 1359 (1995): 245–49, https://doi.org/10.1098/rspb.1995.0087.

179 **theoretically via pheromones:** S. Craig Roberts et al., "MHC-Correlated Odour Preferences in Humans and the Use of Oral Contraceptives," *Proceedings of the Royal Society B: Biological Sciences* 275, no. 1652 (2008): 2715–22, doi:10.1098/rspb.2008.0825.

179 **from their own:** Roberts et al., "MHC-Correlated Odour Preferences in Humans."

179 **spotting:** "IUD Aftercare Instructions," University of Washington Department of Obstetrics and Gynecology, accessed February 11, 2025, www.uwmedicine.org/sites/stevie/files/2018-11/IUD-Aftercare-Instructions.pdf.

179 **bloating:** Megan M. Freeland, "Do IUDs Cause Weight Gain?" GoodRx, accessed February 11, 2025, www.goodrx.com/conditions/birth-control/do-iuds-cause-weight-gain.

179 **mood changes:** U.S. Food and Drug Administration, Mirena (levonorgestrel-releasing intrauterine system) prescribing information, revised May 2020, accessed February 11, 2025, www.accessdata.fda.gov/drugsatfda_docs/label/2020/021225s040lbl.pdf.

180 **"body on her own":** Katinka Locascio, conversation with the author, December 11, 2025.

180 **"shortcut":** Locascio, conversation, December 11, 2025.

183 **inflammation:** Ellen B. Gold et al., "The Association of Inflammation Markers with Premenstrual Symptoms," *Journal of Women's Health* 25, no. 9 (2016): 865–74, doi:10.1089/jwh.2015.552.

183 **nutrient deficiencies:** Nahid Fathizadeh et al., "Effect of Magnesium and Vitamin B6 Supplementation on Premenstrual Syndrome: A Randomized Trial," *Iranian Journal of Midwifery Research* 15, no. 1 (2010): 401–5.

183 **thyroid dysfunction:** P. J. Schmidt et al., "Thyroid Function in Women with Prospectively Confirmed Premenstrual Syndrome," *The Journal of Clinical Endocrinology and Metabolism* 76, no. 3 (1993): 671–77.

183 **endometriosis:** Ryan Heitmann et al., "Premenstrual Spotting of ≥2 Days Is Strongly Associated with Histologically Confirmed Endo-

metriosis in Women with Infertility," *American Journal of Obstetrics and Gynecology* 211, no. 4 (2014): 358.e1–358.e6.

183 **uterine fibroids:** Antonia Navarro et al., "Understanding the Impact of Uterine Fibroids on Human Endometrium Function," *Frontiers in Cell and Developmental Biology* 9 (2021): 633180.

185 **egg:** David F. Katz, "Human Cervical Mucus: Research Update," *American Journal of Obstetrics and Gynecology* 164, no. 5 Pt 1 (1991): 1984–86, https://pubmed.ncbi.nlm.nih.gov/1755453. (Mucus admits, filters, nurtures, and stores sperm for transport.)

187 ***Joyful:*** Ingrid Fetell Lee, *Joyful: The Surprising Power of Ordinary Things to Create Extraordinary Happiness* (Little, Brown Spark, 2018).

187 **"infantilize us":** Ingrid Fetell Lee, conversation with the author, August 5, 2025.

188 **Naisha Ahsian:** Naisha Ahsian, *The Crystal Ally Cards: The Crystal Path to Self Knowledge* (Heaven & Earth Books, 1997).

189 **"other cycles":** Ahsian, *The Crystal Ally Cards,* 201.

CHAPTER 12

193 **mother and baby:** William A. Grobman et al., "Labor Induction Versus Expectant Management in Low-Risk Nulliparous Women," *New England Journal of Medicine* 379, no. 6 (2018): 513–23, https://doi.org/10.1056/NEJMoa1800566.

194 **pelvic outlet:** Jing Huang et al., "A Review and Comparison of Common Maternal Positions During the Second Stage of Labor," *International Journal of Nursing Sciences* 6, no. 4, (2019): 460–67, https://doi.org/10.1016/j.ijnss.2019.06.007.

194 **birth canal:** Annemarie Lawrence et al., "Maternal Positions and Mobility During First Stage Labour," *Cochrane Database of Systemic Reviews* 2013, no. 10 (October 9, 2013), doi:10.1002/14651858.CD003934.pub4.

195 **uterine contractions:** Tine Wrønding et al., "The Aesthetic Nature of the Birthing Room Environment May Alter the Need for Obstetrical Interventions: An Observational Retrospective Cohort Study," *Scientific Reports* 9, no. 1 (2019): 303, doi:10.1038/s41598-018-36416-x; Michael H. Walter, "The Role of Oxytocin and the Effect of Stress During Childbirth: Neurobiological Basics and Implications for Mother and Child," *Frontiers in Endocrinology* 12 (2021): 729011.

195 **deepens fear:** Grantly Dick-Read, *Childbirth Without Fear: The Principles and Practice of Natural Childbirth* (Heinemann, 1942).

195 **labor progression:** Caroline A. Smith et al., "Relaxation Techniques for Pain Management in Labour," *Cochrane Database of Systematic Reviews* 3, no. 3 (2018): CD009514, doi:10.1002/14651858.CD009514.pub2.

195 **recent years:** "Births—Method of Delivery," National Center for Health Statistics, www.cdc.gov/nchs/fastats/delivery.htm; "Cesarean Deliveries," percentage of all live births that were cesarean deliveries by state, National Center for Health Statistics, www.cdc.gov/nchs/state-stats/births/cesareans.html#cdc_data_surveillance_section_1-percentage-of-all-live-births-that-were-cesarean-deliveries.

195 **United States:** "Health at a Glance 2023: OECD Indicators," OECD, 2023, https://doi.org/10.1787/7a7afb35-en. (See figure 9.16: Caesarean section rates.)

195 **risks like asthma:** Ziwei Zhong et al., "Association of Cesarean Section with Asthma in Children/Adolescents: A Systematic Review and Meta-Analysis Based on Cohort Studies," *BMC Pediatrics* 16, no. 1 (2023): 571, doi:10.1186/s12887-023-04396-1.

195 **allergies:** Xiaowu Liu et al., "Risk of Asthma and Allergies in Children Delivered by Cesarean Section: A Comprehensive Systematic Review," *The Journal of Allergy and Clinical Immunology: In Practice* 12, no. 10 (2024): 2764–73, https://doi.org/10.1016/j.jaip.2024.06.022.

195 **gut flora:** Francesco Inchingolo et al., "The Impact of Cesarean Section Delivery on Intestinal Microbiota: Mechanisms, Consequences, and Perspectives—A Systematic Review," *International Journal of Molecular Sciences* 25, no. 2 (2024): 1055, https://doi.org/10.3390/ijms25021055.

195 **autoimmune conditions:** Christopher R. Cardwell et al., "Caesarean Section Is Associated with an Increased Risk of Childhood-Onset Type 1 Diabetes Mellitus: A Meta-Analysis of Observational Studies," *Diabetologia* 51, no. 5 (2008): 726–35, doi:10.1007/s00125-008-0941-z.

195 **eczema:** Ziyu Xiong et al., "Prevalence of Eczema Between Cesarean-Born and Vaginal-Born Infants Within 1 Year of Age: A Systematic Review and Meta-Analysis," *European Journal of Pediatrics* 181, no. 6 (2022): 2237–47, doi:10.1007/s00431-022-04436-5.

195 **six-year-old with asthma:** Mette Tollånes et al., "Cesarean Section and Risk of Severe Childhood Asthma: A Population-Based Cohort

Study," *The Journal of Pediatrics* 153, no. 1 (2008): 112–6, doi:10.1016/j.jpeds.2008.01.029.

195 **celiac disease:** Kim Kristensen et al., "Cesarean Section and Disease Associated with Immune Function," *Journal of Allergy and Clinical Immunology* 137, no. 2 (2016): 589–90, https://doi.org/10.1016/j.jaci.2015.07.040.

195 **pelvic floor issues:** Judith H. Poole et al., "Adhesions Following Cesarean Delivery: A Review of Their Prevalence and Clinical Relevance," *Women's Health* 9, no. 3 (2013): 291–301, doi:10.2217/whe.13.45.

195 **maternal mortality:** Xiao-Ming Shi et al., "Effect of Primary Elective Cesarean Delivery on Placenta Accreta: A Case Control Study," *Chinese Medical Journal* 131, no. 6 (2018): 672–76.

195 **cesareans:** Hong-Tao Hu et al., "Association Between First Caesarean Delivery and Adverse Outcomes in Subsequent Pregnancy Including Risk of Repeat CS," *BMC Pregnancy and Childbirth* 18, no. 1 (2018): 18–95.

195 **abdominal surgeries:** Ihab Ihab Mohamed El-Nashar et al., "Effect of Multiple Repeat Cesarean Sections on Intra-Abdominal Adhesions," *The Egyptian Journal of Hospital Medicine* 89, no. 1 (2022): 4500–506, doi:10.21608/ejhm.2022.258480.

196 **asthma:** "Childhood Asthma Prevalence in the U.S.," U.S. Environmental Protection Agency, December 2024, www.epa.gov/system/files/documents/2024-12/ej-indicators-asthma.pdf.

196 **eczema:** T. E. Shaw et al., "Eczema Prevalence in the United States: Data from the 2003 National Survey of Children's Health," *Journal of Investigative Dermatology* 131, no. 1 (2011): 67–73, 69. https://doi.org/10.1038/jid.2010.251.

196 **autoimmune disease:** "Autoimmune Diseases," National Institute of Allergy and Infectious Diseases, National Institutes of Health, www.niaid.nih.gov/diseases-conditions/autoimmune-diseases.

196 **exhausted physicians:** Howard Markel, *Literatim: Essays at the Intersections of Medicine and Culture* (Oxford University Press, 2020), 272.

197 **safety outcomes:** Shyamkumar Sriram et al., "Midwife-Led Versus Obstetrician-Led Perinatal Care for Low-Risk Pregnancy: A Systematic Review and Meta-Analysis of 1.4 Million Pregnancies," *Journal of Clinical Medicine* 13, no. 22 (2022): 6629, https://doi.org/10.3390/jcm13226629.

201 **mastitis:** Abbey Rose, "Managing Plugged Ducts, Mastitis When Breastfeeding," Mayo Clinic Health System, accessed March 4, 2025, www.mayoclinichealthsystem.org/hometown-health/speaking-of-health/managing-plugged-ducts-mastitis-when-breastfeeding.

202 **anxiety:** Chenlu Yang et al., "Association Between Dietary Quality and Postpartum Depression in Lactating Women: A Cross-Sectional Survey in Urban China," *Frontiers in Nutrition* 8 (2021): 705353, https://doi.org/10.3389/fnut.2021.705353; Juliana dos Santos Vaz et al., "Dietary Patterns, n-3 Fatty Acids Intake from Seafood, and High Levels of Anxiety Symptoms During Pregnancy: Findings from the Avon Longitudinal Study of Parents and Children," *PLOS One* 8, no. 7 (2013): e67671, https://doi.org/10.1371/journal.pone.0067671.

CHAPTER 13

204 **"generativity versus stagnation":** Erik Erikson, *Identity and the Life Cycle* (International Universities Press, 1959).

204 ***All Fours* illuminates:** Miranda July, *All Fours* (Riverhead Books, 2024).

207 **anthropological research:** Anthropologist Sarah Hrdy discusses alloparenting in her book *Mothers and Others*, in which she explains how humans evolved to rely on extended kin networks and non-kin helpers to raise children. Sarah Blaffer Hrdy, *Mothers and Others: The Evolutionary Origins of Mutual Understanding* (Belknap Press, 2009).

208 **motor industry lobbyists:** General Motors streetcar conspiracy: General Motors, along with other companies such as Firestone and Standard Oil, was convicted in 1949 of conspiring to monopolize the sale of buses and supplies to National City Lines, which bought streetcar systems and converted them to buses in numerous U.S. cities, and conspiring to own or control transit systems—contributing to the decline of streetcars. "General Motors Streetcar Conspiracy," Wikipedia, https://en.wikipedia.org/wiki/General_Motors_streetcar_conspiracy.

208 **"As a country becomes":** Trevor Noah, host, clip from *What Now? With Trevor Noah* (podcast), Instagram reel, www.instagram.com/reels/DLKgFZiTG5w/.

CHAPTER 14

213 **menopausal years:** Jean Shinoda Bolen, "Intersection of the Timeless with Time: Where Two Worlds Come Together," address to Annual ATP Conference, Monterey, California, August 6, 1988.

214 **reproductive fitness:** Joan B. Silk et al., "The Benefits of Social Capital: Close Social Bonds Among Female Baboons Enhance Offspring Survival," *Proceedings of the Royal Society B: Biological Sciences* 276, no. 1670 (2009): 3099–104, https://doi.org/10.1098/rspb.2009.0681. Silk et al. demonstrate that close social bonds among female baboons significantly improve offspring survival, highlighting the evolutionary importance of affiliative behaviors in reproductive success.

214 **grandmother effect:** James G. Herndon, "The Grandmother Effect: Implications for Studies on Aging and Cognition," *Gerontology* 56, no. 1 (2010): 73–79, doi:10.1159/000236045.

215 **"on the planet":** Beth Berry Coaching, Facebook post, November 4, 2024, www.facebook.com/revolutionfromhome/posts/as-with-so-many-of-the-cultural-narratives-were-surrounded-by-the-midlife-crisis/1099536168206874/. 2021, www.facebook.com/revolutionfromhome.

216 **osteoporosis:** Samruddhi H. Charde et al., "A Comprehensive Review on Postmenopausal Osteoporosis in Women," *Cureus* 15, no. 11 (2023): e174518, doi:10.7759/cureus.48582.

216 **increased risks of dementia:** Annette J. Dobson et al., "Menopause Age and Type and Dementia Risk: A Pooled Analysis of 233,802 Women," *Age and Ageing* 53, no. 11 (2024): afae254, doi:10.1093/ageing/afae254.

216 **cardiovascular disease:** Samar R. El Khoudary et al., "Menopause Transition and Cardiovascular Disease Risk: Implications for Timing of Early Prevention: A Scientific Statement from the American Heart Association," *Circulation* 142, no. 25 (2020): e506-e532, doi:10.1161/CIR.0000000000000912.

217 **Women's Health Initiative:** "Women's Health Initiative (WHI)," National Heart, Lung, and Blood Institute, National Institutes of Health, 2024, www.nhlbi.nih.gov/science/womens-health-initiative-whi.

217 **key factor was timing:** Louise Lind Schierbeck et al., "Effect of Hormone Replacement Therapy on Cardiovascular Events in Re-

cently Postmenopausal Women: Randomised Trial," *BMJ* 345 (2012): e6409, https://doi.org/10.1136/bmj.e6409.

217 **emerging brain-imaging research:** Lisa Mosconi et al., "Menopause Impacts Human Brain Structure, Connectivity, Energy Metabolism, and Amyloid-Beta Deposition," *Scientific Reports* 11 (2021): 10867, https://doi.org/10.1038/s41598-021-90084-y.

218 ***Call of the Wild:*** Kimberly Ann Johnson, *Call of the Wild: How We Heal Trauma, Awaken Our Own Power, and Use It for Good* (Harper Wave, 2021).

218 ***Hormone Intelligence:*** Aviva Romm, *Hormone Intelligence: The Complete Guide to Calming Hormone Chaos and Restoring Your Body's Natural Blueprint for Well-Being* (HarperOne, 2021).

CHAPTER 15

223 **"nature of reality":** Dené Logan, *Sovereign Love: A Guide to Healing Relationships by Reclaiming the Masculine and Feminine Within* (St. Martin's Essentials / Sounds True, 2024), 118.

225 **"values of science":** Brannon Braga, dir., Neil deGrasse Tyson, host, *Cosmos: A Spacetime Odyssey*, Season 2, episode 9, "The Lost Worlds of Planet Earth," National Geographic Channel, May 4, 2014.

225 **"truly rely":** David R. Hawkins, *Power vs. Force: The Hidden Determinants of Human Behavior* (Veritas, 1995), 177.

226 **Sharks:** Bryan A. Keller et al., "Map-Like Use of Earth's Magnetic Field in Sharks," *Current Biology* 31, no. 13 (2021): 2881–86.

226 **species of birds:** Thomas Alerstam and Göran Högstedt, "The Role of the Geomagnetic Field in the Development of Birds' Compass Sense," *Nature* 306, no. 5942 (1983): 463–65.

226 **"limits of physics":** Erick Godsey, "Forgiving Hierarchy: Honing the Blade of Mythic Play," blog post, February 10, 2023, ErickGodsey.com/blog/forgiving-hierarchy-honing-the-blade-of-mythic-play.

226 **irreverent bit:** Oren Brimer, dir., *Pete Holmes: I Am Not for Everyone*, Rocket Science Pictures, 2023.

227 **"going crazy":** Malcolm Ocean (@Malcolm_Ocean), X post, August 6, 2025, 8:40 P.M., https://x.com/Malcolm_Ocean/status/1953254972524773704.

228 **one interpretation among many:** Jeffrey J. Kripal, *The Flip: Epiphanies of Mind and the Future of Knowledge* (Bellevue Literary Press, 2019).

228 **forced to reconcile:** Kripal, *The Flip.*

228 **"more than that":** Ky Dickens, host, *The Telepathy Tapes* (podcast), Season 1, episode 6, "Scientific Evidence for ESP That Shatters the Materialist Paradigm," October 14, 2024, https://podcasts.apple.com/us/podcast/ep-6-scientific-evidence-for-esp-that-shatters-the/id1766382649?i=1000672943214.

228 **William James:** William James, *Human Immortality: Two Supposed Objections to the Doctrine* (Houghton Mifflin, 1898).

228 **Aldous Huxley:** Aldous Huxley, *The Doors of Perception* (Harper & Brothers, 1954).

228 **"space-time":** Jeffrey J. Kripal, conversation with the author, October 23, 2025.

229 **"awareness":** *The Telepathy Tapes,* Season 1, episode 6.

229 **"impossibility of the impossible":** Kripal, conversation, October 23, 2025.

229 **"little bit broader":** *The Telepathy Tapes,* Season 1, episode 6.

229 **"look stupid":** Ky Dickens, host, *The Telepathy Tapes* (podcast), Season 1, episode 5, "Teachers Break the Silence About Telepathy," October 7, 2024, https://podcasts.apple.com/us/podcast/ep-5-teachers-break-the-silence-about-telepathy/id1766382649?i=1000672033413.

230 **"scientific endeavor":** ASPIRE Poland, "Rupert Sheldrake, *The Science Delusion,*" posted May 31, 2018, YouTube, www.youtube.com/watch?v=hO4p3xeTtUA. Talk given at TEDx Whitechapel, January 12, 2013.

232 **"connects us":** Sam Harris, host, *Making Sense with Sam Harris* (podcast), "Silence and Pilgrimage: A Conversation with Pico Iyer," August 29, 2023, www.samharris.org/podcasts/making-sense-episodes/336-silence-and-pilgrimage.

232 **closest confidant:** *The Gospel of Philip: Annotated and Explained,* trans. Andrew Phillip Smith (SkyLight Paths Publishing, 2005), 53.

233 **sexual shame:** *Reading the Gospels with Gregory the Great: Homilies on the Gospels,* trans. Santha Bhattacharji (Petersham, Mass.: St. Bede's Publications, 2002), 21–26.

233 **own right:** Jean-Yves Leloup, *The Gospel of Mary Magdalene: Translation from the Coptic and Commentary,* trans. Joseph Rowe (Rochester, Vt.: Inner Traditions, 2002), 39.

233 **"almost any *how*":** Viktor E. Frankl, *Man's Search for Meaning* (Beacon Press, 2006).

234 **"unwilling heart":** Diane Duane, *So You Want to Be a Wizard* (Harcourt, 1996), 6.

234 **"magnificence":** C. Sreechinth, *Extracted Wisdom of Alan Watts: 450+ Lessons from a Theologist* (UB Tech, 2017), 51.

236 **"into the answer":** Rainer Maria Rilke, *Letters to a Young Poet*, trans. M. D. Herter Norton (W. W. Norton, 1954).

237 **"grow sharper":** Eden Phillpotts, *A Shadow Passes* (Cecil Palmer & Hayward, 1918), 19.

CHAPTER 16

241 **"Do not try to take":** Madeline Miller, *Circe* (Little, Brown, 2018), 374.

242 **startling clarity:** Penny Sartori, *The Wisdom of Near-Death Experiences: How Understanding NDEs Can Help Us Live More Fully* (Watkins, 2014).

243 **crucial guidance:** Elisabeth Kübler-Ross, *On Life After Death* (Clarkson Potter/Ten Speed Press, 2008).

243 **hearing their voice:** Joshua Black et al., "The Bereavement Experience: Dreams and Waking Experiences of the Deceased," *Dreaming* 35, no. 2 (2025): 184–89, https://doi.org/10.1037/drm0000291.

243 **"grief hallucinations":** Karina Stengaard Kamp et al., "Bereavement Hallucinations After the Loss of a Spouse: Associations with Psychopathological Measures, Personality, and Coping Style," *Death Studies* 43, no. 4 (2019): 260–69, https://doi.org/10.1080/07481187.2018.1458759.

CHAPTER 17

245 **"the love we had":** Glennon Doyle, *Love Warrior: A Memoir* (Flatiron Books, 2016), 210.

247 **long-term mental health:** Petra Persson and Maya Rossin-Slater, "Family Ruptures, Stress, and the Mental Health of the Next Generation," *American Economic Review* 108, nos. 4–5 (2018): 1214–52.

250 ***Rules of Inheritance:*** Claire Bidwell Smith, *The Rules of Inheritance: A Memoir* (Plume, 2012).

250 ***Missing Stage of Grief:*** Claire Bidwell Smith, *Anxiety: The Missing Stage of Grief—A Revolutionary Approach to Understanding and Healing the Impact of Loss* (Balance, 2018).

251 ***Signs:*** Laura Lynne Jackson, *Signs: The Secret Language of the Universe* (Dial Press, 2020).

256 **"the future":** Hermann Hesse, *Siddhartha* (Wellfleet Press, 2023), 158.

FIFTH PRACTICE

259 **"front of everything":** Esther Perel, conversation with the author, January 14, 2026.

CHAPTER 18

264 **"tree without a root":** Richard Alan Krieger, *Civilization's Quotations: Life's Ideal* (Algora, 2002), 260.

264 **"Afro future":** David Smith, "'A Temple of Liberation': Behind the Unwavering Rise of the National Black Theatre," *The Guardian*, September 27, 2024, www.theguardian.com/stage/2024/sep/27/national-black-theatre-new-york-expansion.

265 **"weakened by her departure":** Maya Angelou, untitled poem read at Barbara Ann Teer's funeral service, New York, July 28, 2008. Shared with the author via personal communication from Sade Lythcott, March 20, 2025.

265 **"the other side":** Sade Lythcott, conversation with the author, March 20, 2025.

266 **"your freedom":** Lythcott, conversation, March 20, 2025.

267 **"Black imagination":** Lythcott, conversation, March 20, 2025.

267 **across cultures:** Simon Hanseung Choi et al., "The Impact of Perceived Relationship to Ancestors on the Association Between Self-Transcendence and Psychopathology: A Cross-Cultural Examination," *Transcultural Psychiatry* 62, no. 4 (2025): 461–77, https://doi.org/10.1177/13634615211049072.

268 **ancestral connections:** Choi et al., "The Impact of Perceived Relationship to Ancestors."

268 **"social identity":** Thomas Hübl, *Attuned: Practicing Interdependence to Heal Our Trauma—and Our World* (St. Martin's Essentials/Sounds True, 2023), 158.

268 **grandmother's experiences:** Bastiaan T. Heijmans et al., "Persistent Epigenetic Differences Associated with Prenatal Exposure to Famine in Humans," *Proceedings of the National Academy of Sciences* 105, no. 44 (2008): 17046–49, https://doi.org/10.1073/pnas.0806560105.

269 **"light our way":** Sade Lythcott, conversation with the author, January 12, 2024.

271 **"'What are you doing for others?'":** Dr. Purushothaman, *Words of Wisdom: 1001 Quotes and Quotations*, vol. 5 (Centre for Human Perfection, 1987), 155.

273 **"single brush-stroke":** Iris Müller-Westermann, "Paintings for the Future: Hilma af Klint—a Pioneer of Abstraction in Seclusion," in *Hilma af Klint—a Pioneer of Abstraction*, ed. Iris Müller-Westermann and Jo Widoff (Moderna Museet; Ostfildern: Hatje Cantz, 2013), 38.

CHAPTER 19

277 **the womb:** Paraphrase after Max Stossel's retelling of Wayne W. Dyer's twins-in-the-womb story in Wayne W. Dyer, *Your Sacred Self: Making the Decision to Be Free* (HarperCollins, 1995), 1.

280 **Laura Lynne Jackson:** Laura Lynne Jackson, *Signs: The Secret Language of the Universe* (Spiegel & Grau, 2019).

280 **loved one:** Jackson, *Signs*, 192.

281 **"one element of faith":** Paul Tillich, *Paul Tillich: Theologian of the Boundaries*, ed. Mark Lewis Taylor (Fortress Press, 1991), 220.

CONCLUSION

290 **"struggle":** Elizabeth Gilbert, *All the Way to the River: Love, Loss, and Liberation* (Riverhead Books, 2025), 209.

ABOUT THE AUTHOR

Ellen Vora, MD, is a holistic psychiatrist, acupuncturist, and yoga teacher, and the author of *The Anatomy of Anxiety*. She takes a functional medicine approach to mental health—considering the whole person and addressing imbalance at the root. Dr. Vora received her BA from Yale University and her MD from Columbia University, and she is board-certified in psychiatry and integrative holistic medicine. She lives in New York City with her husband and daughter.

ellenvora.com
Instagram: @ellenvoramd

ABOUT THE TYPE

This book was set in a Monotype face called Bell. The Englishman John Bell (1745–1831) was responsible for the original cutting of this design. The vocations of Bell were many—bookseller, printer, publisher, typefounder, and journalist, among others. His types were considerably influenced by the delicacy and beauty of the French copperplate engravers. Monotype Bell might also be classified as a delicate and refined rendering of Scotch Roman.